Domestic Sources of Foreign Policy

Domestic Sources of Foreign Policy

West European Reactions to the Falklands Conflict

Edited by

Stelios Stavridis and Christopher Hill

BERG

Oxford / Washington, D.C.

First Published in 1996 by
Berg Publishers Limited
Editorial offices:
150 Cowley Road, Oxford, OX4 1JJ, UK
13950 Park Center Road, Herndon, VA 22071, USA

© Stelios Stavridis and Christopher Hill, 1996

Library of Congress Cataloguing-in-Publication Data
A catalogue record of this book is available from the Library of Congress.

British Library Cataloguing-in-Publication Data
A catalogue record of this book is available from the British Library.

ISBN 1 85973 088 4 (Cloth)
ISBN 1 85973 089 2 (Paper)

Printed in the United Kingdom by WBC Bookbinders, Bridgend,
Mid Glamorgan.

Contents

Contents

Preface

In 1981–2, the non-British editor to this volume happened to be in London. In early April 1982 he was taken aback by the Argentine invasion of the Falkland Islands and by the British reaction to it, which eventually culminated in armed conflict and the loss of 1,000 lives.

The Falklands crisis was his first experience of living in a country mobilizing for war, and it left its mark. As a student of European and International Politics at the time, his interest was not limited to the rights and wrongs of the conflict but extended to an analysis of the way in which the other European states reacted. This eventually led to an MSc. dissertation on the Spanish position on the war which, although finished in September 1984 (at the London School of Economics and Political Science), was only published, in a slightly revised form, in November 1992 as an Occasional Paper of the *Centre for Mediterranean Studies* at the University of Bristol.

In the meantime, although the literature on the Falklands had vastly expanded, not much had been written on the implications of the war in the South Atlantic for European foreign policy, despite the fact that the crisis had evidently been a significant case in the development of European Political Cooperation, particularly in relation to the ability of member states to maintain solidarity over a policy of economic sanctions.

Thanks to the interest expressed by all the contributors to this volume and of course by the other editor, this book then began to take shape. The Editors are grateful to all the contributors for their cooperation in what is inevitably a complex, multi-national project.

It is hoped that this case-study will offer the reader a better understanding of how foreign policy decisions are taken in Europe, as well as adding another dimension to our picture of what happened in those dramatic months of 1982.

Stelios Stavridis
Christopher Hill

Notes on Contributors

Esther Barbé is Professor of International Relations at the *Universitat Autónoma de Barcelona.*

Dimitris Bourantonis is Lecturer in International Relations at the Athens University of Economics and Business.

Michael Clarke is Executive Director of the Centre for Defence Studies at King's College London (University of London).

Geoffrey Edwards is the Alderson Director of Studies in the Centre of International Studies at the University of Cambridge and a Fellow of Pembroke College.

Christopher Hill is Montague Burton Professor of International Relations at the London School of Economics and Political Science (LSE).

Cees Homan is Head of the Department of Naval Studies at the Netherlands Defence College in The Hague.

Henrik Larsen is a diplomat at the Danish Foreign Office in Copenhagen.

Elfriede Regelsberger is Deputy Director of the *Institut für Europäische Politik* in Bonn.

Domitilla Savignoni is a Rome-based free-lance journalist and researcher who specialises in Italian defence problems.

Stelios Stavridis is Lecturer in International Relations and European Politics at The University of Reading, and holds a Jean Monnet Chair in the Internal Dimension of European Integration.

Ben Tonra is Lecturer in Political Science at Trinity College in Dublin and Adjunct Fellow in International Politics at the Center for Strategic and International Studies in Washington D.C.

Notes on Contributors

Panos Tsakaloyannis is Research Associate in the Volkswagen Research Project, Department of Political Science, University of Jena.

Sophie Vanhoonacker is Lecturer at the European Institute of Public Administration in Maastricht.

Introduction: The Falklands War and European Foreign Policy

Christopher Hill

The war of the Falkland Islands burst onto the scene of world politics in April 1982 like an exploding shell. Although the islanders themselves and the people of Argentina had long been concerned about the dispute over ownership and sovereignty, in Britain, the metropolitan power, it was an arcane subject even for foreign policy specialists. For Britain's partners, whether in Western Europe, North America or the Commonwealth, rapid research was required to discover why Argentina had decided to invade the Falklands on 2 April, and why, only three days later and after an emergency Saturday session of Parliament, a large combined task force was embarking from Portsmouth on the long journey towards combat in the South Atlantic.

For most of 1982 and half of 1983 the Falklands – first the sharp, dramatic war which ended in June 1982 and then the political and military fall-out, affecting not just the two adversaries – held the attention of international public opinion. The Soviet military were said to be studying intently the performance of weapons systems and strategies in this classic amphibious operation. The United States lost a Secretary of State (Alexander Haig)[1] and paraded severe internal differences as it struggled to patch up the relations with Latin America which had been damaged by its ever more obvious support for Britain. The political debates worldwide over colonialism, self-determination and the use of force were reinvigorated within and between a wide range of states.

The war and its aftermath remained, nonetheless, little more than a shooting star in the wider universe of international politics. It did not threaten the stability of the international system as a whole, and few third countries stood to gain or to lose much from the conflict, whatever its outcome. After the clear-cut British victory, the *status quo ante* gradually reasserted itself, albeit at a slightly higher level of salience, whereby Britain and

---

1. The failure of Haig's mediation over the Falklands was not the only reason for his fall from grace, but it was his own view that 'my efforts in the Falklands ultimately cost me my job as Secretary of State'. See A. M. Haig, Jr., *Caveat: Realism, Reagan and Foreign Policy*, London: Weidenfeld & Nicolson, 1984, pp. 298–308.

Argentina reiterated well-worn and incompatible positions on the fundamentals, and fenced ineffectually over various possibilities for compromise. If in London and Buenos Aires the issue was beginning by 1984 to slide back down the foreign policy agenda to its normal lowly position, this was even more true in states such as France, Italy and Germany, Britain's main partners in the European Community (EC) system of foreign policy coordination known as European Political Cooperation (EPC).

On the face of things, the issue of the Falklands crisis and its aftermath seems best suited to an historical analysis, either by specialists like Peter Beck[2] or by generalists prepared to spare a chapter, a page or perhaps just a footnote for this highly distinctive and self-contained episode of international conflict. Yet this supposition has already been proved wrong; political scientists, especially those working in international relations, have already shown what a fascinating laboratory the Falklands crisis provides for the study of a number of important questions. Lawrence Freedman and Virginia Gamba-Stonehouse, for example, have narrated the course of the crisis so as to lay bare for subsequent analysis the problems of communication and signalling which afflicted both sides, while G. M. Dillon and the team of Greenaway, Smith and Street have used the Falklands case as one entry point into the analysis of British politics and policy making.[3] Even the Franks Report on how Britain became embroiled in the crisis, which tends to obscure as much as it elucidates, contains a good deal of tantalising policy analysis on such imponderables as the role of intelligence and the setting of priorities in foreign policy.[4]

The present book sets out to build on this body of analytical work, with three particular aims in mind: to illuminate further the Falklands crisis as an historical event by looking more widely into Britain's relations with the rest of the European Community; to examine the nature and variability of domestic constraints on national foreign policy by examining the circumstances of sovereign states of a similar type which are confronting similar problems; and to provide a detailed empirical investigation, through the case study method, of the ability of the member states of the Euro-

---

2. Peter Beck is Britain's leading expert on the history and diplomacy of the Falklands problem. See *The Falkland Islands as an International Problem*, London: Routledge, 1988.

3. L. Freedman and V. Gamba-Stonehouse, *Signals of War: The Falklands Conflict of 1982*, London: Faber & Faber, 1990. The title of this absorbing account can be misleading, as the book contains no theoretical discussion of signalling in foreign policy. See also G. M. Dillon, *The Falklands: Politics and War*, London: Macmillan, 1989; J. Grenaway, S. Smith and J. Street, *Deciding Factors in British Politics: A Case-Studies Approach*, London: Routledge, 1992, especially Chapter 5, 'The Falklands War'.

4. *Falklands Islands Review: Report of a Committee of Privy Counsellors, Chairman the Rt. Hon. the Lord Franks*, Cmd 8787, London: HMSO, 1983. See also W. Wallace, 'How Frank was Franks?', *International Affairs*, vol. 59, no. 3, 1983, pp. 453–8, and L. Freedman, *Britain and the Falklands War*, Oxford: Basil Blackwell for the Institute of Contemporary British History, 1988.

pean Community to produce and maintain coherent foreign policy positions in EPC. It is hoped that this volume will therefore be of interest to students and scholars in the distinct areas of contemporary international history, foreign policy analysis and EC external relations. In the 1990s, when we have groped to understand why countries which call for more intervention or solidarity in great events like those of the Gulf War and the disintegration of Yugoslavia cannot always deliver what they themselves recommend, it is of particular importance to look closely at the recent experiences of states trying to balance an interest in multilateralism with the pressures for particularity deriving from their domestic environments. For the members of the EPC system, the Falklands crisis was a classic case in point.

To this end, the book begins with the outline of issues and purposes which is the province of this introduction, and continues in Chapter 1 with a detailed examination of the theoretical area from which most of the book's concerns grow, foreign policy analysis. The body of the book, an analysis of the main players involved in European reactions to the Falklands crisis and to Britain's involvement in it, then follows. The collective responses, through the Community institutions as well as EPC, are dealt with first, followed by country studies of all the 1982 EC member states and their domestic politics with the exceptions of Britain, which as one of the two protagonists was more part of the problem than the response,[5] and of Luxembourg, which with a population in 1982 of 365,000 was too small to justify separate treatment, particularly as Belgium and the Netherlands have formal responsibilities for looking after, respectively, the economic and political interests of the Grand Duchy in countries where Luxembourg does not possess its own missions.[6] Spain, although not a member of the EC until 1986, is included here as a special case. Its status in 1982 as an important Western European state with both clear aspirations to join the Community and EPC, and a special relationship with Latin America (to say nothing of the parallels between Gibraltar and the Falklands) makes Spain's inclusion in the present project imperative. Although Spanish entry into NATO on 1 June 1982, in the middle of the war, denotes its desire for general acceptability in the West, Spain is cast as the 'external dissenter' as the result of its being torn between the desire to go along

5. Although the question of Britain's reactions to the reactions, that is of how London responded to the varying positions on the Falklands War taken by the other EC states, is important, and will be dealt with in the Conclusion.

6. Such arrangements rest fundamentally on the BENELUX (Belgium, Netherlands, Luxembourg) customs and commercial union set up in 1944, but specifically derive from bilateral agreements signed in 1964-5. See C. Franck, 'Une Présidence Benelux du Conseil? Une Hypothèse de Travail plus qu'une idée magique', paper for a conference on 'The Community, the Member-States and Foreign Policy: Coming Together or Drifting Apart?', Florence: European University Institute, 1-3 July 1993.

with the European majority and its need to listen to voices at home and in Latin America which were demanding opposition to Britain. In this it is grouped with the 'internal dissenters', Ireland and Italy, who for different but comparable reasons found that they could not sustain support for EPC's generally pro-British line.

Naturally some judgements have had to be made as to priorities. France and the Federal Republic of Germany have been paired together, as they so often choose to act jointly in EPC, and in harness they were clearly capable of setting the tone of the Community's response to Britain's decision to fight. Equally, Belgium, the Netherlands and Greece have been grouped together in a single chapter as states with active and important foreign policies, but also with a limited capacity to influence events outside their own immediate region. Denmark, by contrast, which otherwise falls into the same category, has been given a chapter to itself, not because it was a dissident on policy like Ireland but because its attitude to collective sanctions was highly distinctive, in insisting on a national rather than a Community basis of authorisation.

All of the contributors to the book have been asked to consider the same broad questions, although they have also enjoyed the freedom to construct the answers according to the peculiarities of the country in question. In this way the authors have attempted to avoid the familiar trap of incoherence for collective books, without at the same time imposing a straitjacket on the country specialists. Contributors were provided with an outline of the content of the theoretical chapter on foreign policy analysis, and against that background they were asked to describe the positions taken by the country in question on the main issues involved in the Falklands crisis, to consider the degree to which they were distinctive, and then to *explain* why the state either diverged or conformed. In line with the possibilities evident within the literature of foreign policy analysis, it was suggested that explanations should at least be related to the various 'domestic politics' and decision-making theories available, so that the final conclusions could consider the extent to which foreign policy does 'begin at home' and also the meaning of, in Sophie Vanhoonacker's words, 'the truism that when there are serious domestic pressures, solidarity among the EC member states is severely tested'.[7] It should also be noted that while contributors were asked primarily to concentrate on the 1982 crisis, with its heightened tensions and visible conflicts of interest, they also undertook to provide some analysis of the descent from war over the decade after 1982, with particular reference again to the question of solidarity within EPC and of the domestic pressures (if any) on the foreign policy professionals responsible for formulating positions on the Falklands dispute. Clearly once the war was over the Falklands was a major issue

7. See Chapter 4, p. 85–6.

only for Britain among the twelve (from 1986) member states, but it remained a delicate test of diplomacy for the others who sought to balance loyalty to a partner-state against diverse national interests and pressures, domestic and external.

National Foreign Policy and the Domestic Factor

It is perhaps the defining characteristic of foreign policy analysis, and certainly its major achievement, that those who study international relations now rarely make the error of supposing that state behaviour can be understood solely by reference to the external realm of power balances, geopolitics and the anarchical society, important as all these things remain. The domestic sources of foreign policy, previously only highlighted by historians in such apparently exceptional cases as Germany's pre-1914 'reach for world power'[8], are now widely assumed to be in a condition of perpetual dynamic tension with those deriving from beyond the state's frontiers. A full explanation of foreign policy must take full account of constitutional structure, bureaucracy, political parties, linkage with domestic issues and political culture, not forgetting the media and public opinion; and this despite the evident difficulties which most parliaments have in imposing accountability on foreign policy makers. Foreign policy is now no longer (if it ever was) insulated from society by a glass wall of presumed expertise and confidentiality. However erratically and indirectly, it is coloured by the economic, political and cultural life of the people in whose name it functions.

But what does it mean, more precisely, to talk of the domestic sources of national foreign policy? If, as many tend to assume, national diplomacy is less and less distinctive in both style and substance as interdependence exerts pressures towards multilateralism and convergence, then surely national governments have an ever narrower range of choices from which to make decisions and take distinctive stances? It follows that whatever the apparent domestic turbulence surrounding (particularly) democratic decision makers, domestic factors can do little more than complicate the implementation of strategies largely determined by global or at least regional forces. When it is further argued that domestic groups

8. This is the literal translation of F. Fischer's famous *Griff nach der Weltmacht* (1961), watered down in its English translation to *Germany's Aims in the First World War*, London: Chatto & Windus, 1967. Fischer's work became famous for arguing, against the conventional wisdom of the time, that the Kaiser's foreign policy did differ from that of the other states in the European balance of power and that its driving aggression was rooted in the character of the Prussian state. See also J. Joll, *The Origins of the First World War*, London: Longmans, 1984.

are themselves increasingly influenced by the direct impact of transnational relations, with their aspirations, tactics, and even identities being
shaped as much by functional ties, the global market and the electronic
media as by their own national traditions, it seems inevitable that the
case for the importance of the domestic 'sources' of foreign policy must
be restricted to the level of coalition building and its problems; that is,
in the management of interdependence, there will always be difficulties
associated with collective action, achieving consensus and then maintaining the critical level of support for it over time when many individuals and groups see, for one reason or another, an interest in defecting.[9]

This sort of approach may be termed 'international structuralism', in
that it explains major developments through structures which are observed
at the international level, subsuming individual states and what goes on
inside their borders. Such a structuralism may be neo-realist, of the kind
associated with Kenneth Waltz (who explicitly disavowed the need for
his purposes to take into account the differentiation of states),[10] as well as
neo-liberal, of the type associated with notions of transnationalism and
interdependence. These two otherwise rival schools of thought share
an inherent disregard for *das primat der innenpolitik* explanations. The
liberals' emphasis on economic and social forces sometimes obscures this
point, but it holds nonetheless; their conceptualization subordinates the
state to the international system no less than that of the neo-realist.[11]

9. These problems have been widely discussed since (if not before) the publication of
M. Olson's, *The Logic of Collective Action*, Cambridge: Harvard University Press, 1965.
But as Robert Keohane rightly warns us, both 'Prisoners' Dilemma [from game theory] and
the problem of collective action ...warn us against the fallacy of composition, which in world
politics would lead us to believe that the sources of discord must lie in the nature of the
actors rather than in their patterns of interaction...[they] both suggest, on the contrary, the
power of 'third image' explanations, which attribute causality to the nature of the international system rather than the nature of states'. R. O. Keohane, *After Hegemony: Cooperation and Discord in the World Political Economy*, Princeton: Princeton University Press,
1984, p. 69.

10. 'National politics consists of differentiated units performing specified functions. International politics consists of like units duplicating one another's activities'. K. Waltz, *Theory
of International Politics*, Reading, MA: Addison-Wesley, 1979, p. 97.

11. This is even true of the traditional realist like Morgenthau, whose stress on the national interest can lead both to the supposition that national idiosyncrasy is the basis of explanation in international relations (criticized by Waltz, *Theory of International Politics*, p. 64)
and to the billiard ball assumptions of most realists which, allied to notions of a predominant balance of power system, are fundamentally structural and provide a logical jumping-
off point for the neo-realists. See R. Little's insightful analysis of 'Structuralism and
Neo-Realism', in M. Light and A. J. R. Groom (eds), *International Relations: A Handbook
of Current Theory*, London: Pinter, 1985, pp. 74-89. It should be noted that Morgenthau
complained bitterly of misrepresentation, and argued that 'the obsolescence of the nation-
state and the need to merge it into supranational organisations of a functional nature was
already one of the main points of the first edition [of *Politics Among Nations: the Struggle
for Power and Peace*] of 1948'. See the preface to the third edition of his famous book; New
York: Knopf, 1960.

This somewhat cavalier approach, not just to the state but to the political lives of the billions who live within them (that is, the entire world's population), runs up against at least five fundamental objections. The first is that even the collective action problem conceded by international structuralists is not a trivial matter. Realists have long been aware of the problems of alliance cohesion, and liberals of the weaknesses of international cooperation through intergovernmental organizations (it is not surprising then that there is some confusion as to the distinction between neo-realism and neo-liberal institutionalism in the contemporary debate on international relations theory).[12] States find it genuinely difficult both to reach agreement on group strategies and then to hold to these strategies once agreements are reached. Historically, solidarity is the exception rather than the rule and even in Western Europe, the region most self-consciously determined to overcome interstate anarchy after 1945, the 'limits of integration' (in Paul Taylor's phrase)[13] are perpetually manifested. Moreover, the reasons for fragmentation are not simply those of a low-level Machiavellianism, or the increasing mathematical odds against interests coinciding as the size of a group enlarges. From where do divergent national interests come? They stem partly from particularities of position, historical legacy and capability, but also from the ways in which the current generations of living and breathing people which make up the 'nation (state)' interpret their position, legacy and capability. Given that they usually have a powerfully specific sense of their collective identity and community, this will significantly compound the problems in the way of agreement which would confront autistic rational actors, playing the hand of national interests as if in a game of poker. There is, in effect, a dual problem of collective action: first in any negotiation, a number of actors will see the advantages in defection or free riding, and second, every negotiating government is engaged in its own process of collective deliberation, with its component parts (bureaucratic politics) and political hinterland (democratic pluralism).

This brings us to the second objection to international structuralism, and by the same token to another reason for paying serious attention to the domestic genesis of foreign policy. This is that much of the analysis which elevates systemic or structural explanations (the distinction is not always evident, and for the purposes of this discussion it is not crucial) is based on little more than over-simplification and assertion. It is not in the nature of things easy to investigate such a high-level issue empirically;

12. See R. O. Keohane, 'Institutional Theory and the Realist Challenge after the Cold War', in D. Baldwin (ed.), *Neorealism and Neoliberalism: The Contemporary Debate*, New York: Columbia University Press, 1993, pp. 269-300.

13. The phrase is P. Taylor's, from *The Limits of European Integration*, London: Croom Helm, 1983.

writers like Waltz recognize this in making their first priority the construction of a parsimonious *a priori* statement which can stand as a testable hypothesis.[14] This is a reasonable procedure, but it is no less reasonable to point to those aspects of international politics which cannot be accounted for by, for example, a theory of bipolarity, and to show, whether logically or empirically, how these in turn may have very significant consequences even for international systems. Even if they do not reach so far, these aspects will probably help to explain the behaviour of any single state among the 180 plus which now exist, rather more satisfyingly than a remote, high-level theory of the system as a whole, elegant in proportion both to its tendency to simplify and to the strength of its underpinning assertions. That these assertions are central may be seen by the way in which both realist and interdependence generalizations prove brittle under the challenge of events, tending to ebb and flow according to relatively ephemeral occurrences such as the OPEC oil embargo or the invasion of Afghanistan. The bases of most overarching paradigms of global politics are as likely to be simple articles of faith as they are tightly argued interpretations of a mass of human experience: this is because most of them are ahistorical.[15]

The third counter-argument to the various strands of international structuralism is that they never fully address the question of the variety of states. For neo-realists variety is important insofar as it relates to degrees of power and consequently to positions in the hierarchy of states. Structuralist liberals tend to downplay the role of states as such, but this is to miss a very large amount of actual politics. States vary on many more dimensions than that of power, even allowing that power subsumes such things as wealth, size and development, which are by no means always isomorphic to each other; their age or youthfulness, governability, ethnic heterogeneity, constitutionality, openness to cooperation with neighbours, relationship to major religions *et al.* vary enormously, and the combinations of possible characteristics are endless. This indeed is what makes each state distinctive and inimitable.[16]

Moreover, it is hardly less than perverse to overlook such factors when constructing explanations of how the world comes to work in the way that it does. Even to pose the question is to raise the level of analysis problem: what is it that we are trying to explain? Waltz faces this with admirable clarity and economy of thought, but he is almost alone: and even with his limited *problematique*, of understanding the fundamental character of the international system and the nature of dominance within it, Waltz has found

14. For example, K. Waltz, *Theory of International Politics*, pp. 122–8.

15. A point made by an important recent attempt to carry theory forward from neo-realism. See B. Buzan, C. Jones and R. Little, *The Logic of Anarchy: Neorealism to Structural Realism*, New York: Columbia University Press, 1993.

16. See J. Mayall, 'The Variety of States', in Cornelia Navari (ed.), *The Condition of States*, Milton Keynes: Open University Press, 1991, pp. 44-60.

it difficult to convince his critics that, in neglecting the internal character of even the great powers, he is not giving an incomplete picture and denying himself a powerful predictive tool.[17] If one shifts the level of explanation downwards to why particular actors behave in the way that they do, or why certain events happen, the case for focusing on the interplay of domestic and international politics becomes even more unanswerable.

This is not a matter of old-fashioned, tautologous statements about states following their own, varying interests; rather, it is about accepting that while domestic society is not fully autonomous, neither is it completely lacking in significant autonomy. Although any fair-minded observer who stopped to reflect for a moment would agree that the truth is that most states are semi-autonomous, it is remarkable how many analyses of macrointernational relations simply sweep past the issue altogether, presumably on the magisterial assumption that such domestic distinctiveness as remains has few important consequences for other states or for the system as a whole (apart from foreign policy analysis, perhaps only neo-Marxists, discovering both the state and international relations in recent decades, are the honourable exceptions here). What is important, *per contra*, is to analyse the dialectical relationship between external and internal forces, and to show how that is important for both 'inside' and 'outside'.[18] Some parts of domestic society will undoubtedly be shaped by international influences, but not all, and not always in the same ways. Furthermore, any homogenizing effects that external forces exert are bound to be relatively superficial compared to the pull of community represented by the state (or even the region within the state). Common institutions, laws, values, myths and educational systems, usually backed up by language, are a great deal to set in the balance against the global market and mass media in the liberal perspective, and against the balance of power in the realist one. Admittedly, the latter is attempting only to explain what states can or cannot do in the international system, not their internal characteristics;[19] no amount of domestic distinctiveness will enable Switzerland, for example, to become a superpower. But it is often the case that the particular tracks that a state and society run on historically, their own internal logic, can interact dramatically with the rest of the international system, in a way that an

17. See, for example, Buzan, Jones and Little, *The Logic of Anarchy: Neorealism to Structural Realism*, pp. 24-8, and R. O. Keohane (ed.), *Neo-Realism and its Critics*, New York: Columbia University Press, 1986.

18. The terms are, of course, those used by R. B. J. Walker in his illuminating *Inside/Outside: International Relations as Political Theory*, Cambridge: Cambridge University Press, 1993, although I am using them with some of the very modernist assumptions he wishes to transcend.

19. But there is, even here, a possible link. See P. Gourevitch, 'The Second Image Reversed: the International Sources of Domestic Politics', *International Organization*, vol. 32, no. 4, 1978, pp. 881-912; also Hintze, cited in Little, 'Structuralism and Neo-Realism', p. 84.

analysis of geopolitics and capability would not predict. Prussian militarism is the best-known example, but British pacifism in the 1930s or almost any state in a revolutionary or pre-revolutionary condition are also illuminating cases.

The fourth reason for finding structuralism insufficient, at least in its international variant, is the fact that states not infrequently exert their existential capacity for defying the apparently irresistible pressures from the structure, or history, or whatever label one wishes to attach to the whole outside the individual political constituency. At the least this means that some states prefer the role of Canute to that of fellow-traveller with the *zeitgeist*;[20] at the most it means that they can delay the apparently inevitable for a surprisingly long period, as Portugal did with African decolonization in the 1960s and 1970s, and as the Swiss population has continued to do with its rejection of UN membership in 1986 and then the European Economic Area agreement in December 1992. Many states of course continue to defy with impunity the growing normative groundswell in favour of common standards of human rights; the only plausible explanation of such behaviour is that national decision makers, in varying degrees of harmony with their own societies, are interpreting their position in the international system in a distinctive way. That distinctiveness, where it does not come from their own personal madness or tyranny, derives from domestic impulses (note how modern Italian conservatives are now seeking to rehabilitate Mussolini by claiming that Italian fascism was much milder than its Nazi counterpart).[21]

The fifth and last of our counterblasts against structuralism canalso be dealt with briefly, notwithstanding its importance. Much of the literature we have been referring to is based, too narrowly, on rationalist assumptions. This is true both of statespersons making decisions about the necessary strategy for coping with an anarchical society, and of individuals making functional choices about consumption, employment and political loyalty, but it is also true of a good deal of writing on the domestic environment, which is otherwise presented here as a way of producing complementary explanations to those deriving from external sources. Many pluralists writing on foreign policy analysis (which is a subject dominated by pluralists) essentially operate on rationalist assumptions, to the effect that they reproduce the Waltzian model inside the state: if decision makers have to take notice of domestic pressure groups by virtue of the latter's power in the political process then they will do so, but not other-

20. For non-British readers, Canute was a Danish King of England in the early eleventh century who ordered the waves to retreat. Not surprisingly, he was disappointed.
21. 'La festa della liberazione' on 25 April 1994 drew crowds estimated at 300,000 to the centre of Milan to demonstrate against this rewriting of history. See *La Repubblica*, 26 April 1994.

wise. Equally, domestic groups and individuals will be activist to a level broadly in proportion to the degree that their self-interests are engaged.

It should by now be clear that the present author sees this as a somewhat impoverished view of politics in general and the domestic environment in particular. It is of central importance to analyse foreign policy in the light of domestic as well as international considerations, but it is just as necessary to go beyond interest group pluralism in doing so. For example, concepts such as those of elites, agenda setting and the mobilization of bias help us to realise that the nature of decision making is often about far more than bargaining, coalition-building and trade-offs. It can be about particular classes subordinating both foreign policy and the democratic process to their sets of values and interests; beyond this it can also be about competing visions or sets of beliefs about politics, ethnicity, senses of history or of destiny, and what in today's language might be termed 'embedded practices' (i.e. traditions).

These are the kind of things to which studies of the domestic sources of foreign policy need to be alert, as well to the nature of decision making in a more conventional institutional or pluralist sense. Of course this book will hardly neglect the conventional approach. The roles of the major elements of the state apparatus in determining positions on the Falklands issue and coordination with partners will be important in most cases. The literature on bureaucratic politics, group-think and bounded rationality is a fertile source. Some attention will also naturally be paid to the conditions of crisis in which some of the decisions during the period May-June 1982 were made, bearing in mind the problem of the perception of crisis, that is, for who else in Europe (other than Britain) was this a crisis; and in what sense? The most significant political parties and groups involved in debate on the Falklands question within these various countries will also go under the microscope. If pluralism is not enough, it is certainly an indispensable part of a comprehensive treatment of the domestic environment.

European Foreign Policy

Part of the argument thus far has been that a concern with national foreign policy is not incompatible with a wide range of possible theoretical positions about decision making. It is just as true that an approach to European foreign policy cooperation which emphasises the continued importance of the member states and their foreign policies does not have to involve taking up realist stances on the European Union in particular or on international relations in general. Any explanation of EPC or of the CFSP which does not include the national dimension is fundamentally flawed. But avoiding that error does not mean denying that state foreign policy is engaged in an interesting process of change by virtue of immersion in EPC, or that Johann De Vree was right in 1985 when he said that if the Western Europeans 'wished to be taken seriously in international decision making they must do their utmost to generate more power, specifically: to attain a level of power which is at least comparable to that of the superpowers of today.'[22] The truth is that EPC has been a process more than a set of outputs or principles ordained from the outset, a process in which individual states, sub-groups of states, and the forum as a whole have interacted both amongst themselves and with external stimuli to produce a gradually accumulating *coutumier* of practices and positions that has to be taken into account on the next occasion for decision.

What is always interesting at any given time is the capacity which EPC has reached for collective action and solidarity, and the impact which a particular problem has on the *coutumier*.[23] This could be strengthened or weakened, according to the nature of the event (not always a crisis) and of the EC's response to it. Equally, the legacy from the past will shape possible responses to a new problem. In this light, the Falklands crisis was an important event for European Political Cooperation, quite apart from its other ramifications. The record of EPC up to 1982 made it natural for Britain to expect some concrete assistance from its European partners as a group: compare the secret bilateralism of Anglo-French diplomacy over Suez. And the Falklands was one of the toughest tests of unity in EPC's brief history, certainly the most dramatic since the Yom Kippur War and its aftermath in October 1973, when the newly enlarged European Community had split apart under the twin pressures of an Arab oil embargo and pugnacious American diplomacy.

What then was the state of EPC in early 1982 as it faced up to this sudden and serious new test? The brief answer is that it had just begun to show some signs of revival after a year or so of setbacks, which had themselves followed on from five years of unspectacular consolidation. After the initial period of activism, from 1969–74 when EPC was set up and first tested, there was a quieter time in the second half of the 1970s; this was partly fortuitous, thanks to détente and an unnerved, post-Watergate

---

22. J. K. De Vree, P. Coffey and R. H. Lauwaars (eds), *Towards a European Foreign Policy: Legal, Economic and Political Dimensions,* Dordrecht: Martinus Nijhoff, 1987.

23. The term *coutumier* is actually used within the EPC system to denote a volume of confidential documents on past practices and stances, which evidently goes beyond those codified in the Single European Act and in the Treaty of Maastricht. The use of the term here is wider and more metaphorical and should not be taken to indicate a reference to any documentation. Interestingly enough, great care was taken to exclude from public statements any mention of the *coutumier* until the drafting of the Foreign Ministers' 'Decision' adopted on the occasion of the signing of the Single Act, when some reports have it that the word was accidentally not cut out before a text was released. Needless to say, the citadel of state (or Brussels) power has not crumbled as a result.

USA. In these years there were no major calamities for EPC and (perhaps not coincidentally) no serious attempts to carry it further institutionally. At the end of 1979, however, came the Soviet invasion of Afghanistan, and the mute inability of European diplomacy to react. In practice the paralysis lasted for little more than a month, as under the stimulus of Lord Carrington and later the German and Italian foreign ministers, energetic efforts were made to develop the system of EPC. Moreover the EC was not significantly divided on Afghanistan; the problem was largely one of actorness. It was therefore not difficult to galvanize EPC to produce the London Report of October 1981, with its various sensible procedural innovations.[24]

Setbacks continued, however, on the policy front, partly because by this time expectations of what EPC should be able to achieve had begun to rise beyond its immature capabilities. The proposal for the neutralization of Afghanistan, which EPC came up with in February 1980, fell on stony ground; Lord Carrington suffered a disdainful dismissal when he took further collective proposals to Moscow in July 1981. In early 1980 the EC prevaricated painfully over whether to impose sanctions on Iran over the taking hostage of the staff of the US embassy, and in doing so succeeded in alienating both Washington and Tehran. During the Polish crisis of 1981–2, EPC took a back seat to NATO in the coordination of Western diplomacy, and the Europeans were furious at what they saw as the humiliation of insufficient American consultations over sanctions after the proclamation of martial law in Poland. East-West relations in general continued to deteriorate, with the Europeans seemingly powerless to save détente. Genscher and Colombo failed to carry their partners with an ambitious plan to graft defence cooperation onto EPC, to cope with the more dangerous environment.

There were things to set against this disappointing record. The EC came up with what is still its best-known foreign policy position, the Venice declaration of June 1980 on the need to move towards an even-handed Arab-Israeli settlement (even if the new Mitterrand government temporarily disavowed the policy in public one month after agreeing the London Report).[25] The EC representatives persisted, through exhausting diplomatic shuttles, in attempts to bring the parties together, despite a lack of support from either superpower. EPC itself survived despite the active scepticism of the superpowers as the Cold War returned.

24. On the London Report, see S. Nuttall, *European Political Cooperation,* Oxford: Clarendon Press,1992, pp. 175-80, and C. Hill, 'Changing Gear in Political Cooperation', *Political Quarterly,* vol. 53, no. 1 1982, pp. 47–60.

25. See F. de La Serre and P. M. Defarges, 'France: A Penchant for Leadership' in C. Hill (ed.), *National Foreign Policies and European Political Cooperation*, London: Allen & Unwin, 1983, p. 68.

It remained true that, as 1982 got underway, coordination over foreign policy inside the European Community seemed at a critical juncture. Was the momentum for reform and development evident in the London Report and the Venice Declaration to be sustained, breeding an enhanced capacity to deal with the great international questions of the day, or would the system lose all credibility amidst rebuffs and internal dissension? The Argentinian invasion of the Falklands Islands, everywhere unexpected,[26] was immediately a crisis for Britain. It would not have merited more than a passing statement in EPC had not Britain then decided to deal with what it perceived as an urgent threat to vital interests by launching an expedition to retake the islands by force. Thus the problem became a crisis for the other eight member states, and for the mechanism of EPC, because a turning point had to be faced: if Britain became involved in a war its European partners could either distance themselves from London and make strenuous efforts to end the conflict, or they could support Britain as a *de facto* ally.[27] Doing nothing, and/or leaving responses up to individual member states was a theoretical third option, but it would have exposed EPC as an ineffectual sham. The first two options also carried considerable risks; dissociation from Britain would alienate one of EPC's most active supporters and probably lead to enduring schisms (it is, of course, possible to argue that such a stance could also have had a salutary shock effect on Britain by forcing it to face up to the need to win the support of its European partners). On the other hand, support for Britain risked the EC being judged in the outside world as an accessory before the fact of whatever measures Britain deemed it necessary to take once the war began. It was, as events were in fact to show, a recipe for internal disputes and institutional crises further down the road.

The *problematique* therefore, in terms of the analysis of European foreign policy in this book, is in large part about the impact of the unfolding Falklands crisis on the capacity of EPC to produce coherent and sustained collective positions. The case is untypical, but it is also revealing in that it involves reacting to the decisions taken by a partner state which, because vital interests and lives were at stake, was basically prepared to act unilaterally first and ask for support second. Although British diplomacy made strenuous efforts to ensure the backing of its European partners, not least because of the effects that such support could have on both Argentina and

26. It would be interesting to know – but it is of course impossible to find out – whether Spanish or French intelligence had picked up evidence of a coming invasion any earlier than MI6 had done.

27. Not *de jure* because EPC was never, of course, a military alliance or treaty of mutual guarantee. Even under the 1993 Maastricht Treaty the CFSP does not extend so far. Moreover the North Atlantic Treaty of 1949, to which 7 of the 8 subscribed, only applies to 'Europe and North America' and to 'the islands under the jurisdiction of any party in the North Atlantic area north of the Tropic of Cancer' (Article 6).

on the United States, there were inevitably many moments when London either did not have time or could not afford the security risk of consulting with the other eight EC member states of varying views and degrees of importance. There was therefore a significant 'take on trust' factor for both Britain and the rest of the EC during the development of the crisis; and on various occasions trust failed.

An extra dimension to the issue for EPC was the *post bellum*. Even if the Falklands soon stopped being a formal agenda item at the Conference of Foreign Ministers and a significant concern for most member states, it continued to preoccupy the British government. By extension, London was very concerned to get support from its European partners at the United Nations, and in such terms to ensure that the regrowth of their bilateral relations with Buenos Aires would not make the British position unnecessarily difficult. For their part no other EC member particularly wanted to take an individual and exposed position on the Falklands. One of the main motivations behind EPC has always been the safety which lies in numbers. The degree of European solidarity on the Falklands therefore continued (and continues) to be of significance in relation both to national foreign policies and to EPC in the decade or more after the war ended. This aspect is also dealt with in the chapters which follow.

There are two more aspects of European foreign policy making which naturally arise from studying the Falklands case: linkage politics and the principles of foreign policy. By linkage politics is meant here the making by governments of connections, deliberate or otherwise, between distinct issue areas, and also between the work of different international organizations. In the particular context of Europe and the Falklands this involves, for example, the relationship between the external relations of the European Economic Community (i.e. formal treaty-based activities, largely in trade and development) and the high politics of EPC. As the Copenhagen Report of July 1973 on EPC had recognized with its assertion that 'for matters which have an incidence on Community activities close contact will be maintained with the institutions of the Community',[28] there was an intrinsic problem of coordination between these two parallel but separate sets of common policies, often to the frustration of insiders and the confusion of those outside. As Geoffrey Edwards shows in Chapter 2, the Falklands created an important new precedent with the Community by acting as the basis for the rapidly-agreed sanctions against Argentina, despite the manifestly political nature of the problem. But the story was to become more complicated because of the decision to renew sanctions

28. *Second Report of the Foreign Ministers to the Heads of State and Government of the Member States of the European Community of 23 July 1973, Part II, para. 12(b), in European Political Cooperation – EPC*, 4th edn, Bonn: Press and Information Department of the Federal Government, 1982, pp. 43–55.

on a monthly basis, and the unhappiness of some member states with either the form or the substance of what had been done. A further twist came from the intertwining of the debate on Falklands policy with that over farm pricing under the Common Agricultural Policy. EC states normally try to compartmentalize conceptually distinct issues such as these and dislike crude attempts to trade them off against each other, as Henry Kissinger was perceived to have done in the early 1970s. But on this occasion it was Britain which wanted to hold out on the CAP while expecting support on the Falklands, and it discovered, to paraphrase Kissinger himself, that sometimes there are 'linkages in reality'.

It is also interesting under this heading to consider the indirect linkages that existed between the European forums of cooperation and that of NATO. These were indirect because there was no institutional link between the two organizations and because Ireland as a neutral EC member was very sensitive about the civilian status of EPC. But the very lack of a defence dimension to the Community (and even security had only just become a legitimate subject of discussion in 1982) meant that in crises such as this, the Europeans inevitably looked towards the United States, partly out of concern for the direction which American policy would take, and partly for the technical infrastructure which the Pentagon commanded. Britain certainly turned straight to Washington for help with fighting the war and, as was subsequently revealed, received decisive aid in the form of intelligence and logistics. Given the possible use of NATO facilities this entailed and other connections such as French and German arms sales to Argentina, it is clear that European foreign policy on the Falklands could not have been made in a vacuum, untouched by the NATO dimension. Naturally such considerations did not appear in public statements, but it is possible that in relation to individual states, defence questions were entangled with the Falklands affair and that both were affected by domestic politics.

The United Nations was a public arena where an obvious overlap occurred between policies on the Falklands and stances on other issues. It was as well that Britain succeeded in obtaining Security Council Resolution 502 in its support so quickly, because the criticisms always latent of British 'colonialism' in the General Assembly soon emerged and began to embarrass those EPC members such as Denmark, Greece, Ireland, and the Netherlands who tended to associate themselves with the Third World. This was always likely to be a significant factor in the formation of public opinion in such states, where the United Nations is usually perceived as the voice of both liberal conscience and the world community. On the other hand, the relationship between the various different issues was by no means uncomplicated. On the one hand it was clear that powers like France or the United States, with their own overseas territories or military bases, would always find it difficult to come out directly in criticism of Britain, whatever coalition might be formed between their own opinion at home and groups in the General Assembly; on the other, there were some Third World small and micro states which were grateful for the strong British response to Argentina's invasion, bearing in mind their own vulnerability to powerful neighbours. This was particularly true of the Commonwealth Caribbean states such as Belize and Trinidad and Tobago.[29]

The last aspect of European foreign policy which the Falklands case promises to illuminate is the 'principles of foreign policy'. By this is meant the underlying values or criteria behind foreign policy. National experience shows that these are usually defined empirically, on a case-by-case basis, without even a very great self-awareness as to what philosophical stances are being taken. But gradually, over time, a sense emerges of what the sticking points are for each country and what is the culture in which particular decisions are made. Thus Britain has been long associated with a strong emphasis on national sovereignty and on a 'pragmatic' method; Germany has had a historical preoccupation with continental systems and with abstract ideas. By contrast to both these examples, EPC has hardly been able to build up a corpus of traditional positions, although in the 1970s great play was made with the notion of civilian power. In the infancy of EPC, events like the Falklands crisis were bound to be crucial in determining both the external view of European foreign policy and the Europeans' own self-image. These events were part of the process of creating a collective memory based on shared myths, out of which whatever principles came to be important to EPC could be read back; this was particularly the case with the Falklands because Argentina's invasion was the first time (and it remains the only example to date) that territory belonging to a member state had been attacked.

Such events make very clear the extent and the limits of such common values as exist at a particular time. This is particularly so when domestic interest is alerted, since public opinion naturally looks at foreign policy from a more overtly moral position than that of decision makers, constantly aware as the latter are the source of pressure for compromise and for national security. Opinion was certainly exercised on the question of the varying principles at stake during the Falklands crisis, including those of sovereignty, territoriality, self-determination, imperialism, justice, nationalism, peace or loyalty.

29. As noted during the crisis by the Foreign Secretary, Francis Pym, and by his FCO officials in their evidence to the Foreign Affairs Committee of the House of Commons on 10 and 17 May 1982 respectively. See *House of Commons Papers, 48 (iii), Minutes of Evidence of the Foreign Affairs Committee 10 May 1982*, Session 1981-82, vol. 12. The transcript of evidence taken on 17 May is only available in the House of Commons Library.

Conclusion

Studying foreign policy naturally draws us to the interplay between the domestic and the international. When that interplay is given a third dimension by the issue of the solidarity of a particular group of states, the analysis becomes both more fascinating and complicated in equal measure. This three-dimensional effect is not uncommon in the study of modern international relations. Many states belong to particular groupings, whether regional or ideological, and most to a range of universal institutions. In the case of the European Community, however, the problem is most sharply defined. How can the attempt to build a common foreign policy survive not only the centrifugalism of nine (or twelve, or fifteen) governments, competing hard-headedly to promote national concerns, but also the extra strains of the same number of domestic environments, pulling on their own governments while simultaneously acting on a transnational level in ways which do not always promote a European level of decision making? It seems logical to expect to reach realist conclusions, with major obstacles being identified to persistent cooperation. However, study of the EC and of EPC leads us also to identify clear patterns of systematic cooperation, developing over time and managing to overcome some of the aforesaid obstacles. Perhaps European foreign policy is being pulled between two powerful forces, with predictable final results; or perhaps the process is yet more complex, with domestic factors not simply acting to reinforce national interests and collective institutions not solely promoting a European identity. It is this conundrum, and others like it, that the chapters which follow will try to elucidate.

Foreign Policy Analysis: A Theoretical Guide

Michael Clarke

Foreign policy analysis (FPA) has detractors and supporters in the academic world, and vociferous exchanges occur between them. Within the discipline of international politics, the study of foreign policy has made considerable theoretical strides, and therefore has come to embody both the virtues and vices of applied theory. Arguments about FPA are often reflections of deeper debates about theory and methodology within the discipline as a whole, and such arguments should be seen in this wider context. To be useful, therefore, any guide to the theories of FPA must confront some of the major methodological questions at the outset. FPA is built on a series of models that have been refined and reinterpreted over almost thirty years, so the most immediate major question concerns the use that can be made of such models.

What is the Use of Models?

Models are a deliberate simplification of complex realities, which is precisely why they are used. If social science were ever to achieve the impossible and create a model that was as complex as the reality it was trying to study, we would be none the wiser: the model would be as confusing to us as the world already is. Only by the very process of simplification and the exclusion of more complex variables can models be of any service to the student.[1]

As wilful simplifications, therefore, academic models serve two general purposes. The first is that they force us to be explicit about the key variables we think are likely to affect the outcome in a given situation, and they force us to remove some of the clutter of reality and experiment

---

1. See M. Broadbeck, 'Models, Meanings and Theories', in M. Broadbeck (ed.), *Readings in the Philosophy of the Social Sciences*, London: Collier Macmillan, 1968, pp. 579–86.

with the interactions of what we suspect are the major forces at work. Thus the construction of a model makes intellectual demands which forces us to make explicit what would otherwise tend to remain implicit. Critics of social science models, on the other hand, normally argue that such an exercise is not worth the effort involved: good analysts do this anyway, and are already engaged in a constant process of explicating what is otherwise implicit.

Second – and more important – models are intended either to create (by suggestion or deduction) useful hypotheses, or else to test an existing hypothesis. Models are therefore part of the more general intellectual process of arriving at, and testing, hypotheses. This is the essence of scientific method: to produce 'falsifiable hypotheses' which can be tested, falsified, refined and re-tested in a constant reiteration of knowledge. On this point, the critics argue that the hypotheses involved in foreign policy modelling are either intuitively obvious or trivial (either way, not worth the effort of modelling), or else incapable of being validated to any worthwhile extent by as simple a device as a social science model. Why do we need a model, they argue, to tell us that in foreign policy crises there is likely to be a greater flow of information? That is simple common sense. And if the FPA modeller is suggesting something more complex – for example in time period t^2 of a crisis the information overload will so confuse leaders that they will come to rely less on clear interpretations and more on national stereotypes of their opponents – then such a hypothesis is simply unreliable when confronted by the infinite variety of crisis situations and the human diversity among decision makers.[2] The technique of modelling in the natural sciences, the critics point out, may work successfully in this way – in producing, testing and refining hypotheses – but the fact remains that human and social entities are far more complex than most other phenomena in the natural sciences and are not susceptible to so crude an analytical tool. In the eyes of the critics, foreign policy models, unlike scientific models, have not – and will not – take us beyond intuition.

But students of FPA argue that our understanding of the subject has already gone some way beyond the intuitive insights of thirty years ago precisely because a series of theoretical models have successfully been articulated and developed into what have been termed 'middle range' theories. From the grand theory that foreign policy can be defined as a system, and analysed as such, it has been possible to derive a number of subordinate theories which develop their own hypotheses. Such theories include 'group-think', 'belief systems', democratic decision-making theo-

2. See C. Bell, *Conventions of Crisis*, London: Oxford University Press, 1971. See also C. F. Hermann (ed.), *International Crises: Insights from Behavioural Research*, New York: Free Press, 1972.

ries and the celebrated theory of 'bureaucratic politics'.[3] The essence of this advance therefore lies in the simultaneous use of multiple models of foreign policy which each encapsulate a different theoretical emphasis. To understand the value of models it is necessary to move away from any assumption that different models in some way compete with each other for accuracy or truth, and accept instead that complementary models can be used simultaneously in a process of constant reiteration to arrive at better understandings of the mysterious processes by which political decisions are made.

Let us imagine that the phenomenon in which we are interested – foreign policy decision making – is an unknown sculpture in a room that is completely dark. More than that, it is a sculpture which tends to change its shape at irregular intervals; it is a mystery to us at any given moment. We cannot enter the room and we have no prospect of lighting the whole area to view it *in toto*. Nevertheless, our analytical method represents one small torch which can be shone into the room from the outside, and our models represent windows arranged around the room through which the torch can be shone. The first beam from the torch will illuminate the sculpture in a certain way. The picture it shows us is true but incomplete, and it may be distorted by shadows thrown up by the angle of the beam. Another torch beam from a different angle will show a different image of the mysterious object, no less true but also incomplete. Images derived from beams shone at some angles may tend to confirm each other as we gradually sense the shape of the sculpture; others may contradict our previous view, indicating perhaps a deep irregularity in the form, or else one of its periodic changes. In this way we approach more closely – though never to achieve absolute proximity – to the reality of the mysterious form. This is the way foreign policy models work. They all reveal some aspect of the truth but they are not capable of providing complete illumination of so complex a business as collective human behaviour. They have to be applied both simultaneously and constantly if the phenomenon of decision making is to be observed carefully. And they should be judged not according to whether they are 'right' or 'true', but rather whether they are useful. The trick for the foreign policy analyst is not to dismiss the power of intuition and experience but rather to use it in making a judgement as to which models – which vantage points around the room – are worth spending more time on, according to the questions being investigated.

---

3. On middle range theories and FPA see S. Smith, 'Foreign Policy Analysis and the Study of British Foreign Policy', in L. Freedman and M. Clarke (eds), *Britain in the World*, Cambridge: Cambridge University Press, 1991, pp. 42–73.

The Explication of FPA Variables That Make Up a Model

Many groups of variables go into the construction of foreign policy models. Some variables, however, will tend to be common to them all and represent a core of inputs that provide an effective checklist of the most often used building blocks of FPA models.

The first and most obvious set of variables is the domestic constitutional frameworks of the decision-making systems in question. The constitutional 'power map' of any state will tell the analyst something about the locus of decision in any system, whether it be a presidential system, a cabinet, or a dictatorial system. Such a power map must be overlaid with an awareness of the more dynamic way in which the system works. If we are looking at a presidential system, for example, on whom does the president rely for influential advice? If we are considering a cabinet system, to what extent are coalitions within the collectivity likely to be relevant on foreign policy issues? The analyst, in other words, has to try to determine where decision-making power lies, among how many people, among which institutions, and how widely it is dispersed? The domestic constitutional framework, therefore, must always be viewed in the light of the broader domestic forces that impact upon it, such as parties, interest groups and the forces of international business.

A second group of variables concerns the political culture of a society. Political culture is a wide and elusive phenomenon and affects foreign policy decision making in many ways. For our purposes, however, the most immediate and tangible way in which decision making is affected by political structure is through the socialization of decision makers. The socialization of leaders and officials will have a major effect on their general perception of the international environment which confronts them. Since the realities of international relations have to be perceived before they can be regarded as decision-making variables, the process through which inherent and long-standing perceptions are shaped in the minds of leaders and advisers is likely to be a major part of most FPA models.

History plays a major – though by no means exclusive – role in the development of political culture. All societies, even within a similar general culture (Western European Christendom, for example) have unique histories that will tend to condition the outlook of political elites from which their decision makers are drawn. The fact that Britain emerged from the Second World War as a victor with global responsibilities, for example, created a very different socialization process for the maturing British elite of the 1950s, compared with their counterparts in Germany whose experience of the 1940s imbued them with a desire for political rehabilitation and economic reconstruction. The French political elite could also count themselves as victors in the war, but the inheritance of the collapse of 1940 and all that flowed from it cannot be overestimated in accounting for their perception of post-war Europe and of France's natural role within it.

A third set of variables flows from this, the beliefs of decision makers.[4] If we regard political culture as a framework for deep perception, then beliefs may be thought of as the framework for cognitive perception, the process whereby decision makers rationalize and analyse their situation according to what they consciously believe about the world. A good deal of work has been done on the effect of beliefs on decision making, particularly where 'beliefs' can be interpreted as an ideology or a religious code, by definition a neat and relatively coherent arrangements of beliefs. Thus studies have concentrated on the effect of authoritarian, fascist, communist and liberal capitalist beliefs on leaders, and more recently on the influence of Islam and Hinduism.

Two major questions arise in relation to beliefs. The first is what a belief system holds to be true of the international world. Fascist and communist ideologies maintain relatively clear views of the nature of international politics; liberal capitalism does so rather less, since it arose through a more pluralist historical process. Most belief systems, however, cannot be characterized so simply as 'ideology' and in reality are shifting aggregations of other beliefs. Nevertheless, certain major premises often emerge with clarity. Belief systems tend at the very least to establish a pattern of adversaries, since societies define themselves and others to a large extent according to what they believe and what they assume other societies believe. During the Cold War, for example, the principal great power players assumed that whether a society was 'communist' or 'capitalist' was the most important single fact of its international posture. That this became increasingly untrue after 1960 is a tribute to the power of beliefs in keeping the distinction meaningful for so long afterwards.

The second relevant question is to what extent beliefs affect decision makers in the day-to-day process of shaping policy. For all the elegance of an ideology, does not sheer human pragmatism emerge when leaders are confronted by the prosaic difficulties of real political decision making? The answer is not obvious. Certainly, pragmatism is an impressive motivator of human decision makers and most religions and ideologies allow plenty of room for interpretation. There is at least as much pragmatism as fundamentalism in contemporary Islam, for instance, which allows Islamic states to accommodate their behaviour to an international system that is still dominated by the West and, more importantly, to an international economic system that is now thoroughly market-led after the collapse of

4. See R. Neustadt and R. May, *Thinking in Time*, New York: Free Press, 1986.

the Bretton Woods regime in the early 1970s.[5] The same was true of the major powers of the communist world, who behaved in a highly pragmatic manner in the international system. Their ideological commitment was manifested most strongly in the domestic sphere and it was the source of their ultimate downfall that their international pragmatism was not matched by a similar approach to social and economic organization at home.

And yet, beliefs do matter as a decision-making variable. Within the general pressure that events put on decision makers to be pragmatic, individuals still have to interpret what they see in the outside world. Beliefs provide frameworks of perception which act as filters of information that guide decision makers as to what should be regarded as relevant and what should not. The communist Soviet Union, for example, had more intelligence information – both overt and covert – about Western powers and leaders than any society in history has ever possessed about its adversaries, yet its choice of relevant information and the interpretations made by Soviet leaders of that information proved to be gross distortions of reality. They placed far too much emphasis on the social inequalities and economic crises of Western societies instead of on some of the underlying strengths, apparently because that generation of Soviet leaders believed Western societies were primarily driven by institutionalized inequality. Equally, Western leaders overestimated the pragmatism of Soviet military planners. During the Cold War NATO had absolutely no plans, and little real ability, to launch a 'bolt from the blue' aggressive strike against the Warsaw Pact, and Western planners assumed that since this was demonstrably the case, Soviet leaders could not genuinely fear such an attack: their protestations that they did were only propaganda. But it is now clear that this is exactly what senior military leaders in the Soviet Union did believe. Since the West was believed to be an adversary which would become more aggressive in its final social decline, NATO was perceived as a genuine threat to the Warsaw Pact. NATO's assumption that pragmatic common sense would prevail between military professionals on both sides who could see and evaluate what was there and how it would be used in battle simply did not do justice to the power of beliefs – particularly collective beliefs – in filtering the selection and interpretation of information.

A fourth set of variables concerns the psychological processes that are embodied in decision making. The most popular work on this aspect of the study has been done on the psychological processes of key political leaders in times of crisis. But in fact, some understanding of psychological processes in decision making is vital at all governmental levels. The psychology of a lowly official who fails to perceive or transmit some vital

5. See J. Piscatori, *Islam in a World of Nation-States*, Cambridge: Cambridge University Press, 1986.

piece of information, or the officer who suppresses doubts on the reliability of equipment, or the adviser who has conflicting personal interests
in an issue, may be just as important as the psychology of the leader to
the whole process. Psychological variables apply throughout the decision-
making system.

The essence of the psychological variable is to try to get closer to the
internal logic of decision makers as they repond to stimuli. Particular
concerns include the ways in which certain types of personalities react to
external or internal pressures. Most decision makers, for example, will
tend to try to avoid conflict, but some decision makers positively promote
it since it is part of their personality type; conflicts offer the prospect of
resolving issues in their favour and confirm their power. British Prime
Minister Margaret Thatcher, in contrast to her predecessor, Edward Heath,
offers a classic case of a personality type which regarded confrontation
as a fundamentally important way of making progress; a factor that
became highly relevant in the circumstances of the Falklands conflict.[6]
Other factors include the definition of 'operational codes' by which officials and leaders will tend to see the world; these are concerned mainly
with the perception in decision makers' minds of the relationship between
different factors. Leaders who saw Soviet military developments as a part
of a Kremlin master plan to further the influence of the communist world,
for example, were operating on a different set of operational codes to those
who saw such military developments as evidence of internal inertia and
a defence production system running effectively on autopilot. Or again,
leaders who see militant Islam in the 1990s as a conspiracy against the
West – even part of a 'Confucian-Islamic connection' – are working on
different operational codes to those who see the phenomenon primarily
as a reaction to the internal dynamics of those societies. In this respect,
decision makers will respond differently to certain types of stimuli. Political leaders are also likely to be greatly moved by various symbols and
stimuli which pertain in the domestic political setting; most political leaders have one eye on the next election and certain symbols will, for them,
be much more powerful than for officials who do not have a domestic
political constituency to appease.

A further set of psychological issues concerns the ways in which decision makers reconcile conflicts in their own operational codes. A good
deal of work has been done on the problems of cognitive consistency and
cognitive dissonance: studies of cognitive dissonance in particular concentrate on the ways in which decision makers handle information which
may be inconvenient or contradictory to their view of the world and the
operational codes on which they base their decisions. It is possible for

6. See H. Young, *One of Us: A Biography of Margaret Thatcher*, London: Pan Books,
1990.

decision makers to use quite contradictory facts and information to bolster a particular view of the world, and there are many ways in which inconvenient material can be shown to be a double bluff, an exception which proves the rule, or to emanate from unreliable sources. This is particularly important when decision makers are under pressure, since one of the most observable psychological patterns in a crisis is where decision makers become confused and anxious at the overload of information and therefore become more committed to one course of action. There seems to be a premium on consistency in a crisis, and fearing that they will be left behind by the sheer speed of events, leaders often become stubborn and tend to fit contradictory information neatly into a consistent but increasingly artificial picture which bolsters their instinct rather than any rational calculation as to the course they should adopt.

There are, therefore, many psychological processes which should be taken into account in constructing foreign policy models. Though the tendency in FPA has been to concentrate on psychological processes under the pressure of international crises, psychological processes in routine foreign policy are arguably more important since they will dominate the day-to-day workings of policy. The need of officials, for example, to deal with enormous amounts of routine paperwork results in 'satisficing', whereby they do not look for the best or optimum solution to their problems but merely the first satisfactory solution that is available. Given that there is a tendency for most officials to regard their job as completed once the relevant piece of paper has left their desk, they will tend to take the option which most rapidly passes the matter on to another department rather than consider some of the wider or optimum implications for policy output as a whole, which would be more time-consuming and would possibly exceed their own authority. The phenomenon of 'satisficing', therefore, tends to produce minimally acceptable policy outcomes as opposed to good policy outcomes. In a perfect world, the search for optimum solutions as opposed to 'satisficing' solutions should be generated from the top down, but in reality the top of the decision-making hierarchy is so conditioned by what is done lower down that the technique of 'satisficing' is ubiquitous throughout most decision-making systems. And, of course, administrative cultures differ, so that what will 'satisfy' officials in one system as an acceptable level of performance may not be regarded as satisfactory in another.

A fifth set of variables builds on these ideas and addresses what may be termed the 'group dynamics' of policy making. At the most superficial level, there is the well-understood process of 'group-think' whereby it becomes psychologically difficult for an individual to argue something that is contrary to the collective views of a group. Indeed, where a group asserts that something is the case – even the observation of a physical phenomenon – individuals will think they see things which may simply not be there, or will discount clear observations they themselves made where other members of a group failed to make them; or worse, where they deride anyone who claims to have seen the phenomenon. In short, there is abundant scientific evidence to support the psychological reality of the fable of the emperor's new suit of clothes. The group-think phenomenon is not so much that a policy system will make it difficult for a dissident voice to be heard, but rather that the voice will simply lose its dissidence as an individual questions his own judgement from within.

The more complex processes of group dynamics which affect policy processes concern the ways decision-making groups can work, their implicit rules of procedure and seniority, their ability to filter out inputs which do not conform to a type with which they are familiar, and the sheer power of consensus in groups which meet for more than one purpose. This latter dynamic is most important, for the vast majority of policy-making groups – cabinet committees, meetings of officials, presidential adviser lunches – meet for more than one purpose, or to consider more than one issue. This means that very few issues indeed will ever be considered strictly on their intrinsic merits; all will be reflections of a continuum of debate in which, to some extent, victories on one issue will have to be paid for with defeats on another. This is one reason why consensus is so powerful in a regular policy-making group. Consensus does not imply that everyone agrees on an issue, but rather that no one disagrees strongly enough to be prepared to pay the price of dissent; conversely, lack of consensus in a decision-making group (though far less common, because leaders do not willingly surround themselves with divisive groups unless for a purpose of their own) may not indicate that there is disagreement necessarily on that issue, but only that there is disagreement; the issue may simply be the focus of it. Almost all policy-making groups tend towards a kind of operating consensus. Where groups habitually disagree they will tend to become moribund, as the members who do agree will meet elsewhere or will find ways of bypassing the effects of the disagreement. This is as true of the 'national salvation councils' beloved of dictators as it is of cabinet committees set up to work by consensus.

The dynamics by which a system arrives at consensus, maintains it, reinforces it and then uses it, are of great interest to the student of foreign policy. It has often been observed, for example, that during the Second World War Churchill had greater personal power at his disposal in Britain than Hitler had in Germany, precisely because the British governmental system was, from top-to-bottom, more consensual than that of Nazi Germany and when it finally resolved itself to war – not until April 1940, in the event – the Prime Minister had immense personal power. Equally, nothing will so quickly hobble a decision-making process as competition between groups who naturally tend towards consensus within themselves but who then compete on a roughly equal basis in a horizontally-structured system which does not organize their different views into a usable consensus. In extreme cases, government becomes little more than an arena for a bureaucratic contest; this happened to major aspects of Japanese military planning during the latter years of the Second World War, to the defence and foreign policies of the French Fourth Republic after 1945, and in some policy areas, at various times, in post-war US defence policy. It also happened between leaders of the different branches of the armed forces within the Argentine military during the Falklands War. Group dynamics can therefore be regarded as the structural manifestation of many other variables already mentioned, especially socialization, beliefs and the psychological processing which gives tangible expression to both: all these affect the terms on which groups will operate, their versions of consensus and how much consensus will affect those 'groups of groups' which make up a whole foreign policy system.

A sixth, and final, major set of variables is the information processing characteristics of any system. Earlier works on the development of cybernetic and computing processes have proved particularly useful here. Information is the single most vital ingredient in a decision-making system, and the way it is processed, sifted, redirected, interpreted and summarized is of critical importance in understanding the performance of any system. At its simplest, information has to go from the bottom of the decision-making system to the top – for example, from embassies to prime ministers – while constantly being filtered and summarized. Each level of the system aims to give some added value to the information, to summarize it, add supporting information or simply decide who needs to see it. At every stage, the bottom-to-top process is filtering ambiguity out of the raw material and making it conform to a pattern. And that will coincide with another flow of information which constitutes instructions going downwards, from top-to-bottom. At each level the instructions – for example, from the prime minister – will have to be made more explicit, expanded and developed as each level in the system thinks about how to honour the spirit of a request when the prime minister clearly did not specify quite how a new civil project was to be developed, or how youth orchestra exchanges were precisely to be handled.[7]

Needless to say, this is a highly idealized view of information processing which takes no account of deliberate motives for mishandling information, or the problems of sheer overload where information is inadvertently mishandled. There is a wealth of literature on the well-known mishaps and tragedies caused by the deliberate or inadvertent mishandling of infor-

---

7. On the wealth of literature on this topic see A. Dunsire, *Implementation in a Bureaucracy*, Oxford: Martin Robertson, 1978.

mation at critical moments,[8] and for each such tragedy there are a thousand inconveniences which are not made public. This must be accepted as a fact of policy-making life.

More interesting for our purposes, however, is the view of information handling not so much as sequential (up and down) but rather as a simultaneous process which constitutes the lifeblood of bureaucracy. In reality, it is difficult to see a single piece of information go 'up' through the system and emerge in its filtered and processed form at the top (even though there are some celebrated examples of this happening). More typically, any given piece of information forms part of the circulation of information lifeblood through the system: it can be rejected, transformed, absorbed and so on. There are so many personal and systemic influences on the quality, amount and circulation of this lifeblood that we have to regard it as an indispensible variable in the construction of any foreign policy model.

The majority of information will tend to be handled by the use of cybernetic triggers; that is, if information is perceived to be 'about' two or three topics – a perception usually triggered by key words or phrases – then the system will react by sending the information automatically to the persons responsible for those particular matters. At some stage, information may be handled with a high degree of personal discretion as its deeper implications are appreciated, but it will already have gone through a number of semi-cybernetic triggering processes to reach that particular responsible individual, and by then it will be batched and packaged with other information as the bureaucratic lifeblood thickens. Information, in other words, can be handled in an infinite number of ways, and judgements on what constitutes good and bad information processing depend first on the specification of what a decision-making process is designed to achieve. This brings us to the next stage, where it is necessary to specify some of the most relevant policy models.

The Articulation of Foreign Policy Models

There are many different types of foreign policy models, some more complex than others; some make full use of the various nuances involved in the types of variables specified here, while others are very parsimonious with them. All such models share a common strand in that they are attempts to represent foreign policy action, the ever-changing and mysterious process by which policy systems stimulate collective human behaviour. For the sake of clarity, three types of foreign policy model can be identi-

8. N. Dixon, *On the Psychology of Military Incompetence*, London: Futura Books, 1976.

fied, all of which have originated a number of particular variants and middle range theories.

The first type can be characterized as 'rational actor' models of foreign policy.[9] These represent the most instinctive type of policy modelling; it seems natural to assume that policy is not conducted in an irrational manner, but it must represent something. In fact, the term 'rational actor' is something of a misnomer, for it does not assume that the foreign policy system will act in a rational way – that is, in a correct way, or in a way in which optimal outcomes are achieved. Policy may proceed in a rational actor fashion and yet be a complete failure, or be transparently self-defeating. All that is implied in rational actor models is that the behaviour of the policy system is purposeful. To be more precise, it assumes that decisions are taken by those individuals who are supposed to take them; that the decisions are meaningful and not merely rubber stamps of something done elsewhere; that the leaders have some sense of what their policy objectives are; that the situation surrounding the decision has been consciously assessed and alternatives have been mapped out; that one of those alternatives is adopted; and that the effects of the decision in the outside world are then monitored and measured against the original objectives. Whether or not the choice turns out to be   it, it follows from an act of rational analysis by the system's 'brain'. In other words, rational actor models treat the policy-making system as if it were a card player, facing each trick of the game and making intelligent – if not necessarily very precise – choices.

In arranging the variables outlined above, rational actor models assume that power maps are generally congruent with reality. Whether or not the system is democratic, those leaders who think they are taking key decisions are in fact doing so. The socialization process and the power of personal beliefs allows those leaders to have a clear sense of their various objectives and helps them to arrange multiple objectives into a hierarchy of preferences. Psychological processes are given less prominence, and it is assumed that whatever pressures decision makers are under, they nevertheless continue to engage in a process of analysis even though psychological pressures may make the analysis progressively faulty. Information is processed in an essentially 'up-down' manner and is used to articulate a range of choices, and group pressures build consensus around a relatively small range of options from which the choice is eventually made.

All decision-making systems would like to believe that they work in this way, and the essential hypotheses that these models yield are that the

9. See M. Clarke, 'The Foreign Policy System: A Framework for Analysis', in M. Clarke and B. White (eds), *Understanding Foreign Policy*, Aldershot: Edward Elgar, 1989, pp. 27–59.

preferences of leaders – singly or in groups – will determine outcomes in the real world of foreign policy. But of course, life is never as neat and tidy as a card game. Rational actor models represent something of an ideal against which actual policy making can be measured. It was the failure of rational actor models to explain key features of observable policy making that led analysts to articulate different types of foreign policy models. In his seminal work on rational actor models, Graham Allison concluded that US behaviour in the Cuban missile crisis was characterized by a great deal of rational action;[10] this was such a dramatic and brief crisis that the US presidential system worked in a way which was as close to the rational actor ideal as we were ever likely to see. And yet even in this situation, critical aspects of the crisis could not be accounted for by rational actor assumptions alone. How much more insufficient, therefore, must the model be in less dramatic or in purely routine settings? There has thus been a major impetus to develop different angles from which to view the mysterious sculpture in the dark room.

But, however limited rational actor models may be, they are remarkably ubiquitous, especially among those who do not believe in the use of models. The model represents what we would like to believe normally happens, which is the most instinctive of foreign policy assumption to make. Just as those who claim not to be interested in politics are almost always intuitively conservative, so those who eschew foreign policy models are invariably – and implicitly – 'rational actorists'. If nothing else, models expose the assumptions that agnostic academics make.

The second type of foreign policy models may be described as administrative process models. These concentrate not so much on leadership but rather on the standard operating procedures of the administration as a whole. Power maps are less important as a variable than administrative mores, and the psychology of groups and the power of collective beliefs, because they critically affect the ways in which information is handled, are given greater prominence than individual preferences or the inclinations of political leaders. Such models assume, therefore, that the momentum built up by administrators behind certain analyses of a situation, or behind the articulation of choices, becomes the real decision maker. The typical hypotheses yielded by such models are that in most cases of decision making, feasible alternatives may not be put because they have been filtered out by the system before the leadership considers them; that the system may not even know there are other alternatives because its receptors simply do not recognize what they see; or that the system may simply be unable to articulate

10. G. Allison, *Essence of Decision*, Boston: Little Brown, 1971. For a summary of the critiques of the theory see S. Smith, 'Perspectives on the Foreign Policy System: Bureaucratic Politics Approaches', in M. Clarke and B. White (eds), *Understanding Foreign Policy*, pp. 109–34.

choices because it is preoccupied with internal administrative problems. All of these hypotheses yield outcomes which account for much real foreign policy behaviour; things happen not so much because of a purposeful act of choice by the system as a whole, but more because of its standard operating procedures.

These administrative characteristics take a number of specific forms. One of the most generally recognized is that of incrementalism. This is a general term which summarizes the tendency of all administrative systems to make decisions in a series of small, sequential steps; officials within the system deal with their own portion of a matter, and necessarily do not consider implications that fall outside their remit. By incremental progression, therefore, major decisions are effectively made at low levels of political responsibility by officials who are not aware of their real role in them. By the time senior leaders *appear* to take the decision they may have little genuine discretion left to exercise, beyond that of presentation. Incrementalism therefore exists to some extent in all decision-making systems, and is generally regarded as the enemy of the individual leader.

Another administrative characteristic which is built into such models is the operational process of the foreign policy system in question. Some administrations are highly centralized while others are quite decentralized; some will take a certain amount of time to process a standard piece of information, regardless of how urgent it is, while others will be able to react more quickly. All administrations have their own peculiar characteristics, and an understanding of these is vital to the workings of this type of model. Some writers have tried to codify these operational characteristics into the study of what they have called 'bureaumetrics', a classification of operational modes within British central government which helps account for the ways in which different ministries and departments make policy.[11] Such studies can apply to any level of administration: at an international level, the operational processes of the European Commission are very different to those of Whitehall, as they work within a different structure and a more gallic administrative culture and have many more constraints on their actions. At a sub-national level, it can be observed in many Western societies that police forces have different administrative and operational characteristics from the security services with whom their work overlaps, causing frequent difficulties between them.

Yet another well-observed administrative characteristic is that of bureaucratic politics. This is a rather specific process – most prevalent in decentralized policy-making systems – whereby different sections of the administrative machine knowingly compete with each other for the ear of decision makers and try to engineer foreign policy decisions which explicitly benefit their own part of the bureaucracy. The most prevalent

11. A. Hood and A. Dunsire, *Bureaumetrics*, Farnborough: Gower, 1981.

example of bureaucratic policy processes arises in the case of the natural competition between the armed forces in developed societies. In this model it is assumed by arms control agencies that the best way of ensuring the security of the country is through more arms control while the military, by contrast, assume that the best option is more military hardware; and within the military, as one might expect, the navy (or the army or the air force) assume that more hardware for their own service is the best guarantee of the country's security. The result of such competitive administrative drives in these models is that leaders may simply be unable to take clear decisions, or else may take compromise decisions which fail to address anyone's concerns fully. The particular hypotheses yielded by bureaucratic approaches in administrative models are that where there is conscious competition between administrative agencies over the course of policy, a significant – even a predominant – explanation of the outcome will lie in the result of this internal competition rather than in a decision taken in response to the external foreign policy issue itself.

Aside from a case of straight illogicality, or simple madness on the part of dicatorial leaders, bureaucratic politics represents the antithesis of the rational actor model. The notion of bureaucratic politics has attracted a great deal of attention over the last quarter century and has been both lauded and denounced; its value is generally well-appreciated. Bureaucratic politics can be presented as a trite model of foreign policy action, which nevertheless contains vital insights into some of the ways foreign policy systems work some of the time; the rational actor model is also trite which is why they are both useful models. There are elements of bureaucratic politics, just as there are elements of rational action, in most foreign policy decision making. The interesting questions concern which systems, and which types of issues within those systems, tend to validate one explanation as opposed to another.

A final category of models is that concerned with the implementation of policy. It has been acknowledged only comparatively recently that the implementation of policy had been neglected in FPA and that it requires the articulation of distinctive models to explicate the processes involved.[12] Implementation has to be seen as part of the whole decision-making system; it is not the epilogue to a foreign policy decision, or the end of the matter. Decisions and their implementation form a constantly flowing continuum and the experience of implementation feeds into the thinking behind future decisions and further implementation. All the characteristics of decision making can therefore apply to the implementation stages since implementation requires a series of subordinate decisions as the policy is translated into specifics. Incrementalism, rational action and opera-

---

12. S. Smith and M. Clarke (eds), *Foreign Policy Implementation*, London: Allen & Unwin, 1985.

tional processes all have their place in implementation models, but such models are built on certain assumptions specific to the business of implementing major decisions.

One assumption of implementation is that not all foreign policy decisions require action, in the generally understood sense of the term. Some decisions are self-implementing in that they are enacted in the very act of being made, while other decisions are known and understood to be impossible to enact – or at least to enact immediately – but are made nevertheless. Only a certain proportion of what we can define as discrete foreign policy decisions require action to follow from them. Implementation models thus begin by asking what can be expected to happen as the result of a policy decision, and then trace lines of causation back to the central authorities from whom the decision flows. Implementation models also assume that lower-level officials in any system are more important than is commonly imagined; not because they wield formal power, or even because they might overtly disagree with their leaders, but rather because of their inate ability to prioritize between different functions they have to perform, their tendency to marginally delay the enactment of new policies so that multiple minor 'administrative' tardiness becomes a major policy delay and the importance of their professional morale to the overall working of the policy machine that along with many other characteristics, are typical manifestations of the incremental power of the implementers.

Yet another assumption of implementation models is that sheer complexity of action is not merely a hurdle to foreign policy action but is rather a political factor in its own right. In order to overcome what has been called 'the complexity of joint action', it is necessary for political authorities to form effective coalitions of implementers, and hold them together for long enough to get the policy enacted. Thus in these models the nature of implementers' coalitions – the way they are formed, the bonds which hold them together, the ways in which they reform in response to change and the political strength it takes to break them – are critical to an understanding of foreign policy outputs. Some systems will allow the formation of new implementation coalitions more easily than others,while some coalitions will only hold together for as long as certain key personalities are involved in them.

At the most extreme, implementation models would deny to decision makers any genuine influence over action. There is, said Tolstoy, a flow of events in which leaders and military commanders are the least important people. Only those commanders, like Kutuzov in *War and Peace*, who can sense the flow of events and go with them can be successful.[13] Human affairs are dominated by the accretion of an infinite number of individual human decisions: the most that leaders can do is to influence the way they

13. L. Tolstoy, *War and Peace*, London: Penguin Books, 1957, pp. 896, 1420–1.

are presented. Again, however, an extreme implementation model is trite, yielding hypotheses that decisions are really made from the 'bottom up' according to what most suits the officials; this is not true in the real world, at least not in such a stark form, but the models do explicate a number of characteristics of foreign policy which suggest, for example, the importance of the policy learning process from one decision to the next, how resistant to change systems can be from the top, and how politicized foreign policy systems can be down to even low levels.

The Application of Foreign Policy Models to the Falklands Crisis

This chapter has attempted to sketch out the rationale and the most important contributions FPA can make to the understanding of foreign policy in general; individual analysts will apply some of these perspectives in their own thinking to the Falklands crisis of 1982; examples of everything that has been mentioned so far can be found in the various foreign policies that collectively make up the 'Falklands issue'. Four major forms of application of FPA models can be outlined: these concern the differential use of models to illuminate the way a foreign policy issue changes; the adding of an extra dimension of comparison between national actors to that which is normally intuitive; the provision of a heuristic device to ask appropriate questions of detail and compare the answers, and the provision of a framework in which the domestic politics of the most relevant actors can be analysed.

The first general pattern worth noting is the use of different models in order to better understand the way the changing situation in 1982 – from peace to war – affected policy-making processes. During peacetime, the Argentine government seemed to be operating on predominantly rational actor principles in its policy of trying to force and then control a 'Malvinas crisis' during 1981–2.[14] On the basis of a purposeful calculation, there was every reason to believe that if a successful invasion could only be mounted then Britain would not try to retake the islands, and the world would feel sufficiently sympathetic, or indifferent, to Argentine claims to let a *fait accompli* stand. Though this analysis turned out to be wrong, it was a rational calculation with which independent observers would have agreed. During the same period, however, British policy towards the issue can best be explained as a system running on political autopilot while administrative processes dominated the policy output. The government failed to

14. L. Freedman and V. Gamba-Stonehouse, *Signals of War: The Falklands Conflict of 1982*, London: Faber & Faber, 1990.

address the issue at cabinet level on three separate occasions between 1979 and 1982, while other departments were pursuing policies on different issues – cost-cutting, new immigration rules, United Nations diplomacy – which had the side effect of giving an impression that Britain's commitment to the Falklands was rapidly waning.[15] At best, British Falklands policy prior to March 1982 could be described as 'benign neglect'.

Once the invasion had taken place, however, and the situation rapidly altered from peace to the prospect of war, British policy making became almost classically rational actor. The decision-making system became highly consensual at all levels; although it was directed by a small war cabinet at the very top of the system, the direct influence of that group was exerted deep down the implementation chain, so that particular orders – such as the sinking of the *General Belgrano* – were issued, and even reconfirmed, from Downing Street. During the same period, however, the pressures of the impending war seem to have opened up critical bureaucratic fissures within the Argentine leadership which, in the event, adversely affected both policy making and its implementation. Though the form – the 'power map' – of the Argentine government remained the same, the working of it became impaired by the pressures of the situation, and while British administrative consensus grew, that within the Argentine system declined.

Similar distinctions can be made, if less dramatically, between the ways in which allied and neutral governments reacted to the move from peace to war. The government of the United States in particular began by reacting to the crisis in a disaggregated way: President Reagan tried to keep his options open and to avoid having to choose between two different allies, while the Defence Department under the leadership of Caspar Weinberger gave Britain immediate military support for its planned operation. This support did not explicitly contradict the presidential approach, but it certainly threatened to undercut it. Once a conflict had become unavoidable, however, US policy was more unified as the President was forced to support his NATO ally rather than a less important ally in South America. The difference between 'normality' and 'crisis', and between 'crisis' and 'conflict', are to a significant extent determined by the way decision-making systems react to what they perceive. In this case, the US government entered a 'crisis' mentality some time after the government of Argentina and Britain, after which its choices were more constrained. The European allies, on the other hand, never entered the crisis phases since they were at a greater distance from the problem and always had significantly more room for manoeuvre.

---

15. *Falkland Islands Review: Report of a Committee of Privy Counsellors, Chairman the Rt. Hon. the Lord Franks*, Cmnd. 8787, London: HMSO, 1983.

A second insight concerns the different foreign policy systems embodied in all the governments concerned. While governments articulated their national positions on the issue, their different types of foreign policy systems also conditioned the ways in which they were able to react to a fast-moving situation. Though it is intuitively important to understand that the Spanish and Italian governments, for example, were more naturally sympathetic to a South American country and that this made their support for the British position more tentative, it is also important to analyse their difficulties in reacting to a crisis which went swiftly from peace to war and which was thereafter quickly concluded. Similarly, the reactions of Italy at least (Spain was not then a member of the EC) had to be coordinated through a complex politico-bureaucratic arena within the European Community and – for both Spain and Italy – through NATO, which built in competing pressures and incentives to compromise which all added to the difficulties these countries had in expressing a purely 'national interest' over the conflict. To put it another way, the British were both skilful and lucky once the invasion had taken place: skilful in being able to manage the growing crisis and stealing a march on their potential critics both diplomatically and militarily, and lucky in not meeting any major technical or military hitches which would have prolonged the conflict and allowed diplomatic support to ebb away as casualties mounted. Having allowed themselves to be presented with an Argentine *fait accompli* in the invasion of the islands, the British government in effect presented its allies with another *fait accompli* by retaking them within two months.

Thirdly, an awareness of FPA models should be used to ask the right questions about the fine detail of national responses to the crisis. Argentine information-processing and the interpretation of intelligence emerges as a major area of concern when trying to understand why after the invasion the Argentine leadership failed to perceive the nature of their opposition, and psychological process explanations will offer some hypotheses as to why the leadership's position atrophied once conflict became a likelihood. Similar questions should be asked of the British policy system. This had all the information required to make an accurate assessment of Argentine intentions; indeed, parts of the policy machine made very accurate predictions, but the system as a whole failed to interpret the information correctly, in part because of deep psychological pressures towards conservative interpretations of the information inputs. In the event, the psychology of Mrs Thatcher and her determination to retake the islands by force if necessary proved to be a dominant explanatory factor in the way her government handled and interpreted all subsequent inputs after 2 April 1982.

To understand the early US response more deeply, one needs to ask questions that derive from administrative process models of foreign policy behaviour. Britain and Argentina had fairly concrete ideas as to what they wanted from the crisis; both had clear – and irreconcilable – goals. The US response was much more ambiguous. It should be asked, therefore, whether this was because the US had genuinely ambiguous national interests in the crisis which were distilled through the position of the president (the rational actor explanation), or rather whether it was because different agencies in the US foreign policy system – the White House, the Department of Defense, the State Department, the US mission at NATO, the US ambassador at the UN – took differing views of what was at stake for the US and were given the freedom to compete with each other in a relatively decentralized policy system. Similar questions could be asked about most aspects of the outputs of all the countries involved in the crisis.

The final type of application for FPA models in the case of the Falklands crisis concerns the importance of the domestic context in the determination of the policy positions of all the relevant actors. The role of elites, parties, interest groups and particular economic circumstances looms large in determining why a policy system works in a particular way at a given time. France, for example, is generally characterized by a centralized state, but this does not automatically make the state all powerful in the face of domestic interests, and there may be as much competition within the different *corps* of the bureaucracy as between the bureaucracy and the private sector.[16] Most of the governments of Britain's European allies during the conflict were under pressure from domestic interests of various sizes and strengths, which militated against rational actor decision making. The aggregation of separate interests into a 'national interest', still less a 'European interest', was difficult to maintain for those actors on the periphery of the issue.

For Britain and the United States, and most especially for Argentina, the domestic context was critical in certain contexts. It affected the personal perceptions and reactions of General Galtieri, President Reagan and Prime Minister Thatcher. In their cases, there is little evidence that they were subjected to the pressures of organized interest groups – the crisis was too short for these to come into play – but their perceptions of what the wider public expected of them and the ways in which these expectations might affect the party machinery (and in the case of Galtieri, the lower echelons of the armed forces whose support was crucial to the survival of the *junta*) reduced their room for manoeuvre and tended to force them to rely on instinct rather than analysis.

In short, all of the types of model outlined here raise relevant questions about the foreign policy behaviour of the actors in the crisis. Analysts will look for those areas of policy making in which different models offer

16. See E. Ritchie, 'France', in M. Harrop (ed.), *Power and Policy in Liberal Democracies*, Cambridge: Cambridge University Press, 1992, pp. 42–4.

complementary or at least consistent answers, and they will want to probe further those areas of behaviour where different models yield contradictory hypotheses. In such cases the fault may lie either in the quality of the information available to answer the questions posed by the model, or in the articulation of the model itself and its applicability to the Falklands issue. Whether implicitly or explicitly, the analyst constantly makes such judgements. This dialectical relationship between information and model remains one of the sounder tools of social science analysis.

– 2 –

Europe and the Falkland Islands Conflict[1]

Geoffrey Edwards

Introduction

The Falkland Islands conflict marked an important step for both the European Community (EC) and European Political Cooperation (EPC), the system by which the EC member states sought to coordinate their foreign policy. It revealed that the then ten member states could react quickly and decisively in a crisis, albeit one that involved a clear breach of international law and aggression against the territory of one of their own members. It indicated too the interlinkage of economic (Community) and political (EPC) instruments of foreign or external policy; when more than simply the coordination of diplomatic measures such as declarations and *démarches* were wanted, Community instruments including sanctions became necessary. The crisis thereby suggested a new multilateral framework for foreign policy, one that, potentially at least, gave additional international weight and a complementary dimension to national policy even if at the same time it brought the possibility of added costs and necessary compromises in other areas of policy.

At the same time, the Falklands conflict also revealed clearly the limits to any common action and agreement. Once the diplomatic crisis gave way to war and the UK resorted to the unilateral use of force, the consensus of the Ten came under ever greater strain. For the British, the Falklands crisis may have reinforced their view that the EPC/EC remained a somewhat limited supplement to national policy; for others, it suggested the potential as well as perhaps the dangers of cooperative ventures and common policies. Certainly it showed the importance of the role of the United Nations in providing legitimation for any such action, as well as the

---

1. This chapter is based largely on an article by the author that first appeared in the *Journal of Common Market Studies*, vol. 22, no. 4, 1984, pp. 295-313, under the title 'The European Community and the Falkland Islands Crisis'.

continued significance of the United States and the need for at least its tacit support.

The Community and its member states have rarely moved with such speed as they did in the Falklands case. It was perhaps fortuitous that the Political Directors of the Ten happened to be meeting in Brussels on 2 April 1982, debating *inter alia* the possibilities of extending foreign policy cooperation to security issues within the Genscher-Colombo Initiative.[2] Argentina's invasion of the Falkland Islands was condemned immediately by the member states of the European Community. This display of solidarity was followed rapidly by agreement on an arms embargo. This was of particular importance given the quantity and sophistication of the arms being exported by Community member states to Argentina; France was supplying *Super Etendards* and *Exocet* missiles, Germany had already sold two submarines and was building frigates, and Italy was supplying aircraft and helicopters. The readiness of member states to introduce an arms embargo was evident and, individually, they imposed one within the first week of the conflict.

The response to Britain's call for an import embargo on Argentinian goods took only a few days longer to complete. The Committee of Permanent Representatives (COREPER) met on 6 and 7 April; the political directors met again on the morning of 9 April, Good Friday, and COREPER met the same afternoon and again on Saturday, 10 April. The imposition of a month-long import ban was then announced by foreign ministers. The precise texts of the embargo were agreed on 14 April and entered into effect two days later.

In taking their decisions, the Ten were strongly influenced by moves made at the United Nations and in Washington. The 2 April declaration, for example, included a reference to the call from the President of the UN Security Council for restraint to be shown and for negotiations on the future of the Falklands to be continued. Of even greater importance was Security Council Resolution 502 agreed on 3 April (drafted by Sir Anthony Parsons, the UK Ambassador to the UN), which called for the immediate withdrawal of Argentinian forces and for both parties to seek a 'diplomatic solution to their differences and to respect fully the purposes and principles of the Charter of the United Nations'.

The role of the UN remained of considerable importance as a reference point both for the Ten, including the UK, and for the United States. Clearly the American administration was regarded as the only government likely to have any influence with the Argentinian *junta*, if it chose to use it. Inevitably, therefore, the Community was only one centre of UK attention, and once

2. For a discussion of the Initiative, see G. Bonvicini, 'The Genscher-Colombo Plan and the "Solemn Declaration on European Union" (1981–3)', in Roy Pryce (ed.), *The Dynamics of European Union*, London: Croom Helm, 1987, pp. 174–87.

the imposition of sanctions against Argentina had been agreed the Community became very much subordinate to the USA; that is, until support among the EC member governments began to deteriorate, a fact not wholly unrelated to this lack of attention. Yet focus on the United States was perhaps inevitable given initial American ambivalence and the division within the administration between 'Europeanists' and 'Latinos',[3] the subsequent attempts by Secretary of State Haig to bring about a settlement through shuttle diplomacy, and the importance of US military assistance to the British effort. The failure to maintain EC solidarity had no particular impact on the British war effort, though it had some costs in terms of other British concerns within Europe, and sanctions were continued by eight member states; the fact that the sanctions were continued by the majority in the middle of an armed conflict and when pressures for a ceasefire were considerable cannot itself be considered wholly unsuccessful.

The Issue of Sanctions

If action at the Community level has necessarily to be seen against a background of frenetic diplomatic activity in Washington and at the UN, the issue of economic sanctions as such was not new to the Community. As members of the UN, the member states had imposed sanctions against the illegal white regime in Rhodesia; at the behest of the Americans they had also introduced restrictions on trade with Iran after the seizure of the hostages and, again largely thanks to an American initiative, sanctions were the subject of considerable debate in the aftermath of the Soviet invasion of Afghanistan, though those that resulted were of a very limited character. Limited sanctions were introduced against the Soviet Union after the imposition of martial law in Poland in December 1981, again largely at the behest of the United States. As a result, it has been suggested[4] that the fact that there was no pressure from the United States over the Falklands made decisions on Argentina easier to take.

It was considered of fundamental importance that the Ten should be seen as active and in concert. After the Argentine seizure of the Falkland Islands, the British had unilaterally imposed an import ban, but British trade with Argentina was small, with Argentina ranking only forty-second among the UK's trade partners.[5] The act was therefore very much symbolic rather than injurious and an embargo by Argentina's largest market, the

3. See L. Freedman and V. Gamba-Stonehouse, *Signals of War: The Falklands Conflict of 1982*, London: Faber & Faber, 1990, p. 155.

4. S. Nuttall, *European Political Cooperation*, Oxford: Clarendon Press, 1992, p. 207.

5. See J. Pearce, 'Economic Measures', *The Falkland Islands Dispute: International Dimensions*, London: Royal Institute of International Affairs, April 1982, p. 14.

European Community, was seen as being much more significant. Some 27.7 per cent of Argentina's imports were from the EC and 31.7 per cent of its exports went to the Community. However, sanctions themselves were not expected to have an immediate economic impact; they only suggested the potential expense of the venture. What the Ten hoped was that their concerted action would have real political and psychological impact on the *junta*. It was hoped too, especially by the British, that EC sanctions would also have an impact in the United States and not just in Argentina, and encourage the US administration to take the European side and exercise whatever influence it could with the Argentinians. This dual purpose meant, however, that a rapid and complete display of European solidarity was even more imperative.

In view of past negotiations on sanctions, there was some pessimism that solidarity could be easily achieved or that it could be expressed in more than simply pious declarations. Some in England became suddenly acutely aware that the UK had not always endeared itself to its partners on EC matters, but there was the hope that since the situation was clearly one whereby the territory of a Community member state – territory explicitly linked to the Community under Part IV of the Treaty of Rome – had been attacked, the other member governments of the EC would agree to sanctions of some sort.

Fortunately, this was a position readily accepted by others within the Community. Emmanuel Gazzo, the widely read and respected editor of *Agence Europe,* took up the general point: 'It is clear that since the Falklands are part of the overseas territories associated with the Community, it is the Community which has been attacked.'[6] The European Commission made the same point in its declaration of 6 April when it condemned the Argentinian invasion and called for an Argentinian withdrawal. The declaration may have raised some eyebrows among the more legalistic officials in Whitehall, preoccupied with questions of Community competence, but it was hardly considered politic to do anything but welcome the statement. A second widely held view was expressed by the French Foreign Minister who declared: 'What is clear is that since last Friday there has been an aggression, unprovoked, uncalled for by the peoples of the Falkland Islands; then a Security Council development...and the invader did not heed it. We are on the side of those who defend international law and decisions. All the more so in the present case as the attacked party is our ally.'[7] *Die Zeit* added a further point: 'Britain is exercising its right to self-defence against unprovoked aggression. What the West and the overwhelming part of the Third World did not allow the Russians to do with

6. *Agence Europe*, 5–6 April 1982.
7. *Agence Europe*, 13–14 April 1982.

impunity in Afghanistan should not be allowed to General Galtieri.'[8] This was a particularly pertinent point in the debate within the USA.

A number of other parallels were also drawn which favoured solidarity among the Ten. Condoning aggression through inaction was regarded as an especially poor precedent: '"If you abandon 1800 Falkland Islanders", said a friendly German at this weekend's Konigswinter Conference at Cambridge, "What will 2 million West Berliners think?" The cases are scarcely comparable but it was none the less a telling point.'[9] In a somewhat similar way, attitudes in Greece were influenced by its scattered and vulnerable islands as well as, of course, the situation in Cyprus. The French too could hardly be unaware of the vulnerability of some of their remaining overseas territories, as well as being influenced by their own interventions in former colonial territories for which they had on occasion sought Community support.

Moreover there was, initially at least, a sense of moment, of participating in an important common venture. The symbolism of sanctions has been considered by others, but as Johan Galtung has suggested: 'There is the value of at least doing something, of having the illusion of being instrumental, of being busy in times of crisis.'[10] In the Falklands crisis, the illusion was magnified by the conscious feeling of acting together as a Community. As one German official was reported as saying: 'I have not had the same feeling for a long time. Here was a case where we were doing something for the Community with no national profit to be gained, in fact quite the opposite. But all governments could see that the issue of protecting territory against acquisition by force was of great importance. A Community response could not be avoided and no one wanted to avoid it.'[11]

The speed with which the initial declaration condemning Argentina's aggression was agreed was itself of no little symbolic importance and set the tone and the direction of subsequent action. Translating the declaration into an economic commitment, however, was a major achievement. There was more than an element of pure symbolism in the application of sanctions; as *The Economist* put it, 'the decision, taken after some high level arm-twisting was eased by the belief that the Falkland Islands dispute will be over before the sanctions have an economic bite rather than a purely diplomatic one.'[12] Such a view was reinforced by the exclusion of all goods in transit or for which contracts had been agreed before the actual date of the decision. In fact, non-exclusion of such goods may have

8. *The Economist*, 17 April 1982.
9. *Sunday Times*, 4 April 1982.
10. Quoted in J. Barber, 'Economic Sanctions as a Policy Instrument', *International Affairs*, vol. 55, no. 3, 1979, p. 381.
11. *Financial Times*, 27 April 1982.
12. *The Economist*, 17 April 1982.

rendered the Community liable to actions for compensation from traders suffering material loss. But since sanctions were not expected to last long, neither the Commission nor the member governments expected any difficulties or costly commitments to check and prevent the exploitation of any loopholes.

It was none the less clear that a good deal could go wrong between the agreement to condemn Argentinian aggression and the imposition of an economic embargo. In their efforts to win support, the British were helped enormously by the position taken by the Belgian government, which held the Presidency of the Council of Ministers between January and June 1982. Leo Tindemans, the Belgian Foreign Minister, was not only a staunch European (and author of the Report on European Union of 1976), but he was keen to exploit the provisions of the London Report on European Political Cooperation that had been agreed only in October 1981. He and his officials were able, at least temporarily, to sweep aside many of the sensitivities that still existed as to the legal and institutional proprieties of crossing and recrossing the boundaries between EC and EPC matters. At a more practical level, the fact that the Belgians held the Presidency allowed officials to simply move up and down the rue de la Loi between the Belgian Foreign Ministry's Palais d'Egmont and the Council of Ministers' Charlemagne building. In addition, as recommended by the London Report, a British official (representing the immediate past Council Presidency) had been seconded to the Belgian Foreign Ministry as part of the so-called Troika support team, and he was able to act as an additional, informal source of information and as a channel of communication between London and Brussels.

One issue that created an immediate obstacle was that of the Treaty base for the introduction of an import embargo. The British, on practical rather than ideological grounds, were initially in favour of using Article 224 of the Treaty of Rome whereby member states gave effect to common action through national legislation. The Iranian embargo was considered the most useful precedent for action. The idea was to avoid the arguments used before, particularly by the Danes, that as an embargo was clearly a political act rather than a part of trade policy, it should be the responsibility of national parliaments to implement and not the Community. However, the Belgian Presidency, the West Germans and the Irish were especially insistent that Article 113 should be used. The Belgian rationale was that the action was a trade matter, that common action was necessary in order to preserve the unity of the market, and therefore Article 113 was the appropriate instrument. The Germans were particularly concerned with the need to avoid any legal divergences on implementation as well as with the need for urgency. The Irish position was somewhat different as they had few economic interests involved, rather, the imposition of sanctions under Article 224 was seen as posing a political test, which threatened wholly unnecessary political difficulties for the Irish government. Article 113, on the other hand, defused the situation by making sanctions more of a Community responsibility, which somewhat distanced the government from the actual decision.

At that initial stage, the disagreement over the legal base for the embargo did not mask any more substantive opposition. However, little headway was made in COREPER despite strenuous efforts on the part of the Belgians and the British to secure agreement. It all seemed so much easier in EPC but, as it became increasingly clear, the weight of precedent, of past conflicts and package deals, was considerably less in EPC than in COREPER. And EPC did not have to decide how precisely to implement the decision that had been agreed in principle so easily; COREPER did. On 10 April, COREPER had echoed the agreement in principle that had been arrived at the day before in the meeting of political directors in EPC, but as the Danes continued to block the use of Article 113, ministers were able only to continue to declare their solidarity with the UK and point out the alternative bases for action. It was not until 14 April, after the Danes had referred the issue back to the Folketing, that they were able to agree to the Commission's proposed text. Regulation 877/82 was then adopted by the Council through its written procedure and came into force on 16 April. Significantly, the Regulation in its recitals refers to the discussions held in EPC in an order, in Nuttall's words, 'which implies that these discussions provide the necessary grounds for the Community decision.'[13]

The decision to impose an embargo on Argentinian goods had been taken within only two weeks of the invasion. *The Times* saw a particular importance in the decision when it was set against the irritation caused by Britain's budgetary claims, adding: 'In this case it is the Europeans who have reacted with a global perspective while the response of the United States has been made ambiguous by regional considerations. It is a neat turning of the tables in the trans-Atlantic debate.'[14] Given the later problems of renewing sanctions, and the interrelationship between them and the budgetary issue, it was a somewhat premature conclusion.

The Consensus Under Strain

Once sanctions had actually been agreed, there were many in the Community who felt a certain surprise that the Ten had proved so ready to take such a decision so quickly. Thus while British attention inevitably reverted

13. S. Nuttall, *European Political Cooperation*, p. 263.
14. *The Times*, 19 April 1982.

to the progress of the task force and to Washington and the Haig peace mission, in the rest of the Community there was now a sense of needing to reflect on the wider ramifications of the decision. There was also, of course, the need to deal with the more mundane items on the Community agenda, such as agricultural prices and budgetary contributions, on which the British were also fairly demanding. The linkage between these last issues and sanctions had not been clearly recognized or pressed in early April, in part at least because of the strong position taken by the Belgian Presidency, but it became increasingly apparent as the month progressed. At the same time, as hopes of any compromise faded and the task force approached the Falklands, European minds became increasingly focused on their dependence on the United States and on the United Nations to renew their peace efforts and prevent bloodshed.

What also came to the fore was the inherent ambiguity in the relationship between sanctions and the use of force. The ambiguity was neatly summed up by Barber: 'Whilst some advocates see them [sanctions] as an alternative to force, there is a contrary view that sanctions can only be effective when force is available and ready to be used.'[15] In early April, with the task force weeks away from the Falklands and the Americans active in the search for a peaceful solution, the ambiguities were regarded as of little more than academic importance. Attitudes changed as the task force drew closer to the Falklands; as Hill and Mayall have suggested, 'EPC has always been a diplomatic operation first and foremost and the prospect of being identified with major military operations against a country which could claim membership of the Third World unnerved many governments in the EC.'[16] As other South American governments made clear their position, so Community governments had to weigh up the danger to their economic interests, direct and indirect, real and potential. They also had to take into account the fact that impressive though the Community's solidarity may have been, its impact on the Argentinian *junta* appeared to have been negligible.

The Community's doubts and concerns therefore increased many times with the retaking of South Georgia on 25 April and the sinking of the *General Belgrano* on 2 May. In some ways the sinking marked a turning point for, as Lawrence Freedman has put it, it was 'an important military victory, yet it turned into a political defeat because of the premium that the international community put on the appearance of avoiding escalation. Any military action, which is not self-evidently for defensive purposes, even if it is pre-emptive, becomes an outrage.'[17] As the prospect of further conflict

15. J. Barber, 'Economic Sanctions as a Policy Instrument', p. 367.
16. C. Hill and J. Mayall, *The Sanctions Problem: International and European Perspectives*, Florence: European University Institute, 1983.
17. L. Freedman, 'The War of the Falkland Islands 1982', *Foreign Affairs*, vol. 61, no. 1, 1982, p. 209.

came closer, so Community governments were obliged to acknowledge their lack of impact on Argentina's stance and the potential costs to their interests in South America. Other than attempting to maintain relations with South American governments on a bilateral basis, Community governments collectively could only emphasise the need for conciliation and negotiation; collectively, given the British position, that was all the Community could do. It was a similar case within other fora such as the Eurogroup and NATO, when its Defence Planning Committee met on 6–7 May. Ministers once again condemned the invasion, noted the importance of maintaining the principle that aggression or occupation of territory by force should not be allowed to succeed, and urged the need for a negotiated solution on the basis of Security Council Resolution 502.[18]

However, there was a growing concern that the British government was taking continued expressions of solidarity as a blank cheque in its support. Mrs Thatcher appeared to many in the Community as immovable, and neither personally nor politically disposed towards compromise. The situation was further complicated by the clear distance between the increasingly hawkish Prime Minister and her dovish Foreign Secretary, Francis Pym, which inevitably undermined the latter's credibility as a negotiator and spokesman. Given the British preoccupation with the war, Mr Pym's visits to Brussels tended to be brief; this, and the inevitable secrecy surrounding the progress both of mediation efforts and the military operation, meant that many in the Community believed the British government was leaving them too much in the dark and that their support was being taken for granted, and they resented this.

British officials strenuously denied that they regarded Community solidarity as a one-way street, or that they kept their partners poorly informed. Community briefings in London were sometimes held two or more times a week; political directors met on a number of occasions at the UK's request in order to exchange information and views, for example, immediately after the sinking of the *Belgrano*. Mr Pym himself also took pains, in the margins of the Council and foreign ministers' meetings, to inform colleagues of the course of events and the stage reached in the negotiations. An impromptu foreign ministers' meeting was called on 20 April to explain the proposals of the US Secretary of State, Mr Haig. All this was in addition to the many bilateral meetings and consultations that took place. And yet, despite all these exchanges, the suspicion grew that the Foreign Secretary was not at one with his Prime Minister and that the information he and his officials provided was limited in value. Some within the Community, somewhat uncharitably given the problems of keeping everyone up to date in the middle of a military campaign, held that they

18. *Communiqué of the Defence Planning Committee 6-7 May 1982*, Brussels: NATO Information Service.

could read as much in the press as in the material provided by the Foreign Office. Perhaps what was lacking was a greater sensitivity at the top to win the continued personal commitment of other heads of government.

The almost total preoccupation with the Falklands meant that the British were even less sensitive than usual to Community concerns and opinion. The brevity of his visits meant that Mr Pym was unable to exploit the opportunity to familiarize himself with other Community issues, especially that of the budget, and learn personally the views of his colleagues. What warnings there were from officials about the growing linkage between sanctions, agricultural prices and the British budgetary contribution seem either to have been unheard or rejected. But the idea of the 'indivisibility' of solidarity had grown rapidly in Community capitals and Community institutions; as one French MEP declared during the debate on 22 April: 'We support Britain in this issue [of the Falklands] but European solidarity ought not to be one way. When we are in need of your solidarity [on agricultural prices] we hope it will be there and we hope you will not show excessive nationalism.'[19] Monsieur Galland hoped in vain; Britain's behaviour on both Community issues remained unchanged. Attitudes among the other nine member states were well summed up by *The Economist:* 'there was Europe whistling through trade sanctions against Argentina after the Falklands were invaded; there were France and West Germany holding the line on EC sanctions after the sinking of the *General Belgrano* had rocked their domestic public opinion into questioning the whole Falklands venture; and there they all were with British budget mud kicked into their eyes.'[20]

The British refusal or inability to see any linkage between sanctions and the budget created a very much more difficult atmosphere for discussions on the renewal of sanctions. The British, if they saw the link at all, tended to regard it as little more than blackmail. But many others expected some show of gratitude, preferably expressed in a more conciliatory position on agricultural prices; a number of governments, not least the Irish and the Italian, were coming under increasing political pressure from various quarters to modify their support for the British position. The fact that the British were at the same time holding out against an increase in agricultural prices proved too much, and a majority in the Council of Ministers refused to recognize the British veto on price rises. It was the first time that agricultural prices had been decided by vote, and the first time a member state had been denied recourse to the Luxembourg Compromise. The British reaction was inevitably one of fury and the belief was widespread that, since little sacrifice was involved on the part of the other EC partners, they had simply been taking advantage of Britain's preoccupation

19. *Agence Europe*, 23 April 1982.
20. *The Economist*, 22 May 1982.

with its war effort.[21] *The Economist*, however, was somewhat more balanced, suggesting: 'There is in Mrs Thatcher an incomprehension of what Europe is about... There was little cause for her to bring upon herself the isolation in Europe that has descended on her government at a moment when it can least afford it. That in the process the Europeans behaved badly should not disguise the fact that it was British diplomacy that failed to prevent them doing so.'[22]

Not all governments may have drawn such a direct link between the continuation of sanctions and British isolation on the agricultural and budgetary issues, but it had been made increasingly clear to the British that sanctions were causing political problems. In the immediate aftermath of the sinking of the *Belgrano*, for example, the political directors at a special meeting on 4 May had pressed hard for diplomatic measures to be reactivated, the Irish and others having come to regard sanctions as reinforcing a military solution.[23] That meeting was followed by what became an extremely acrimonious informal foreign ministers meeting on 8–9 May, which left the British under few illusions that the renewal of sanctions was a foregone conclusion. The Political Committee met again on 15 May and failed to agree, as did the foreign ministers when they met in the margins of a meeting of the Atlantic Council on 16 May. Governments were keenly aware of increased public and parliamentary disquiet, especially perhaps, but far from exclusively, in Italy and Ireland. In the European Parliament, for example, support for sanctions fell from 203 – 28 on 22 April to 137 – 79 on 12 May. All that could be agreed on 16 May in the face of the expiry of sanctions on the following day was an extension for one week when the matter could be discussed further at a full Foreign Ministers Council meeting.

The interim agreement, and that of 24 May when sanctions were renewed without a time limit, was finally reached by a majority led by France and Germany, together with the Belgian Presidency.[24] As President Mitterrand was to say on 18 May when in London for the annual Anglo-French summit: 'There are no new facts which could cause us to change our minds. The immediate French solidarity with Britain was a result of Argentine intervention by force. The regrettable logic set in motion by this initial act means that we can give no support to the act of aggression in law or in fact.'

Not all the member states were able to agree and Ireland and Italy withdrew from the common position. At the same time, however, both continued to declare their strong hostility to Argentinian aggression (though

21. *The Guardian*, 25 May 1982.
22. *The Economist*, 22 May 1982
23. *Agence Europe*, 5 May 1982.
24. See *Le Monde*, 23-24 May 1982.

not necessarily their support for British action) and both undertook not to undermine the impact of the sanctions imposed by the rest of the Community by allowing trade to be deflected. The Danish government also took advantage of the collapse of the consensus by reverting to its position on the political use of economic measures and the use of Article 224, agreeing to continue to apply Community measures only until they could be succeeded by national measures. This agreement to differ among the Ten continued after sanctions were renewed indefinitely by seven states on 24 May. Sanctions were finally lifted by the Community, with the exception of the UK, on 21 June upon the effective end of hostilities (although an arms embargo continued). Once again, the procedure was that agreement was reached in EPC before the decision was actually taken by the Council of Ministers.

The disintegration of consensus among the Ten on the question of sanctions was reflected too in the coordination of the position of the Ten at the United Nations. The extent to which the member states had in general been able to harmonize positions with the UN General Assembly had perhaps been disappointing,[25] while the particularly proprietary attitudes of the two permanent members of the Security Council meant that British and French actions had rarely become the subject of EPC discussion. The immediate reaction to the Argentine invasion had been one of unanimity in the Security Council, with France in strong support (and prepared to influence other members such as Togo), together with Ireland, then also a member of the Security Council. However, with the sinking of the *Belgrano* and Britain's seeming intransigence, the position changed. The Irish in particular led efforts to renew attempts at conciliation in what became Security Council Resolution 505, and thereafter, both during and after the cessation of hostilities, there were increasing signs of concern and discontent over the British position. In the General Assembly especially, a growing number of member states tended to abstain on the various Falklands resolutions, seemingly oblivious to Mrs Thatcher's remonstrances.[26] Significantly, no member state voted against the UK on any substantive resolution, though Britain was perhaps fortunate that Spain was not a member of the Community in 1982.

Once the military conflict was over, the EC's role in the UK-Argentinian dispute effectively disappeared. Much of the EC's concern – expressed as early as the end of June 1982 at the meeting of the European Council

25. See S. Nuttall, *European Political Cooperation*, pp. 136-9.
26. Mrs Thatcher in her Christmas message to the Falklands on 25 December 1985 was led to complain after a series of adverse votes in which EC member states had either abstained or even voted against the UK: 'I regret that at the recent General Assembly so many of our friends proved unwilling to face up to the real issues at stake... They were content to have self-determination for themselves, but not all of them were content or prepared to vote for it for the people of the Falkland Islands', *International Herald Tribune*, 26 December 1985.

of heads of state and government in Brussels – was in rebuilding bridges with Latin America and strengthening cooperation between the two regions.[27] The advent of a civilian regime in Argentina made the process a good deal easier, with *inter alia* the European Parliament taking an active role; in October 1984, for example, the Parliament invited President Alfonsín to address it. However, the fact that the British were determined to maintain an embargo in the absence of an Argentinian agreement to an official ceasefire complicated direct EC-Argentinian relations, and even after the UK had lifted its embargo unilaterally in July 1985, Argentina still continued its ban on British imports until August 1989. It was only in February 1990 that an EC-Argentinian trade and cooperation agreement could be signed, thereby in a sense bringing about an end of the Community's involvement in the dispute.

Conclusions

The speed with which the Community had arrived at its decision to impose sanctions against Argentina was impressive. Insofar as the issue was one of aggression against the territory of a member state, it had certain particular features which distinguished it from other crises. Yet the sanctions decision, even though it was implemented for only one month, marked an important step in terms of policy coordination that appeared to reinforce the development of common decision making apparent in the London Report of 1981. The member states may not then have been able to go so far as the Genscher-Colombo Initiative may have wanted in terms of a legal base for EPC or an extension of its remit to include security issues in general, but the Falklands conflict provided an example of a growing habit of common discussion and decision making that allowed the Single European Act of 1986 to fulfil a number of the Genscher-Colombo Initiative's objectives.

Much of the credit for the rapid decision making in the Falklands case was given to EPC; the speed with which political directors reached a consensus was in marked contrast to previous attempts at responding to crises. But it was fortuitous that political directors were already meeting in the *ad hoc* group on the Genscher-Colombo initiative; although the London Report had incorporated provisions for crisis management, they had not

---

27. A. Pijpers et. al. (eds), *European Political Cooperation in the 1980s*, Dordrecht: Martinus Nijhoff, 1988, p. 294. Little seems to have been achieved until 1987 when the Community initiated consultations with the Group of Eight or Rio Group (which included Argentina). See W. Grabendorff, 'Relations with Central and Southern America: a question of over-reach', in G. Edwards and E. Regelsberger (eds), *Europe's Global Links*, London: Pinter, 1990, pp. 92-6.

been needed (and were not in fact to be tested until the Israeli invasion of the Lebanon in June 1982). Yet the British tended to contrast the speed of decision making in EPC with the stickiness of the discussions in COREPER, even after discounting the differences in responsibilities and the need for COREPER to finalize a legally enforceable text. It confirmed their view of EPC as both a means of safeguarding national interests through its emphasis on unanimity and as a useful vehicle for attempting to influence events: even if the consensus had broken down at the first whiff of grapeshot. But, since the British government was still smarting over the decision on agricultural prices, it was not perhaps surprising that the work of 'POCO', as EPC was often familiarly known, had particular attractions. As Mr Pym put it, 'compared with the problems on the economic side of the Community activity, this political cooperation receives less publicity. It might get more if it did not work so well. Its value cannot be measured in tonnes or calculated in millions of units of account. But it is a valuable and important aspect of membership.'[28]

However, the Falklands case proved how vital both the EPC and EC fora had been and how important it was that there was close interaction between them. On the one hand, for example, EPC had been crucial in taking the high road of principle that had eased the path for the Danes in the Community framework in their predicament over Articles 224 versus 113, and the Commission had responded by including references to EPC in the Regulation. On the other hand, the British were fortunate in having an EC Presidency that was prepared to blur the distinction as much as was necessary, allowing in effect joint meetings of the Political Committee and COREPER. That may well not have happened if the Presidency had not been held by the Belgians, which had meant that Political Committee meetings were held in Brussels. As Nuttall wrote in 1983, sanctions helped to create a '*modus vivendi* which, while leaving intact respective competencies and procedures, encourages continued action with a shared objective.'[29] Such joint meetings may not have occurred subsequently until after the collapse of Soviet domination of Eastern Europe, but in a sense the precedent had been set even while the legal proprieties had been met. That situation persists even under the Maastricht Treaty on European Union; while there is now a common Council of Ministers, decision making on common foreign and security policy issues remains based very largely on intergovernmental consensus and unanimity.

The Falklands crisis also clearly reinforced the artificiality of trying rigidly to separate foreign policy from external relations. Of course, the blurring of the distinctions had already been recognized in the London

28. *Hansard*, 26 May 1982, col. 937.

29. S. Nuttall, 'European Political Cooperation: a Survey', in F. G. Jacobs (ed.), *Yearbook of European Law*, Oxford: Clarendon Press, 1983, p. 258.

Report on EPC of 1981, but in the Falklands' case, the need to go beyond merely condemning Argentinian action to use economic policy instruments was clear, despite the reluctance of the Danes. Sanctions marked, however briefly, a joint determination to actually take action, and to take action in effect – despite Irish and Italian misgivings and their later regret – in support of military action being taken by one of the member states. That sanctions were introduced without any pressure from a non-member state gave them a greater symbolic importance as a result, both for the member states and for third countries in that the international profile of the EC was enhanced.

In 1982, EPC was but a dozen years old. Since it was geared to the coordination of foreign policy in the sense of diplomatic interaction, it had often been dismissed as being merely declaratory, or even a procedure substituting for policy.[30] It was regarded by Britain and France in particular as not much more than a sometimes useful supplement or complement to their own efforts.[31] Since it was seen as having been successful, however temporarily, in the Falklands crisis, it has been argued that the conflict marked an important contribution to EPC's further development, not least because the process has been based on incrementalism and precedent. The particular element in the case was the coordination of the policy of the Ten and the Community, that is in showing that EPC and the EC necessarily ran in tandem, and that the totality of the interrelationships had to be taken into account.

Insofar as sanctions also became bound up with internal Community issues such as the budget, the crisis further indicated the growing global quality of the Community system or at least the dimensions of solidarity, something the British have frequently had difficulty in understanding. It suggested the existence of a new wider framework of policy making, in some ways desirable in terms of possible extra international leverage, and in other ways necessary despite some potential costs. But what it also suggested was that the framework was increasingly unavoidable; that even the bigger member states could no longer easily pick and choose which issues were to involve the EPC/EC nexus and which were to be immune. That is not to claim that Community or other member states' concerns had any influence over British policy towards the Falklands War, but there is a difficulty in isolating issues from the wider bargaining process within the EPC/EC framework.

---

30. 'Political Cooperation: Procedure as Substitute for Policy' was the title of one of the earliest studies of EPC, by W. Wallace and D. Allen in H. Wallace, W. Wallace and C. Webb (eds), *Policy-Making in the European Communities,* 1st edn, London: John Wiley & Sons, 1977, pp. 227-48.

31. See C. Hill (ed.), *National Foreign Policies and European Political Cooperation,* London: Allen & Unwin, 1983.

This wider framework does not necessarily have equal impact on all the member states, nor over time even the same impact on any individual member state, but it does have some wider ramifications in terms of policy formulation. National policy may well be the result a highly sophisticated bargaining and coordination procedure among different, sometimes competing national ministries, institutions and other actors. The wider European policy-making framework necessarily means that the positions of the other member states and the EC institutions - including the European Parliament on issues that might be considered particularly sensitive in terms of public opinion – have to be taken into account. This has sometimes meant a particularly difficult ride for foreign ministries which are usually responsible for attempting to explain those other positions,[32] but the latter are ignored sometimes only at the peril of compromising other policies.

It would be easy of course to exaggerate the importance of this factor in providing a new framework for foreign policy decision making. One example was hardly likely to change the situation radically, particularly one where the consensus lasted barely a month. There have been innumerable examples since 1982 where member states have acted unilaterally or held out against a consensus within EPC and prevented either diplomatic or any Community action as a result, without necessarily incurring any particularly disadvantageous compromises in other policy areas.[33] On the other hand, examples such as the Falklands crisis contributed to a growing reflex action among EPC partners to consult, and further to the adoption of a position whereby the member states undertook not to act until they had so consulted. That has not necessarily meant that agreement has always followed consultation; the process continues to be based on unanimity, except in the highly restricted circumstances set out in the Maastricht Treaty where voting may take place on joint actions.[34] But regardless of the legal position (a position in which, of course, the European Court of Justice plays no role), the habit of consultation and cooperation has increasingly disposed governments to agree whenever possible. Moreover, the decision-making process itself, the 'dynamism of discussion',[35] within EPC has tended to contribute to the adoption of a median position rather than that of the lowest common denominator, which might have been expected from a system strictly based on unanimity.

Moreover, those discussions have taken place within a wider framework of growing economic, social and political integration within the

32. For difficulties sometimes faced by the FCO see G. Edwards 'Central Government', in S. George (ed.), *Britain and the European Community; the Politics of Semi-Detachment*, London: Clarendon Press, 1992, pp. 64-90, especially pp. 74-80.

33. Indeed, one could argue that some member states have been clever enough to use their position outside the consensus to exact additional benefits in other policy areas.

34. Article J.3.2 of the Maastricht Treaty on European Union.

35. S. Nuttall, *European Political Cooperation*, p. 314.

Community. Clearly there is interaction between political cooperation and the Community; legally as yet, even under Maastricht, they remain separate – if linked – and, from the standpoint of theory, the balance between economic determinism and political realism remains one for debate. The Single European Act of 1987 called for consistency between the two frameworks, with the Commission and the Presidency of the Council as referees but policy determination largely in the hands of the member states whether within EPC or the EC Council (now merged into a single Council of the Union), although the Maastricht Treaty failed to settle the issue definitively. Nonetheless, the point is clear that the EC/EPC framework that is now subsumed within the European Union has become increasingly central to the member states in pursuit of their international politics. The Falkland Islands crisis played an important, if limited, role in bringing that about.

– 3 –

The Converging National Reactions (I): The Big States – France and Germany

Stelios Stavridis

and

Elfriede Regelsberger[1]

General Introduction

There were a number of similarities and differences between France and Germany in the way they reacted to the Falklands War of 1982, but there are at least two main reasons for examining these two states together. The first has to do with the simple but important fact that France and (West) Germany represent two of the 'Big Four' states in the European Community; of the other two, Britain has been examined in detail in the existing literature (see Introduction), and Italy's reaction is analysed in depth in Chapter 6. The second reason for dealing with France and Germany together stems from the fact that, generally speaking, Paris and Bonn supported the United Kingdom, which was not the case as far as Italy was concerned.

The similarities in the French and German reactions can be summed up by the fact that both governments considered the Argentine invasion to be an unacceptable breach of international law. For different but similar reasons (French overseas territories, West Berlin), the French President and the German Chancellor believed that to have done nothing to reverse the situation created in the South Atlantic by the Argentine *junta*

---

1. The section on France was written by Stelios Stavridis, and the section on Germany by Elfriede Regelsberger.

would have represented a dangerous precedent. Both countries also strongly believed that, as a matter of loyalty, they should give their support to a close ally, not only to a member of NATO and the EEC but also, in the case of France, to the ally of the Second World War.

However, there were also differences between Paris and Bonn. The first had to do with the foreign policy decision making process in each country; the general view that the French system is dominated by the president whereas the German model is more open to the input of non-governmental actors seems in this case to have been vindicated. The second difference thus had to do with the strategy adopted by both countries in the way they reacted to the events in the South Atlantic and subsequently to reactions in London: Paris took a more political stance which, while backing the UK, refused to link it to the *question de fond* (sovereignty) and was quickly drawn into the internal politics of the EEC (farms prices); Bonn, on the contrary took a more realistic line, ignoring to a certain extent the EC linkage question and making sure that, as the main commercial power in Argentina, any sanctions decision would not harm its own economic and commercial interests, which it achieved by limiting both the duration of sanctions and their applicability. A final point worth mentioning at this stage is the post-Falklands War attitude of the United Nations General Assembly. Whereas Germany maintained a clearly pro-British stance during the several votes that took place between 1982 and 1988, France broke ranks in 1985. All of these similarities and differences between the French and German reactions are examined in turn in detail below.

France and the Falklands Conflict[2]

This section of Chapter 3 deals with the French reaction to the Falklands conflict. There were a number of reasons why France's reaction was particularly important, and these are analysed in detail here. It can be argued that the Falklands conflict represented an important test for the then new Socialist administration's foreign policy. The Falklands episode occurred at a time when the rhetoric of socialism was still highly visible and strongly defended, especially by one of Mitterrand's personal advisers (Regis Debray, who had been close to Che Guevara in the 1960s) and by the then Foreign Minister Claude Cheysson, who had always taken a more Third-Worldist, anti-American stance on international affairs than his boss at the Elysée.

2. The author would like to thank Madame Françoise de La Serre (Centre d'Etudes et de Recherches Internationales, Paris) and Dr Neville Waites (Department of French Studies, The University of Reading) for their comments on an earlier draft. The usual proviso about responsibility applies.

In short, France gave its support to the British for a variety of reasons: the attachment to the rule of law and the respect for UN principles and decisions, the existence of French overseas territories,[3] the need to support an ally and belief in the concept of solidarity. The second of these reasons was extremely important because, had France needed European support in a similar case, at some time in the future, it could have pointed to the support given to the UK in 1982.[4]

What follows consists first of a brief examination of the main features of the French foreign policy making process, and second an analysis of France's reaction to the 1982 events in the South Atlantic in more detail. The final section considers the French position since the end of the war.

The Background to the French Reaction

The General Background : The Colonial Past and the Gaullist Legacy – France's colonial past and Gaullist legacy are two of the most important factors that have influenced both the foreign policy process in France and its outcomes. Historically, decolonisation – preceded the setting up of the Fifth Republic with the latters introduction of presidential perogatives in foreign and defence policy. But the question of Algeria's decolonization – the most painful of all decolonization processes for the French – was the catalyst for de Gaulle's return to power. The events of April 1982 were therefore extremely important for France because of the remaining French possessions, which are scattered all over the world;[5] had the Argentine invasion been allowed to succeed, it would have set a dangerous precedent. Incidentally, there was a historical link with the archipelago which the Argentines claim as their own.[6]

In terms of foreign policy-making process, the main feature of the Fifth Republic has been the presidentalization of the French political system, and in particular of foreign and security policy.[7] The concept of a *domaine*

3. Both these aspects of the question were clearly spelt out by Jean-Pierre Cot, the Minister for Cooperation and Development, in answer to an oral parliamentary question on 23 April 1982, *Journal Officiel Débats de l'Assemblée Nationale* (J. O. A. N. C. R. no. 27, 23.4.82), p. 1292.

4. For a different view, see M.C. Smouts, 'The External Policy of François Mitterrand', *International Affairs*, vol. 59, no. 2, 1983, p. 163.

5. There are three types of French overseas possessions: departments, territories, and territorial collectivities. All come under French sovereignty and reflect the international role of France. For more on the DOM-TOM (French acronym for Overseas Departments and Territories) see J. L. Mathieu, *Les DOM-TOM*, PUF, Paris, 1988.

6. The Spanish word for Falklands (Malvinas) comes from the French 'Malouines', the name given to the islands when they were visited by sailors from Saint-Malo in 1690. France also 'gave up' the islands to Spain in 1767 after French settlers had spent three years there.

7. For a recent analysis of this phenomenon, see J. Hayward (ed.), *De Gaulle to Mitterrand – Presidential Power in France*, London: Hurst & Co., 1993, and in particular

réservé for the French president, which has predominated since 1958, was first established by de Gaulle and was made necessary by the special situation which prevailed at the time in Algeria. The emergence of an independent French nuclear deterrent (the 'finger on the button') reinforced the president's role in the mid-1960s, and the continuation of privileged presidential control over foreign and security policy under Pompidou, Giscard d'Estaing and Mitterrand confirmed the president's pre-eminence in those fields. In particular, during the first *cohabitation* experience of 1986-8, and despite his right-wing Prime Minister's efforts to the contrary, Mitterrand clearly dominated Jacques Chirac in all areas of foreign and security policy.[8]

The Immediate Background: The Socialists' International Rhetoric – Before winning the presidential and the subsequent legislative elections in 1981, the French Socialists had been highly critical of French foreign policy, especially with regards to its extensive arms sales abroad, its continuous support for many military regimes around the world and its numerous military interventions, especially in Africa. As for the French nuclear deterrent, although the Socialist leadership had fully accepted the importance of the nuclear dimension in French security policy by the time François Mitterrand went to the Elysée, there was less consensus within the Socialist Party itself. Overall, the new administration in France had emphasised the need to implement socialist principles in French foreign policy.[9] The Parti Socialiste stressed the importance of human rights and North-South economic issues. In 1981, this rhetoric materialized, at least to a certain extent, in the French position at the North-South Summit in Cancún, and in the joint Franco-Mexican Declaration on El Salvador.

At the same time, from 1981 onwards the new Reagan administration in the United States had taken a more vociferous anti-communist approach in foreign policy (stressing the 'Evil Empire's' expansion and putting less emphasis on human rights, contrary to President Carter's policy). The inherent incompatibility between these two visions of world affairs led to a number of problems between Paris and Washington, especially in the early years of the first Mitterrand presidency, and in particular over the Central American conflict.[10]

J. Howorth, 'The President's Special Role in Foreign and Defence Policy', pp. 150-89.

8. Ibid., p. 160.

9. M.C. Smouts, 'The External Policy of François Mitterrand', *International Affairs*, vol. 59, no. 2, 1983, pp. 158 and 166. See also J. Hutzinger, 'La Politique extérieure du Parti Socialiste', *Politique Etrangère*, no. 1, 1982, pp. 33-44. See also N. Waites, 'France under Mitterrand: External Relations', *The World Today*, vol. 38, no. 6, 1982, pp. 224-31. For Mitterrand's own views, see his *Réflexions sur la politique extérieure de la France*, Paris: Fayard, 1986, especially pp. 7-50.

10. It is true that a more Atlanticist view emerged in the Elysée especially after 1983

The French Reaction in 1982

Mitterrand and the Socialist Government – The most significant feature of the French reaction was the full support given by the French administration to the British position once the Argentines had invaded. This was not wholly predictable, and indeed, the Argentines did express their surprise at a Socialist administration supporting a Conservative government on what they perceived as a matter of decolonization.[11] One needs to stress immediately that the French government's stance was limited to condemning the Argentine military invasion of the Falklands; France made it clear from the start that it did not back the British claim to sovereignty.

France expressed its political support for Britain first at the United Nations where its permanent representative, Monsieur Luc de la Barre de Nanteuil, declared that 'the Argentine action is condemnable and should be condemned'. In a meeting of the EPC political directors in Brussels on the day after the invasion, the then French Political Director, Monsieur Andréani, expressed France's support for a country that had been hurt in 'its pride and its honour'. The British Political Director has pointed out that the French intervention made his own role all the easier because it had facilitated the use of such words as 'pride' and 'honour' by Britain itself.[12] Indeed, not to be the first to use such terms made an important difference for the British in their quest for support among the EC member states. The terms 'honour and pride' were repeated by the French Foreign Minister Claude Cheysson in the French Assembly on 8 April 1982, and the French Prime Minister Pierre Mauroy expressed on French television

with the Euro missiles deployment decided by NATO receiving the full support of the French President (see his January 1983 speech at the Bundestag). But, even though one does not have to agree necessarily with the view that there was a 'honeymoon' period with the US in the early stages of the first Mitterrand Presidency (see *The Times*, 2 September 1981; see also *Le Monde* 28 May 1981 and 31 May–1 June 1981), it is possible to argue that there was an apparent dichotomy between East-West relations and Third-World issues. In the latter case a clear anti-Americanism was present. In the former case, changes within other West European countries and an anti-Sovietism *de gauche* combined to make the traditional Gaullist approach towards the USA less of an oddity. See F. de La Serre, 'La Politique Européenne de la France: New Look ou New Deal', *Politique Etrangère*, vol. 47, no. 1, 1982, pp. 125-37; P. Lellouche, 'France and the Euromissiles: the limits of immunity', *Foreign Affairs*, vol. 62, no. 2, 1983-1984, pp. 318-34. See also D. Moïsi, 'Mitterrand's Foreign Policy: The Limits of Continuity', *Foreign Affairs*, vol. 60, no. 2, 1981–2, pp. 347-57.

11. Gerardo Schamis, the Argentine ambassador in Paris, wrote a letter published in *Le Monde* calling on 'Socialist France' to prevent Britain from recovering the Islands (9 April 1982).

12. In the 'External Relations of the EC Seminar' at the London School of Economics, 25 February 1992.

his 'dismay' at this 'act of war'.[13] In the meantime at the United Nations, France had voted in favour of Resolution 502, also voting in favour of Resolution 505 later in the crisis.

France's economic support for Britain materialized when, within days of the invasion and at the request of the UK, it stopped its arms exports to Argentina. The French decision was significant because 'France was the largest single supplier of military equipment to Argentina in the five years preceding the Falklands War'.[14] France also agreed to an EC-wide imposition of economic sanctions against Argentina. In terms of trade, the sanctions affected Argentina more than the EC, but France had a $213 million surplus with Argentina in the years 1978–82;[15] at a time when French domestic economic policies were about to lead to export controls and other restrictions, any action that hindered French exports would have an impact on the French economy (in retaliation for the EC embargo, the Argentines embargoed EC and therefore French goods). France also refused to send Exocet missiles to Peru in June 1982 because it feared these might have found their way to Argentina; in fact, the French helped the British to defend themselves against Exocet attacks.[16] It is interesting to note that, despite French support for the UK, the French Minister for External Trade, Monsieur Jobert, on a visit to South-East Asia in late May 1982 was quite happy to emphasise that the war in the South Atlantic had rekindled interest in French weapon systems in the part of the world he was visiting.[17]

President Mitterrand also supported the continuation of the EC-wide sanctions on both occasions that they were renewed. After a time however, Mitterrand seemed to turn to what he himself described as a more 'fatalistic' view about the turn of events in the Falklands. He also stressed how important it was to 'prepare for the future' by maintaining the links between Europe and Latin America which had traditionally been strong.[18]

13. Cheysson also expressed his 'sorrow' at Lord Carrington's resignation, but he added he was not surprised by the British Foreign Secretary's decision, as he considered him to be 'a man of honour', *Le Monde*, 6-7 April 1982.

14. $575 million out of a total of $1.8 billion, in E. Kolodziej, *Making and Marketing Arms: the French Experience and its Implications for the International System*, Princeton, New Jersey: Princeton University Press, 1987, p. 387; the fact that this was so over the last five years before the 1982 invasion is important because it roughly coincides with the darkest years of the Argentine military *junta's* internal repression (the period of the *desaparecidos*).

15. Over the period 1963-1983, it amounted to a $1,424 million surplus whereas France experienced huge deficits with other Latin American states like Brazil or Mexico. The figures are from M. O. Campos, 'Déséquilibre des Echanges entre la France et l'Argentine', *Revue des Deux Mondes*, May 1985, pp. 349-52.

16. Interviews.

17. See *Le Monde*, 29 May 1982.

18. At a press conference during his African tour in late May 1982, and at a press conference in Paris on 9 June 1982. His Foreign Minister had taken a similar line in the Senate on 18 May 1982, Journal Officiel Débats Parlementaires Sénat, 1982, no. 44S, 19 May 1982, p. 2113.

Sanctions were brought to an end when the conflict was over, and France also resumed military deliveries soon afterwards.

Internal Divisions – It is important to stress that there was a slight divergence between the views of the Quai d'Orsay, and in particular of Claude Cheysson, and Mitterrand's view that Britain had to be supported in a time of crisis. On the one hand, the French President argued that France should help an ally in a time of crisis because of past history (the Second World War) and for reasons of EC solidarity. On the other hand, the French Foreign Minister expressed his dismay at the way the whole situation had been dealt with in London, at the implications for French and European interests in Latin America, and finally at the absence of any evidence by Britain that it would seek a peaceful solution to the conflict. Mrs Thatcher later publicly acknowledged the important role played by Mitterrand in the whole affair in her memoirs.[19]

This divergence of views was exemplified by the 'Dorin note affair', named after the then Director for the Americas in the Quai d'Orsay, who was described by some at the time as anti-British. This note – which was an internal document – was leaked at the end of April to the right-wing *Figaro Magazine*. In fact there were two notes, the original by Bernard Dorin and a cover note written by Cheysson himself. Cheysson's comments were not as unambiguous as those of his Director, but his use of the word *rastaquouères* to describe how he thought the British had viewed the Argentines suggested British racism towards a Latin nation.[20] Dorin's analysis was not necessarily anti-British as such, and the fact that he later became the French ambassador in London tends to confirm that view. In his note, Dorin insisted that the whole affair had been a 'fiasco' because it was the result of a series of misunderstandings and misconceptions by both sides. Dorin also believed that, as a result of the British reaction and its refusal to negotiate, the USA's credibility in Latin America had suffered unnecessarily and that the USSR had gained new possibilities of influence in a region of the world that had been previously out of bounds.

Cheysson claimed that the press (meaning the right-wing papers) were to blame, and emphasised that the analysis applied to events prior to the Argentine invasion rather than after it.[21] More generally, the Socialists complained that this was the third leak from the Foreign Ministry since they

19. M. Thatcher, *The Downing Street Years*, London: Harper Collins, 1993, pp. 182-3. For some caustic comments on Cheysson's behaviour at the time, see J. Attali, *Verbatim*, Paris: Fayard, 1993.

20. The word *'rastaquouère'* has at least two meanings: someone of mixed race, or someone who is flaunting his newly-acquired richness. It is probably the former that Cheysson meant in his note.

21. *Débats Parlementaires Sénat*, 18 May 1982, p. 2111.

had come to power; at about the same time, the daily *Libération* was sent a copy of an official US embassy document criticizing the 'ignorance, vagueness and romanticism' of Mitterrand's foreign policy.[22]

Therefore, despite the fact that Cheysson fully supported the overall French position, he went to great lengths to stress that France had never accepted the British claim over the Falkland Islands and that the French reaction was only a condemnation of the Argentine military invasion of the islands, and not a judgement on who possessed sovereignty. In diplomatic terms, this actually meant that the French Foreign Ministry favoured the Argentine claim. The French President fully agreed with the distinction made by Cheysson between the condemnation of the military intervention and the reservation over sovereignty, but he insisted that France should abstain on the issue in the annual vote on the Falklands at the UN's General Assembly. This was not to Cheysson's liking but, as stated above, he did not question the pre-eminence of the French President in foreign affairs. Ironically, it was only after Cheysson had left the Foreign Ministry that Mitterrand accepted that the French position at the General Assembly should change (see below).

In terms of relations with Britain and the notion of solidarity among EC members, the most controversial dimension to the war was what the French perceived as a lack of 'mutual solidarity' from the British over the setting of CAP prices and the British contribution to the EC budget. Cheysson in particular publicly attacked the UK on this issue, complaining about Britain's unwillingness to obey European law at a time when it was calling for respect for international law. At the same time, the Foreign Minister made it quite clear that the situation was a reflection of a much wider problem, Britain's lack of commitment to the European ideal. Mitterrand echoed his minister's words while on a trip to Hamburg to see the German Chancellor, and reiterated the same point while in Algiers during his African tour. Cheysson also later painted a very gloomy picture of the G7 meeting at Versailles in early June 1982, describing the atmosphere as 'sinister' and complaining that the word 'negotiation' had not been forthcoming 'especially from London'.[23]

As for the famous incident where the British were overruled on their refusal to accept the agricultural prices, despite having used their veto under the Luxembourg Compromise instituted at the time of de Gaulle, it is important to stress that the French immediately issued a statement to express their continued support for the Luxembourg principle. They felt, however,

22. The document written by John Dobrin who had spent some time in the US embassy in Paris in 1977 before joining the US State Department's European desk went on to call Mitterrand 'a little chameleon who had been a leftist, a socialist and an independent', *Le Monde*, 18 May 1982.

23. *Le Monde*, respectively 29 April, 16 May, 20 May and 7 June 1982.

as Mitterrand himself put it, that to use the term 'vital interests' over an exercise that was occurring annually because all states had agreed to do so on a yearly basis amounted to overstretching the *raison d'être* of the Luxembourg Compromise.

The sense of a lack of reciprocity was further reinforced when, despite legal action being taken in a French court, Captain Astiz, an Argentine officer arrested by the British during the war, was returned to Argentina in an exchange of prisoners despite French (and Swedish) objections. Indeed, Astiz was held responsible for, among other human rights violations, the murder of two French nuns and one Swedish girl in December 1977. He was also said to have infiltrated the anti-*junta* opposition in Paris in the mid-1970s. France did not make a major issue of Astiz' case as, in international law, there are certain requirements as to the treatment of prisoners of war, in particular regarding the swift exchange of prisoners; and from a strictly legal perspective, the allegations against Astiz did not concern the war itself but events prior and unrelated to it. Much later, Claude Cheysson simply described the British attitude over the affair as 'not correct'.[24]

France's growing frustration with the British attitude over the conflict in the Falklands and in the EC did not lead to any major shifts in their support for the UK. When on 4 June 1982 another UN resolution calling for an immediate cessation of hostilities was vetoed by the British in the Security Council, France, unlike Ireland, chose to abstain. The official explanation given by the French representative, Monsieur de la Barre de Nanteuil, was that the resolution was too one-sided as it only mentioned one objective, the cessation of hostilities, and said nothing about any Argentine withdrawal.

There were signs of irritation all the same: the beginning of hostilities in South Georgia had led the French Foreign Ministry spokesman to call for 'urgent negotiations', and a deafening silence at the Quai d'Orsay followed the outbreak of war in the Falklands itself. The Minister for European Affairs, Monsieur Chandernagor, 'deplored' these developments and Cheysson constantly stressed the lack of mutual solidarity from the UK with regards to the farm price negotiations.[25] Mrs Thatcher's uncompromising line also contradicted the French Socialists' belief in the limitations of 'gunboat diplomacy', who instead stressed the need to combine military means with political dialogue in order to defend their overseas territories.[26]

---

24. The author would like to thank Monsieur Cheysson for agreeing to give an interview on 1 February 1994. On that particular issue, Cheysson politely refused to elaborate any further than the quotation reproduced here.

25. *Le Monde*, 4, 11, and 16-17 May 1982.

26. Cot in *Journal Officiel Débats de l'Assemblée Nationale* (J. O. A. N. C. R. no. 27, 23.4.82), p. 1293.

Parliament, Political Parties, and Public Opinion – As noted above, French foreign policy falls inside the *domaine réservé* of the executive and especially of the French president. However, some debate over the Falklands took place in the Assembly, as a statement on foreign policy followed by a general debate occurred just after the end of the hostilities in the South Atlantic on 6 July 1982. During the conflict the government also answered a number of oral and written questions on the issue in both the Assembly and the Senate; moreover, the continuation of the Iraq-Iran War in the Persian Gulf, the assassination of the French ambassador in Beirut in late May 1982, and the Israeli invasion of Southern Lebanon in June 1982, meant that foreign policy issues in general had become important in the political debate in France.

Compared to these other international events, and in particular to the crisis in the Middle East, the Falklands did not dominate the parliamentary discussions. It did however provide a means for the various political groups to either support or criticize the overall foreign policy of the Socialist administration. Thus the left supported the government's reaction to the Falklands War ('the government's reaction has been what it should have been'), although some like Lionel Jospin, the then Socialist Party First Secretary, warned against the risk of 'humiliating' the Argentines and by implication the Latin Americans.[27] The right, on the other hand, stressed the lack of consistency with proclaimed Socialist ideals and the absence of a more powerful role for France which was, in their view, the result of Socialist mismanagement which had led to a weak French economy and a weak French voice in the world.[28] Jean Lecanuet, the President of the Senate's Commission on Foreign Affairs, Defence and the Armed Forces, also recalled the fact that Britain had come to France's aid in the Second World War; in his view, France needed to reciprocate although he stressed that he agreed with the government's view that no blank cheque could be given to the UK. He added that the Dorin Affair showed a lack of consistency between official public support and private reservations, and that the latter were in his view unfounded. He did not hesitate to ridicule the leak.[29] Jacques Chirac, the leader of the neo-Gaullist RPR, merely complained about the absence of any French initiative together with other Latin European states, 'which would have saved the honour of everyone' in the

27. The first quote is from Monsieur Guidoni (Socialist) on 6 July 1982, *Journal Officiel Débats de l'Assemblée Nationale* (J. O. A. N. C. R. no. 40, 6.7.82), p. 4239. The Jospin view is from Le Monde, 11 May 1982.

28. For instance, see Monsieur Couve de Murville (RPR)'s comments during the July 1982 debate on French foreign policy, in *Débats Assemblée Nationale*, 6 July 1982, pp. 4230-1.

29. *Débats Sénat*, 18 May 1982, p. 2109

Falklands.[30] In short, there was no real criticism of the principle of solidarity with the UK.

It is always difficult to assess precisely the role played by public opinion and the media. In this case, because the Falklands issue did not directly concern France, there was not much of a debate besides the usual interest generated by a military confrontation. Most of the public's attention was diverted to other international events and domestic political considerations. As for the press, the intensive coverage of the conflict shows there was a great deal of interest. The Falklands rarely left the front page of *Le Monde*, the most authoritative of all French dailies, although at the time the paper was starting to suffer from a lack of constructive criticism towards the government's actions. The French media in general emphasised the rather ludicrous dimension of the conflict and the spiral of events that had led to its military phase.

The French media were also used by the belligerent parties to put their diverging views to the French public. Various solidarity movements with Argentina emerged in Paris, usually associated with anti-*junta* organizations that had been campaigning since the 1976 coup in Buenos Aires. Some papers reproduced a long list of letters, some supportive, some opposed to the Argentine action and to the war, but nothing exceptional really occurred except for the Dorin Affair mentioned above. In order not to make the overall situation worse, and to avoid involving the French public more, a one-month French rugby tour of Argentina had to be cancelled in late May 1982, despite a long tradition of meetings between the two countries.

The French Attitude Since the End of the 1982 War

The difference of opinion between the Elysée and the Quai d'Orsay survived for a number of years. On 27 November 1985, after having abstained on the Falklands vote on all previous occasions, France decided to back what is usually regarded as a pro-Argentine resolution in the UN (the resolution was passed by the greatest majority ever with 107 votes in favour and 4 against, and 41 abstentions).[31] Moreover, two British amendments calling for the right of self-determination to be recognized for the Falklanders were defeated, with France abstaining on both occasions. The French permanent representative, Monsieur Claude de Kémoularia, argued that although France remained 'committed' to the principle of self-determination, there was no need to vote in favour of the British amendments because that particular issue was not really relevant in those two cases.

30. *Le Monde*, 3 June 1982.
31. The 1986 and 1987 votes produced even bigger majorities.

It seems that some frustration with the lack of progress over the possibility of Britain negotiating with Argentina, the existence of a democratic regime in Buenos Aires after 1983, and the need not to undermine it, all combined to set up this change of heart. France was not the only EC country to change its position in 1985, as Italy and Greece did so as well. *Le Monde* summed up the impact of the decision made by France and other EC countries when it called this a 'double defeat' for the UK. However, there was an unexpected bonus from that development in the following year. Having voted against the UK position once, the French stuck to this position as no positive new signs could be found in the sovereignty dispute. One month later, Argentina repaid its due by abstaining in a vote on New Caledonia, an issue which after more than two decades off the UN agenda was now back in focus, mainly through the efforts of Australia and New Zealand (particularly after the 1985 Rainbow Warrior Affair). Although only a handful of non-aligned states followed Buenos Aires' decision, the French government emphasised that it had gained some support from countries that were expected to vote in favour of the resolution, and that the overall result was not as overwhelming as it could have been (89 in favour, 24 abstentions and 11 did not take part in the vote). Instead of following France's 'No' vote on the issue, Britain and a small minority of EC states abstained, probably in retaliation to the French vote on the Falklands. It is more difficult to assess to what extent the New Caledonia vote had an impact on the way France voted over the Falklands in 1985 and 1986, but it is not impossible to imagine some Machiavellian thinking behind such a decision.

Conclusions

The main elements of French foreign policy traditions remained in place after 1981. Arms sales to military dictatorships continued, especially in the Middle East and Latin America. Mitterrand also continued the French tradition of intervening militarily in Africa (Chad in 1983 and again in 1987) despite being highly critical of similar operations in the past. All this led Stanley Hoffmann to wonder whether Mitterrand's Socialist foreign policy amounted to little more than 'Gaullism by any other name'.[32] Moreover, no real change had occurred in France's stance on its own colonial possessions even if some minor changes have taken place (for example the status of New Caledonia) in recent years. The Falklands episode seems, until 1985, to have confirmed that trend; the change of heart in

---

32. S. Hoffmann, 'Mitterrand's Foreign Policy, or Gaullism by any other Name', in G. Ross, S. Hoffmann and S. Malzacher, *The Mitterrand Experiment - Continuity and Change in Modern France*, Cambridge: Polity Press, 1987, pp. 294-305.

1985 is difficult to assess as the Falklands came off the UN agenda only three years later. The Madrid talks which started in 1989 satisfied the French whose position all along, including during the war of 1982, had been that a final settlement to the issue should be negotiated and not imposed.

What can be argued, therefore, is that one of the first foreign policy tests for the then new Socialist administration in Paris reinforced the traditional Gaullist position on international affairs. We can see, perhaps with the benefit of hindsight, that the Falklands was an international precursor of things to come inside France less than a year later.[33]

In terms of the implications of this case study for theoretical explanations of foreign policy making, the episode tends to confirm the view that foreign policy remains firmly in the grip of the executive and especially of the president.[34] There was a parliamentary session on foreign policy which covered the Falklands, but no real scrutiny of the French position took place. In fact, the timing of this general debate simply happened to coincide with the Falklands confrontation; to a certain extent, no real debate could have taken place anyway because of the existence of an overall Socialist majority. What was revealing was the use by the opposition of a foreign policy issue to criticize the domestic record of the Socialist administration. The other point made by the opposition, namely the view that the Socialists' foreign policy rhetoric did not represent the true interest of France, was deeply resented by the Socialist and Communist parliamentarians, who emphasised in their response that they represented the will of the French people.[35] The relevance of this type of incident for foreign policy analysis is to show that even in a country where foreign policy issues are deemed to come under the president's exclusive control, domestic politics nonetheless tend to impinge, especially at a time when a new administration has not fully asserted its legitimacy in the eyes of an opposition which had previously been in power for an uninterrupted twenty-three years.

Germany and the Falklands Conflict

The reaction of the Federal Republic Germany to the Falklands Crisis of 1982 can only be understood in the context of a knowledge of the workings of German domestic politics and of the policy-making process. Germany's support for Britain during the crisis was substantial, but it was also

33. For a general discussion of this point, see M. C. Smouts, 'The External Policy of François Mitterrand', especially p. 155.

34. This view was cleary reinforced by the author's interview with Claude Cheysson.

35. Monsieur Guidoni, *Journal Officiel Débats de l'Assemblée Nationale*, 6 July 1982, p. 4238.

cautious and finessed in ways which owed much to the operation of the domestic environment. In this respect the case was typical of the FRG's handling of the 'high politics' issues in EPC which pose such a challenge to its post-war position and self-image.

Some Fundamentals of German Foreign Policy Making

The FRG's foreign policy process is affected by its federal structure of government and by the political balance of the political scene of the day. The latter can be seen in the division of powers between the chancellor and the foreign minister, and the former is reflected in the different powers attributed to the federal government and the regional states (*Länder*). Both these dimensions, together with the additional inputs of other domestic sources of foreign policy such as pressure groups and the parliament, are briefly reviewed in this section.

According to the Basic Law, the definition and conduct of foreign policy normally falls under the competence of the minister of foreign affairs (the so-called *Ressortprinzip*), with the chancellor only having the right to give global directives (*Richtlinien-Kompetenz*). This division of labour has been widely respected even though there were occasions when the Chancellor himself took the lead during the 1970s. Under the SPD/FDP coalition governments '(1969–82) Chancellor Brandt somewhat uncontroversially claimed *Ostpolitik* as his personal domain, while his successor Schmidt was actively involved in EC-related and international negotiations on economic and financial matters (the creation of the European Monetary System in 1979 is but one example). During that period EC integration, and particularly its political dimensions including the foreign policy cooperation of the EC governments in the framework of European Political Cooperation (EPC), lay broadly in the hands of the Foreign Minister and his staff.

The traditional pattern of the 1970s changed when Chancellor Kohl came to power in October 1982 to continue the government coalition with the Liberal Party. Contrary to his predecessor, he wished and still wishes to be heavily engaged in EC affairs, particularly with regard to the concept of integration and its future development (the Kohl-Mitterrand proposals during the Intergovernmental Conference on European Union in 1990-1 are the most obvious examples of his pro-European commitment). Since the Chancellor finds himself largely in line with his coalition partner – the liberals being traditionally the protagonists of European integration in the former SPD/FDP government – no major clashes of interest or competence have occurred. One can detect a decline in the role of the Foreign Affairs Ministry, which under the former Foreign Minister Genscher (who served between 1974 and 1992) could be regarded as the key player in determining Germany's EC policy, most notably in the 1981 Gen-scher-Colombo proposal.

The principle of decentralized policy making in the horizontal demen-sion has an equivalent in the vertical one in the division of competencies between the federal and the *Länder* levels. Policy decisions therefore usu-ally require a sophisticated network of mutual information and coordina-tion with a large number of participants. The same can be said for foreign policy decisions to the extent that they are of a fundamental nature whi-le the normal diplomatic business is widely the domain of the Foreign Affairs Ministry. It is interesting to note that the parliamentary Foreign Affairs Committee is not the exclusive forum for such topical matters. Ne-gotiations primarily include the leading figures of the government and the majority factions in the parliament. The Foreign Affairs Committee as such is perceived as a nice club of honoured personalities who are satisfied to have regular exchanges of views with the foreign minister without clai-ming directly to control and influence the government's strategy.

Germany's active participation in EPC tends to reduce the possibility of parliamentary involvement and to widen the gap between the knowl-edge and expertise of which the Foreign Affairs Ministry compared to the limited means of a handful of parliamentary foreign policy experts. To a certain extent, however, international issues are domestically politicized, such as human rights questions related to Turkey, South Africa and Cen-tral and Latin American countries, or the domestic debate along the lines of left-wing and right-wing political forces. German diplomacy is tradi-tionally also rather receptive to issues which relate directly to German hi-story, such as relations with Israel or Poland, or those which enjoy the particular attention of major parts of the electorate, which was the case with regard to the Yugoslav crisis, where the German government was forced towards early recognition of the new republics of Croatia and Slovenia in December 1991.

The profile of pressure groups with regard to foreign policy in Ger-many can be described as low. This is true for the business sector, which usually supports the fundamentals of German foreign policy but main-tains a certain distance as long as trade flows and financial markets are not instrumentalized for political considerations. If situations arise which require economic sanctions, the concerned lobby groups, and in particu-lar the entrepreneurs can use these channels to express their positions. This system of quasi-permanent mutual information and consultation mainly affects issues related to domestic policy, the world economy and trade, but it can also be used to highlight concern over foreign policy decisions of a more general nature. The preferred addressees for interest groups are therefore the traditional interlocutors in the relevant ministries and in par-ticular in the Ministry of Economic Affairs, while the Foreign Affairs Ministry is perceived as being in the second rank. Depending on the subject and the given time frame, other factors such as forthcoming elections or the geographical affiliation of the Chancellor's or another minister's constituency may play a role as well.

Thus, the German decision-making process in foreign affairs is decentralized and complex with no clear dominance of any given single actor. The impact of domestic factors on particular decisions is therefore somewhat unpredictable.

The Falklands Conflict: The Low Cost of Solidarity with the United Kingdom

A number of factors affected the way Germany reacted to the invasion of the Falkland Islands. What should be stressed from the start is the way in which Germany's solidarity was highly visible but rather limited in its scope. The reasons for and the kind of support the Germans gave to the UK in 1982 are reviewed in turn in this section.

Germany's almost unconditional support for the British position during the Falkands War was overwhelmingly determined by considerations of international politics. Argentina's invasion completely contradicted international law, the respect of which was of key importance to the German understanding of international relations. Besides, the invaded islands were part of EC territory and, what was even more important, they belonged to one of Germany's closest allies which was also one of the guarantors of Berlin and German unification. Diplomatic circles directly involved in crisis management in 1982 convincingly argued that this course of solidarity had been fostered by the EPC mechanisms; Her Majesty's Political Director at that time had obviously lobbied for the British cause in such a way that his colleagues in the Political Committee could not but close ranks with a distinguished and highly esteemed colleague who 'could not be left alone in the rain'. In the early days of the crisis, the argument that the obvious pro-British stance would harm Germany's relations with South America as a whole, and with Argentina in particular, was not strong.

Right from the beginning of the crisis, the government in Bonn was also willing to demonstrate solidarity with London by economic means. Concerns in the Ministry of Economic Affairs about a trade embargo with Argentina ranked second compared to the political considerations.[36] Germany's trade with Argentina made up only around 0.4 to 0.5 per cent of the country's overall trade; within the EC, however, almost 30 per cent of the Community's trade with Latin America was through Germany, fol-

36. *Frankfurter Allgemeine Zeitung*, 13 April 1982.

lowed by Italy and France. The federal government did not completely ignore the effects of economic sanctions and Germany tried to reduce possible negative effects by favouring a limited period of application of the sanctions: contrary to other suggestions made in the EC Council of Ministers for an unlimited period, Germany preferred a four-week term. An exclusion of the embargo decision for those agreements already in force and those goods which were on the way to Argentina was also seen as appropriate means for limiting the embargo's impact on German firms.

Commensurate with its EC integration philosophy, the federal government supported the use of Article 113 as the legal basis for the Community decision, arguing that this would accelerate the decision-making process and demonstrate to the outside world Europe's capacity to act. Contrary to the dissenting states among the Ten, Germany together with France remained at the forefront of solidarity with the United Kingdom.[37] However, the longer the conflict lasted and the more it turned into a massive military confrontation, the more evident it became that there was growing discontent in Germany with the British position. Germany's call on London to use its power in a proportionate way[38] remained unanswered. Germany also expressed its 'greatest reservations' about the escalation.[39] What was being felt in other EC circles, including the European Parliament, also became obvious in Bonn: a growing disillusionment with an apparently harsh British line and frustration at the limited value of concerted actions by the Western partners in their efforts to influence the government in London.

Similarly the voices of those who expected not only damage to be done to Germany's economy but also a loss of the political credibility of Germany in Latin America and the North-South dialogue became stronger. The Economics Minister's assessment that nobody in the Federal Republic was happy about a prolongation of the sanctions[40] revealed growing concern among the business sector directly involved in the trade with Argentina. What caused even greater concern in the federal government was the fact that Germany's image in the region was deteriorating. In order to counterbalance such negative tendencies, it was decided to send the Minister of State in the *Auswärtiges Amt*, Peter Corterier, on a ten-day journey to the region to explain and promote the German position. This happened in late May, when the British-Argentine confrontation reached its peak;[41] as

---

37. G. Edwards, 'Europe and the Falklands crisis 1982', *Journal of Common Market Studies*, vol. 22, no. 4, 1982, pp. 295-313.

38. See *Europäische Zeitung*, June 1982.

39. These were the words of the Federal Chancellor after a cabinet meeting according to the *Süddeutsche Zeitung* on 26 May 1982, *Bulletin d'informations*, 26 May 1982.

40. *Vereinigte Wirtschaftsdienste Deutschland*, 26 May 1982.

41. *Frankfurter Allgemeine Zeitung*, 29 May 1982.

a response, Bonn advocated a quick lifting of the sanctions upon the end of the hostilities in the South Atlantic[42] and submitted proposals to deepen European-Latin American relations (the San José dialogue, which formally began in 1984, records Genscher's influence, especially during the German Presidency of 1983, as one of its main initiators).

In contrast to France, which soon after the end of the military confrontation also lifted its arms embargo towards Argentina, the Federal Republic followed a more cautious approach. Although the decision to lift the arms embargo was taken by the Cabinet in September 1982, Germany preferred to await the Foreign Ministers' consultations in EPC on 20 December 1982 to be assured that the other EC partners also supported the return to normalcy before it started deliveries. Germany's position could not be criticized, since by then even the United Kingdom had brought the arms embargo to an end, Rolls Royce having delivered its engines for the German shipyard Blohm and Voss which had to contribute to a contract for a frigate for Argentina.[43]

In the aftermath of the military conflict, Germany favoured negotiations between the British and the Argentine government about the future of the Falklands. The Federal Republic followed a moderate course which made itself manifest primarily in the UN debate and voting. Between 1982 and 1988, contrary to Greece and in later years, France, Italy and the Netherlands, the Federal Republic followed the mainstream line of abstaining during the annual General Assembly vote on the Falklands. Britain obviously tried to change this position but without success.

The Actors Involved at the National Level

The way in which the FRG reacted to the Falklands conflict illustrates particularly well the distribution of power among the domestic actors of German foreign policy making. The fact that the conflict in the South Atlantic only lasted for a few weeks undoubtedly reinforced the pre-eminence of the executive arm, including politicians and their officials with access to information on fast-moving events. Departments not directly connected to foreign policy had little choice but to react to the executive. On the other hand, the longer the crisis dragged on, the more opportunities arose for lobbies to mobilize their connections and to exert pressure on the policy of sanctions, if and when the shoe began to pinch.

---

42. As for Germany's progressive stance with regard to the end of the embargo, see *Le Monde*, 22 June; *Frankfurter Allemeine Zeitung*, 22 June 1982.
43. *Neue Zürcher Zeitung*, 20 November 1982.

The Pre-eminent Role of the Government – As in similar situations of an ad hoc crisis management, the government in Bonn established an ongoing working group to deal with the matter at the administrative level. The Arbeitsstab Falklandinseln[44] included representatives from the Foreign Affairs Ministry and the Economics and Defence Ministry as well as the Chancellery. It was chaired by the sub-divisional Head of the Political Division Three of the Foreign Affairs Ministry, who is in charge of relations with Latin America; he was assisted by diplomats from the Economic Division, the Legal Division and the Political Division Two dealing with Germany's relations with the other Western European countries, including the United Kingdom and European Political Cooperation.

The main task of the working group was to prepare the deliberations at the political level, including the EPC and Community discussions. The working atmosphere of the group was described as constructive and free of bureaucratic or personal rivalries. The definition of the joint position was, however, taken at the political level, where Foreign Minister Genscher and Chancellor Schmidt worked hand in hand and shared the same outlook. Formally, the government's position, particularly with regard to the trade embargo and its eventual lifting, had to be approved by the Cabinet.

Another characteristic of Bonn's crisis management was the government's intensive consultation with both the parties at war and other Western European allies. Apart from the EPC framework, the bilateral links with France and Italy played a prominent role. The government's approach was twofold. First, through its traditional bilateral channels with the other EC countries, the government tried to counteract the massive British pressure. The closest partners in this process were France and Italy[45] who were both directly concerned by the affair and were also traditionally privileged interlocuteurs. These channels were also used to prepare the EPC consultations, and they were seen as a useful means of coordinating how to influence British policy.

The second approach by the government in Bonn had as its focus the parties directly involved in the conflict. Since the federal government traditionally maintains a substantial presence in Latin America, it was well placed to receive first-hand information directly from the Argentine government which was complemented by an intense exchange of views with Argentine diplomats in Bonn. The same can be said for the dense network of contacts between German and British officials and political leaders, whether at the British embassy in Bonn or the German embassy in London. The latter had the task of keeping political circles in Bonn informed on the

44. *Frankfurter Allemeine Zeitung*, 8 April 1982.
45. See the various Genscher-Colombo meetings and Franco-German activities, Agence Europe, 10-11 May 1982; *Neue Zürcher Zeitung*, 9-10 May 1982.

mood in the United Kingdom and on the political arguments pursued in the Falkland crisis. When the war broke out, the German Chancellor became annoyed by the constant pressure from the British Prime Minister and somewhat reduced the level of his personal contacts, leaving communication mainly at the level of Foreign Ministers.

The Parliamentary Level – Information Gathering – The involvement of the Deutsche Bundestag in this affair corresponds to that of a traditional observer in the overall conduct of German foreign policy. The parliamentarians did not play an active part, as they initially perceived the affair as a 'peripheral' issue. Subsequently, they interpreted it as falling squarely within the domain of official German diplomacy, but they were satisfied by the regular information given by government representatives, particularly from the Ministry of Foreign Affairs, and did not ask to be more actively engaged.

It was the foreign policy experts in the Foreign Affairs Committee who naturally showed the greatest interest in the Falkands episode, while the majority of members were concerned with other issues. The committee supported the position held by the government in favour of political solidarity with the United Kingdom, and they abstained from criticizing British behaviour and from publicly warning against negative effects on Germany's standing in Latin America. The few parliamentarians interested in the subject also shared the government's view on a rapid end to the embargo measures once the cessation of hostilities was announced. Occasional references in the parliamentary debate to the possible negative impact on Germany's trade with Argentina appear to have been motivated by the lobbying of the enterprises affected by the embargo. Usually, however, the latter directly lobbied the government itself.

Interest Groups, Particularly in the Business Sector: Discreet Lobbying – As indicated earlier, interest groups in Germany particularly those from the business sector, enjoy excellent access to politicians and other government officials. In the Falklands crisis these traditional channels of communication were intensively used. This meant in particular lobbying on the part of the firms directly concerned by the embargo decisions and the Argentine sanctions.

These lobbyists intervened through their traditional interlocutors, i.e. the Ministry of Economic Affairs, and their representatives injected their concerns into the debate at the ministerial and the official levels. Simultaneously, however, the businesses concerned tried to intervene directly, attempting to be forceful and yet discreet. The Chancellor himself and the Minister of Defence were their favourite targets, not only because of the Chancellor's leading position but also because he and the Minister of Defence had their constituencies in northern Germany which was the area most hit by the trade embargo; 40 per cent of German trade with Argentina went through Hamburg, where the Chancellor lived. In addition the firm Blohm and Voss had been charged by the Argentine government with delivering four frigates, which meant that several billions of deutschmarks were directly at stake during the Falklands crisis. Even though German businesses accepted that raw materials in particular could not be exported to a warring party, the various lobbies constantly warned against the generally negative repercussions on trade with Latin America and on the labour market in Germany.

Lobbying at the national level was complemented by similar actions towards the EC institutions. Once more the national approach, through Germany's Permanent Representation to the EC, was the favourite method of the Deutsche Industrie-und Handelstag and the Bundesverband der Deutschen Industrie, as well as that of other individual lobbyists. How fine tuned this network of contacts is, was also illustrated by the fact that representatives of German enterprises in Argentina and of their federations 'on the spot' were in close contact with the German diplomats in Buenos Aires to signal their concern over the sanctions. Fear was particularly expressed over the negative effects of continuing sanctions once other EC partners (especially Italy) left the common EC front.

On balance, German trade with Argentina was but marginally effected by the sanctions. Only smaller firms with short-term contracts were blocked in their commercial activities, due to the fact that the old contracts could continue and because the embargo was limited to the trade sector only. Other sectors such as finance were not included in the sanctions at all. Such a development would have created a much greater burden for those Germans involved in the international financial markets given the difficult financial situation of Argentina at that time.

Conclusions: Partial Solidarity with the United Kingdom

Germany's solidarity with the United Kingdom in the Falklands crisis was mainly based upon political considerations, on the importance Germany attached to the UK as a partner in the EC, as a member of the Atlantic Alliance and (at that time) as a guarantor of Germany's reunification. Economic considerations ranked second. The federal government's reaction, which dominated the decision-making process and the definition of Germany's position, was clearly influenced by these general political considerations, and it was widely backed up by other domestic, political and economic forces.

Such a basic primacy of political principles did not however prevent the sceptics from expressing their concerns. Their views did not remain totally unheard; they were particularly successful with those officials in the sector ministries who worked in favour of limiting the scope of the trade sanctions. In this respect the federal government did all it could, in a quiet way, to prevent too much damage to German business while making its solidarity with the British position constantly public.

Public support did not, however, mean an unconditional acceptance of the British policy, particularly not with regard to the use of military force. Germany, again supported by domestic opinion, tried to counteract possible negative repercussions on its political and economic standing in Latin America through both the Community and EPC policy and through traditional diplomatic means, particularly in the aftermath of the immediate crisis. The time factor, in that the dispute lasted only three months, played an important role. Had it lasted longer, and had the United Kingdom followed the same policies, political and economic solidarity could have been called into question at any given moment both by the political class and by business.

– 4 –

The Converging National Reactions (II): The Smaller States – Belgium, the Netherlands and Greece

Sophie Vanhoonacker,

Cees Homan,

Panos Tsakaloyannis and Dimitris Bourantonis[1]

General Introduction

This chapter consists of three sections dealing in turn with the reactions of smaller EC states, namely Belgium, the Netherlands and Greece. Although the relative importance of small states in international relations remains an open question, one should not take the extreme view that they cannot play any role at all. Indeed, as will be shown below, the smaller states did play an important role during the Falklands War, either by disagreeing with the majority view (Ireland in Chapter 7, below), supporting it (this chapter), or by taking an in between stance over the question of which legal instrument should be used over EC sanctions against Argentina (Denmark in Chapter 5, below). For a variety of reasons, ranging from personal alliances to pro-European views to support for international law, these three states adopted a pro-British stance in line with the two bigger states examined in the previous chapter.

Two further points need to be made at this stage. The first point has to do with the implications of these stances on the European level. Even though

1. The section on Belgium was written by Sophie Vanhoonacker, that on the Netherlands by Cees Homan, and the section on Greece by Panos Tsakaloyannis and Dimitris Bourantonis.

there was no provision for majority voting in EPC (as it then was), the fact that three states backed the UK made the life of the dissenting EC members more difficult because they found themselves in a clear minority (Spain was not a member state at the time). In other words, numbers do make a difference in international groupings.

The second important point has to do with the first of these states examined here, Belgium. The fact that Belgium held the Presidency of the Council made its role in the EC more important than it would have otherwise been considering the international influence of that country. This raises a number of issues over the international standing of smaller states and how difficult it is for them to exercise the Presidency when their turn comes.

Belgium and the Falklands

When, on 2 April 1982, the Belgian population learned that Argentine soldiers and marines had invaded the Falkland Islands, it was for many of them the first time that they had ever heard of this small group of islands in the South Atlantic, and few would have been able to place them on a map. However, even if the Falklands crisis did not stir public excitement or lead to a major debate in the Belgian parliament, a closer look at the Belgian position is nonetheless of interest, as the country was at the helm of the EC in the first half of 1982.[2] Holding the chair of all EC and EPC meetings and being the Ten's spokesman to the outside world, the country played an important role in the formulation of the Ten's response to the events.

The programme presented to the European Parliament in late January 1982 defined four major issues as being on the top of the Presidency's agenda:[3] the tackling of the economic crisis by stimulating investment and improving productivity, the further development of a European Union together with the strengthening of the EC institutions and the Community's decision-making capacity, the promotion of a more visible European presence on the international scene, and support for the idea of a 'Europe of the citizens' by creating a European Foundation.[4]

2. On Belgium and the Presidency of the Council of the EC, see C. Franck, 'Les Présidences Belges 1973-77-82-87', paper delivered at TEPSA Colloquium, Brussels, 3-4 June 1993. M. van den Abeele, 'Rapport national sur la Belgique', C. O'Nuallain (ed.), *The Presidency of the European Council of Ministers*, London: Croom Helm, 1985, pp. 23-49.

3. 'Programme of Action for the First Six Months of 1982', *Europe Documents*, 29 January 1982.

4. The aim of the European Foundation, as envisaged by Tindemans, was to promote a better understanding of a common cultural heritage and of the goals of European unification among the European people.

It is interesting to see how the Presidency translated the third objective, that of fostering more assertive action by the Ten in the foreign policy field, into concrete terms.

Belgium: a Fierce Supporter of a Stronger European Voice in the World

The determination of the Belgian Minister for Foreign Affairs to seize upon the Presidency as an opportunity to stimulate the Ten to play a more active role on the international scene was completely in line with the country's full support for the development of a European foreign policy and its strong commitment to the process of European integration in general. This had been one of the basic pillars of Belgian foreign policy since the end of the Second World War.[5] Being a small country, heavily dependent on external trade, Belgium was very conscious of the fact that, integrated into a supranational framework, its influence could be much more important than if it acted alone. However, as is clearly illustrated by its rejection of the French plans for political union in the early 1960s, the Fouchet proposals, Belgium was wary of coordinating the member states' foreign policies along intergovernmental lines. It reasoned that a European foreign policy based on decisions taken unanimously and from which the EC Commission would be excluded did not offer sufficient guarantees against domination by the larger member states.[6]

As European Political Cooperation (EPC) gradually developed from 1970 onwards, Belgium always reminded its colleagues that a genuine common foreign policy, organized according to the supranational Community method, would have to constitute one of the basic pillars of a European Union. In his famous report which he prepared at the request of the Paris European Council of 1974, the Belgian Prime Minister Leo Tindemans pleaded for an end to the artificial separation between the EC and EPC and to change 'the political commitment of the member states which is the basis of political cooperation into a legal obligation'.[7] In a speech on Belgian foreign policy before the House of Representatives in March 1982, Tindemans, in his capacity as Minister for Foreign Affairs, stated that the only possibility for Belgium to exert influence on developments

5. On the role of Belgium in the process of European integration, see for example M. Dumoulin (ed.), *La Belgique et les Débuts de la Construction Européenne*, Ciaco, 1987; M.A.G. van Meerhaeghe (ed.), *Belgium and EC Membership Evaluated*, London: Pinter Publishers, 1992.

6. On the role of Belgium in the Fouchet negotiations, see S. Vanhoonacker, 'La Belgique: Bouc Emissaire ou Responsable de l'Échec des Négociations Fouchet?', *Res Publica*, vol. 31, no. 4, 1989, pp. 513-26.

7. *'European Union. Report by Mr Leo Tindemans, Prime Minister of Belgium to the European Council'*, Memo from Belgium, Brussels: Views and Surveys Ministry of Foreign Affairs, External Trade and Cooperation in Development, 1976, pp. 15-16.

on the international scene was within the framework of the EC.[8] It is therefore not surprising that after the outbreak of the Falklands crisis, Leo Tindemans, in his capacity as chairman of the Council, did his utmost to come
up with a common Community position. During the Belgian Presidency
of 1982, he was able to count on the full support of Prime Minister Willy
Martens, a convinced European federalist,[9] as well as on his partners in
the liberal coalition.

The Role of the Belgian Presidency[10]

Due to the promptness with which the Ten reacted to the events in the
Falklands, the EC's role in the crisis is often referred to as one of the success stories of EPC. The question of interest here is to what extent this
timely reaction can be attributed to the role of the Belgian Presidency. It
is evident that the Presidency cannot claim the entire credit for the Ten's
concerted diplomacy in the Falklands, and factors such as the direct
involvement in the conflict of one of the EC member states and the fact
that the attack constituted a flagrant violation of international law certainly
positively influenced the facility of the Ten to speak with one voice. One
should also guard against overestimating the room for manoeuvre of the
Presidency, the role of which mainly consists in chairing meetings and
mediating among its colleagues. As decisions in the framework of EPC
are taken by consensus, the Presidency cannot impose its views and the
minister in the chair is to a large extent dependent on the goodwill of his
partners.

Taking into consideration the above-mentioned reservations, the role
of the Belgian Presidency and more particularly of the Belgian Minister
for Foreign Affairs in bringing about an immediate reaction to the crisis
should nevertheless not be underestimated. The confidence which Leo Tindemans enjoyed in European circles, as well as the fact that Belgium did
not have any major interests in Argentina, permitted the country to play
the role of an honest broker. As a Belgian politician accustomed to dealing with the various interests of the three linguistic communities of his
country, Leo Tindemans had developed the skill to formulate compromises,
a capacity which also proved very useful in his function as President of
the EC Council.

It was nonetheless far from easy to convince a country such as Italy,
with a large Italian community in Argentina, to support the condemnation

8. *Annales Parlementaires*, séance du vendredi 23 avril 1982, p. 1418.
9 . H. De Ridder, *Omtrent Wilfried Martens*, Tielt: Lannoo, 1991. Both Martens and Tindemans belong to the Christian Democrats.
10. The author would like to thank H.E. Leo Tindemans for kindly agreeing to give an
interview on 16 February 1993.

of the invasion. The debate over the legal basis for the implementation of sanctions also proved very strenuous. Leo Tindemans radically opposed the Danish proposal to implement the decision of the Political Committee to impose sanctions through individual action by the member states. Being a fervent proponent of further blurring the distinction between EPC and the EC, he convinced his colleagues that despite the fact that sanctions were motivated by political reasons, the instruments of the Community's common commercial policy (Article 113) could be used.[11]

The Belgian Presidency also succeeded in taking full advantage of the favourable climate towards EPC in the early 1980s and in exploiting the new possibilities created for EPC in the London Report adopted by the Ten under the previous Presidency on 13 October 1981.[12] Novelties such as the possibility to convene within forty-eight hours extraordinary meetings of the ministers for foreign affairs in case of a crisis situation, and the introduction of the Troika system requiring the Presidency to be assisted by an official from the previous and succeeding Presidencies, were beneficial for the functioning of both EPC and the Presidency. The fortunate coincidence that it was the United Kingdom which had been at the helm of the EC in the second half of 1981 meant that the Presidency could profit from the presence of a British official in the Belgian Ministry for Foreign Affairs.[13]

The limits weighing on the room for manoeuvre of the Presidency became very clear in early May when the crisis escalated into an armed conflict. After the torpedoing of the Argentine cruiser *General Belgrano*, the member states were faced with a radical shift in public opinion and it proved to be very difficult for the Belgian Presidency to maintain unity amongst its partners. On 17 May, when sanctions were about to expire, the Belgian Presidency, which still fully backed Britain, faced strong resistance to an extension to the embargo from Ireland, Italy, the Federal Republic of Germany and Denmark. They argued that the policy of sanctions initially aimed at exerting pressure on Argentina to come to a peaceful conclusion of the conflict had failed, and they objected to the continuance of the embargo.[14] The final decision of Italy and Ireland not to extend the sanctions constituted a serious disappointment for both European Political Cooperation and the Belgian Presidency, which had been working hard to maintain the consensus.[15] One week later, the Belgian Presidency

11. S. Nuttall, *European Political Cooperation*, Oxford: Clarendon Press, 1992, pp. 208, pp. 261–3.

12. 'Report on European Political Cooperation issued by the Foreign Ministry of the Ten on 13 October 1981 (London Report)', *European Political Cooperation*, Bonn: Press and Information Office, 1988, pp. 1–63.

13. G. Edwards, 'Europe and the Falkland Islands Crisis 1982', *Journal of Common Market Studies*, vol. 22, no. 4, June 1984, p. 301. See also chapter 2 of this study.

14. *Agence Europe*, 17–18 May 1982.

15. *Agence Europe*, 18 May 1982.

received a second blow when the Danes decided to implement the sanctions against Argentina on a national, rather than on the EC level. Any hopes or expectations that the solidarity which the Ten had demonstrated at the outbreak of the crisis might constitute the first step towards a genuine European common foreign policy, were completely dashed.

Initiatives and Public Opinion at the National Level

In addition to the action undertaken in the framework of EPC, Belgium also adopted a number of national decisions, all of them reinforcing the action of the Ten. On 7 April, the Ministry for Foreign Affairs issued a communiqué with a text which was very similar to the earlier declaration adopted by the Ten.[16] Together with several other EC Member States, Belgium recalled its ambassador in Buenos Aires and halted all arms supplies to Argentina.[17] However, the above-mentioned decision could not prevent the further production of weapons such as the FAL and Browning guns which Argentine firms produced under Belgian licence.

Although all the major Belgian newspapers regularly reported on the development of the crisis in the Falklands, the conflict did not spark a major public debate in Belgium. Most Belgian citizens were too preoccupied with the current economic crisis to bother about the conflict over this small group of islands far away in the South Atlantic. This lack of interest was also reflected in the Belgian parliament. During the first month of the crisis, the members of the Chamber of Representatives and the Senate did not consider it necessary to raise the issue in plenary session, nor did they question the policy followed by the Belgian government. When the Minister for Foreign Affairs, Tindemans, briefly referred to the crisis in a session of the Chamber on 23 April and expressed his solidarity with the United Kingdom, none of the parliamentarians commented on this issue.

As in most other EC Member States, this indifference was reversed when the crisis in the Falklands turned into an armed conflict. In both chambers, there were questions regarding the Belgian position towards alleged British aggression and the government was asked how it intended to prevent the further escalation of the conflict.[18] The rather short answers given by the Minister for Defence, Freddy Vreven (Chamber), and the Minister for Justice and Institutional Reforms, Jean Gol (Senate), seemed to have

16. *Déclaration du Gouvernement Belge*, 7 avril 1982, Ministère des Affaires Etrangères, du Commerce Extérieur et de la Coopération au Développement, Bruxelles: Service de Presse.

17. *De Standaard*, 8 April 1982.

18. *Annales Parlementaires*, Chambre des Représentants, séance du mercredi 12 mai, p. 1608; and *Annales Parlementaires*, Sénat, séance du jeudi 13 mai 1982, pp. 1020-1.

satisfied Parliament and a further debate on the issue did not ensue. It was not until the end of May that the Senate, upon the initiative of the Socialist senator Lahaye, adopted a motion calling on the two sides to stop any further bloodshed and to find a peaceful solution to the conflict.[19]

After the capitulation by Argentina on 14 June 1982, the problem of the Falkland Islands and the future of its inhabitants quickly moved to the back of the minds of the Belgian citizens, if it had ever been there. Only when having to cast a vote on the resolutions adopted in the framework of the UN Assembly were Belgian diplomats reminded that no final settlement on the issue had been reached between the United Kingdom and Argentina. On each of the seven resolutions adopted between November 1982 and November 1988, Belgium aligned its position with that of the majority of the other member states and opted for abstention.[20]

Conclusions

Had Belgium not been at the helm of the EC during the first half of 1982, it might barely have been of interest for this study to examine the role of the country in the Falklands crisis. The conflict was not the subject of any public debate, and it took more than one month for the Belgian Chamber and Senate to formulate the first and also the last question on the issue. The neglible role of the parliament does not come as a surprise, but it is another illustration of the very low-key role of the Belgian parliament in the formulation of foreign policy in general.[21] In contrast to countries such as Italy and Ireland, where the governments were under much pressure from public opinion, domestic factors barely played a role in the shaping of the position of the Belgian government towards the crisis. This attitude of public opinion, which can only be described as mere indifference, implied that in the case of Belgium it was the government which was the major actor in the crisis. The Belgian Minister for Foreign Affairs, Leo Tindemans, had much leeway to act on his own and decide how the Ten should cooperate and coordinate their action in the field of foreign policy, and did his utmost to fully exploit this chance. Yet, regardless of the tenacity and the perseverance of the Presidency, Tindemans had in the end to concede that in the framework of EPC, and in accordance with its own rules and capacities, it is ultimately the member states that have the final word. The experience of the Belgian Presidency in the crisis in the Falklands in the spring of 1982 confirms once again the truism that when there

19. *Annales Parlementaires*, Senat, séance du 27 mai 1982, p. 1115.

20. See also C. Franck, 'Belgium: Committed Multilateralism', in C. Hill (ed.), *National Foreign Policies and European Political Cooperation*, London: Allen & Unwin, 1983, p. 97.

21. R. Coolsaet, *Buitenlandse Zaken*, Leuven: Kritak, 1987, pp. 249-51.

are serious domestic pressures, solidarity among the EC member states is severely tested.

The Netherlands and the Falklands Conflict

'Holland, a country whose wealth was built upon naval prowess and internationalism, though it backed EEC trade sanctions, questioned Britain's sanity and sense of proportion over its military enterprise at every level and every stage.'[22] This passage in an editorial of *The Economist* does not do justice to the Dutch attitude to the Falklands War because, in short, there is no such a thing as a Dutch attitude. In a pluriform society like the Netherlands, all kinds of groups and persons have their own different opinions on political affairs. More importantly, however, the Dutch government's position did support the British during the 1982 War.

Before considering the Dutch position in more detail, some general introductory remarks about the foreign policy-making process of the Netherlands are in order.[23] By reference to such statistics as national and per capita income, military expenditure, military personnel, population size, diplomatic network and membership in international organizations, the Dutch foreign policy specialist Voorhoeve showed that the Netherlands should be classified among the twenty or so foremost countries in the world; in that respect the Netherlands can be counted among the smaller middle powers. The geographical position of the Netherlands, in the delta of the rivers Rhine and Maas, offers it the opportunity to be the gateway to Europe. Rotterdam port and Schiphol Airport are among the largest in the world. Transport and distribution and invisible earnings such as services, insurances and capital transactions figure prominently in the economy. The flow of capital leaving the country is to a large extent managed by the four major multinationals, Royal Dutch/Shell, Unilever, Philips and Akzo.

However, the Dutch themselves dislike *grandeur* and chauvinism, and until recently the terms 'power' and 'national interest' were hardly ever used in debates on foreign policy. The political culture of the country dictates a debate in terms of the general values the Netherlands promotes such as democracy, individual freedom and human rights. While the Dutch themselves regard their attitude as decent and fitting for a small country, others discern a streak of hypocrisy. Not every Dutchman thinks his country has a mission in the world, but many think it can at least set a good example to others.

22. *The Economist*, 19 June 1982.
23. Based on P. Everts and G. Walraven (eds), *The Politics of Persuasion, Implementation of Foreign Policy by the Netherlands*, Avebury: Gower, 1989.

It has been possible to notice in the Netherlands a growing politicization of foreign policy, a process of creeping pluralism, especially since the 1960s. Two interacting national factors have reinforced this development: the 'democratic revolution' and the slow disappearance of the denominated segregation based on theology. Even in the area of foreign policy there was a growing challenge to the established authority of leaders and increasing demands for wider participation. This growing public involvement has contributed also to an increase in parliamentary activities. However, a broad consensus has survived on the main lines of foreign policy; this predominant agreement on main issues shows that, unlike some other Western countries, the three largest Dutch political parties, PvdA, CDA and VVD (Labour, Christian Democrats and the 'conservative' Liberals) hold quite similar views on foreign policy. In other words, there was fundamental agreement on such general goals as European integration, a strong international legal order and maintaining a relatively high level of development aid. It was only on more detailed policy goals and the ways of implementing them that greater differences appeared between the political parties; as far as public opinion at the mass level is concerned, there are sufficient data to show a strong continuity of support for the main policy lines.

The Netherlands and the 1982 Conflict in the South Atlantic

The Government – As far as the Falklands conflict is concerned, the Dutch government supported the EEC embargo and UN Security Council Resolution 502.[24] In its opinion the United Kingdom could invoke Article 51 of the Charter of the United Nations, which allows for the right of self-defence. However, the Netherlands government would have preferred a more conciliatory British attitude towards a diplomatic solution. The government also gave support to the UK in the Eurogroup in NATO. In short, during the whole conflict, the Dutch government had no dissenting policy of its own, but supported the actions of the EEC and the United Nations.

Parliament – As became clear during several consultations between the permanent Committee on Foreign Affairs and the Secretary of State, there were a variety of opinions in the Dutch parliament.[25] A common opinion, however, which received the support of all political parties was that everything should be done to find a political solution. The two political parties which participated in the Cabinet, the Christian Democrats (CDA) and the

24. Parliamentary Proceedings 1981–1982, 17100, ch. 5, Ministry of Foreign Affairs, no.81 and no.84.
25. Ibid.

Liberals (VVD), supported in general terms the policy of the government. However, De Boer, the spokesman of the Christian Democrats, contrasted the quick reaction to the occupation of the Falkland Islands to the lack of a communitarian action over the violation of human rights in Argentina. The strongest support for the British action came from Mr Bolkestein, the spokesman for the Liberal party; for him it was very clear that the Argentines had committed agression, while the British were acting in self-defence. Two other issues were widely discussed: the question of sovereignty and the implications for international law.

The opposition, for the most part consisting of the political parties on the left of the political spectrum, was more critical of the Dutch governmental position. The spokesman of the small Pacifist Socialist Party, Van der Spek, considered the British sovereignty of the Falkland Islands to be an anachronism, but recognized the right to self-determination of the local British population; in his view, the character of the Argentine regime was also a factor requiring consideration. In the opinion of Schaper, the spokesman of Democrats 66, the military developments had created their own momentum with the result that the desired effect of sanctions could not be achieved.

Public Opinion – A great deal of attention was paid to Dutch public opinion towards the Falklands War. At the end of April 1982, the Netherlands Institute for Public Opinion put three questions to a national sample of 1,126 men and women.[26] In the first question they were asked if Argentina should withdraw from the islands: 74 per cent answered positively, 13 per cent negatively, while 13 per cent had no opinion at all. In the second question the sample was asked if, when necessary, the British troops should expel the Argentines by force: 31 per cent answered positively, 58 per cent negatively, and 11 per cent had no opinion. The final question asked whether the Falkland Islands should stay British if the population wished so, or whether the islands should be Argentine, regardless of the wishes of the population: 71 per cent expressed the opinion that, if the population wished so, the islands should stay British, while 14 per cent felt that they should become Argentine. 15 per cent had no opinion at all.

The Press – As was to be expected, considerable attention was devoted to the Falklands conflict in the press. Most commentators were in favour of the action of the United Kingdom. In his widely read column in the weekly *Elsevier*, Van Rosmalen stated that he considered the aspect of international security to be even more important than the aspect of international law: 'When international society resigns itself to conquests by the gene-

26. Netherlands Institute for Public Opinion and Marketing Research, Report no.2187, 2 June 1982.

rals, it is Liberty Hall.'[27] He was referring to a potential occupation of the Dutch island of Aruba by Venezuela. Van Rosmalen also put the question as to whether the Dutch government should not, in cooperation with other Western European countries, temporarily withdraw its ambassador from Argentine 'for consultations'.

In an editorial, the daily paper *De Volkskrant* accused Buenos Aires of being responsible for the failure of the diplomatic negotiations.[28] The columnist Neumam questioned the military necessity of the sinking of the *General Belgrano* on 2 May in the *Trouw* :[29] in his opinion the whole conflict was about the question of whether Argentina should get the sovereignty of the Falkland Islands now or in five years time.

The columnist Heldring of the authoritative daily *NRC Handelsblad* wondered if, as a consequence of the Falklands War, British policy towards Europe would change. His observation was based on the fact that British self-confidence had increased and that the number of people who were in favour of leaving the EC had risen from 39 per cent to 61 per cent.[30]

The Peace Movement – The domestic peace movement, the Inter-Church Peace Council, which was very active in the Netherlands at that time in opposing the stationing of cruise missiles in Europe, took no position at all in this conflict. It did attempt in secret to bring the peace movement of Argentina into contact with the peace movement of the UK; however, the latter did not allow the secretary of the Dutch movement to read out a message from the Argentine Nobel Prize Laureate, Adolf Perez Esquivel, during a demonstration against cruise missiles in London.[31]

Business – Dutch business became indirectly involved in the Falklands conflict. The branches of Unilever and Philips in Argentina were criticized in the Netherlands because they supported with advertisments a marathon television program, the proceeds of which were paid in to the account of the 'Patriotic Fund', an Argentine organization which supported Argentina's war efforts financially. The commercial director of Philips in Argentina, Mr Monfils, declared that his organization had nothing to do with politics and that the way in which the ATC television channel spent its profits was not his business.[32]

Two hundred Argentine military personnel were being trained in Holland at the Hollandse Signaalapparaten B.V. to operate electronics which

27. *Elsevier*, 10 April 1982.
28. *De Volkskrant*, 22 May 1982.
29. *Trouw*, 17 May 1982.
30. *NRC Handelsblad*, 25 June 1982.
31. Author's interview with Mient-Jan Faber, the secretary of the Inter-Church Peace Council, on 25 January 1994.
32. *NRC Handelsblad*, 13 May 1982.

the firm had supplied to the Argentine Navy. When asked in Parliament by Mr Van der Spek (Pacifist Socialist Party) if this training should be stopped, the Secretary of State, Mr Van der Stoel, answered first that the export of electronics was not considered to be a breach of the weapon embargo; second, he wondered if the United Kingdom would welcome the return of these Argentine military personnel to their country under the prevailing circumstances.[33]

When, because of the war, a very large natural gas project by a Dutch firm in Argentina was closed down, the Ministry of Foreign Affairs called in the well-known retired diplomat Emile Van Lennep to find a satisfactory solution. However, it took until the end of 1984 for negotiations to begin, and a bilateral agreement was finally signed in New York on 1 December 1986.[34]

Conclusions

In conclusion it can be stated that, generally speaking and quite unsurprisingly, the most important actors in the field of Dutch foreign policy were strongly opposed to the occupation of the Falkland Islands by Argentina. During the whole conflict they were strongly in favour of a political solution, but as a 'faithful ally', official Dutch foreign policy during the Falklands War was always in line with the policy of the majority of the EEC states and of the European members of NATO. The Netherlands also backed the prevailing UN position on the issue. In that respect, the comment by *The Economist* quoted above does not do justice to the Dutch attitude during the Falklands War.

Greece and the Falklands Conflict

On 2 April 1982, the main story carried by most Greek newspapers was the Commission's first cautious reaction to the Greek Memorandum submitted in early March, in which the new government in Athens had presented Brussels with a list of demand ranging from supplementary Community aid to Greece to a request for the retention of tariffs from other EC countries on certain products. Such measures were deemed necessary by PASOK in order to redress the adverse effects of membership on the

33. *Parliamentary Proceedings* 1981–1982, 17100, ch. 5, Ministry of Foreign Affairs, no. 81.
34. *Emile van Lennep in de Wereldeconomie, Herinneringen van eenå Internationale Wereldeconomie*, E.van Lennep, *The World-Economy, Memories of an International Dutchman*, Leiden: Stenfert Kroese, 1991, pp. 290–302.

Greek economy. The details of this story need not detain us here, and the main reason for mentioning it in the context of the Falklands is because Greek attitudes to the EC at the time go a long way towards explaining Athens' surprisingly pro-British stance, especially at the crucial phase between early April and June 1982.

PASOK's pro-British stance on the Falklands is the more surprising in view of its manifest anti-colonial and non-aligned proclivities. Therefore, apart from attitudes to Brussels, some other factors need to be taken into consideration. The first is the 'Cyprus factor'; from the outset of the Falklands crisis, Athens drew close parallels with Cyprus, not least in terms of the strong Greek opposition to the use of force for the invasion and occupation of territory. Similarly, the British line on the Falklands lent credence to an old Greek argument that geographical proximity is of little relevance in determining the sovereignty of islands, especially when it runs counter to the principle of self-determination.[35] Hence the Greek attitude to the Falklands, as Geoffrey Edwards has rightly pointed out, was very much moulded by preoccupation with 'its scattered and vulnerable islands and, of course, by Cyprus'.[36]

Another, less obvious reason for the Greek responses to the Falklands, is personal, namely the warm relationship between Mrs Thatcher and Andreas Papandreou at the time. This may sound incongruous, considering their sharply contrasting political philosophies. Yet such differences were more than outweighed by the striking similarities. To begin with, in domestic and foreign policies both were radicals and 'revisionists', in that they strove to break the mould and to arrest their countries' decline. In domestic politics they had to fight against entrenched interests, the political establishment in Greece, and the 'wets' in Britain, blamed respectively for the decline;[37] similarly in foreign policy, both leaders championed a more assertive nationalistic stance. Neither could be accused of giving in to pressures, or of 'appeasement'.

Last but not least both leaders shared very similar views towards the EC. Incidentally, Mrs Thatcher and Andreas Papandreou were two conspicuous absentees from the ceremony marking the signing of Greek accession to the EC in May 1979, the former because she was otherwise engaged and the latter because his party boycotted the ceremony. Evidently neither thought highly of EC institutions and both were strong opponents

---

35. For the Greek and Turkish arguments on this issue see, for example, *UN General Assembly, Ninth Session, 14 December 1954*, General Assembly, Official Records A/9/PV750, 14 December 1954, paragraphs 67–8 and 105–7.

36. G. Edwards, 'Europe and the Falkland Islands Crisis', *Journal of Common Market Studies*, vol.22, no.4, June 1984, p.303.

37. It should be recalled that although Papandreou originally came from the pre-1967 'Centre Union Party', in 1974 he broke ranks and formed PASOK, whose share of the vote leapt from 13 per cent in 1974, to over 48 per cent by 1981.

of any further encroachments on national sovereignty from Brussels.[38] Therefore as the crisis in the Falklands was reaching a *crescendo*, both Britain
and Greece were at odds with Brussels, the former over its contribution
to the Community's budget and the latter because of PASOK's negative
attitude to Greece's accession. When the above are added to the two leaders' personal styles of decision making, which often bypassed their Cabinet or even the ministers responsible,[39] it becomes easier to explain the
personal rapport between Mrs Thatcher and Andreas Papandreou. This
rapport was also evident in the easy access that the British Ambassador
in Athens, the late Sir Ian Sutherland, had to the Greek Prime Minister's
office in early 1982. It is not fortuitous that soon after the conclusion of
the Falklands War Sir Ian was rewarded with the post of ambassador in
Moscow.[40]

At the same time Mrs Thatcher's resolute and defiant stance on the
Falklands touched a sensitive chord in many Greeks, who saw in her the
Churchillian qualities they had come to admire during Second World War.
Another reason explaining such pro-British sympathies, especially in the
early phase of the conflict, was public ignorance of what the conflict was
about – most Greeks did not know where the islands were situated – as
well as the nature of the political regime in Argentina, which to many Greeks
closely resembled the Greek *junta* which ruled between 1967 and 1974.
While it is impossible to measure the exact weight of such historical-
psychological factors, nevertheless their importance should not be ignored.

Greece and the Falklands: April–June 1982

When, on 2 April 1982, at the request of the British government, the
Security Council of the UN considered the Falklands issue, Greece was
not a member of the Security Council. However, its representative requested that Greece, together with all other EC countries which were not members of the Security Council, be invited to participate in the debate in
accordance with Rule 37 of the Security Council. During the debate Greece
aligned itself fully with the position of its EC partners' and unreservedly

38. For example, on 30 March 1982, Papandreou declared that 'we have no obligation
to stay in the EC should a solution [to the Greek problems listed in the Memorandum] not
be found. We do not accept, for the sake of Community solidarity, decisions which [might
be] harmful to Greek interests', *Kathemerini*, 1 April 1982.

39. For example, Gerasimos Arsenis, the overlord of PASOK's economic policy between
1982-5 (and Minister of Defence in the current Administration) confided in 1987 that the
question of Greece's policies and strategy in the EC was handled exclusively by Papandreou
himself, and that it was never discussed even by the Inner Cabinet, the KYSYM. See G.
Arsenis, *Politiki Katathesi* [Political Testament], Athens: Odysseas, 1987, p. 168.

40. Interviews with British diplomats in Athens in June 1994. They would like to remain
anonymous.

supported Resolution 502 of 3 April 1982. While Greece did not take a position with regard to the substance of the dispute, it nonetheless condemned the armed intervention in the Falklands by Argentina as a violation of Article 2, paragraph 4 of the UN Charter. According to the Greek representative in the UN, 'nobody can negotiate freely and in fairness any international dispute under pressure of military occupation', an argument which must have more than gratified London which was calling for the evacuation of Argentinean troops from the Falklands. On no occasion, the Greek representative argued, 'should a military invasion be condoned'.[41]

Following the adoption of Resolution 502 by the Security Council, London's attention turned to other fora, not least to the EC whose foreign ministers had already issued, on 2 April 1982 a joint declaration condemning the invasion and appealing to the Argentine government to withdraw its troops from the islands. But as this resolution was regarded by London as too woolly and innocuous, pressure was stepped up in the days following for more drastic and tangible action by the Ten, such as the recalling of their ambassadors from Buenos Aires, the blocking of arms sales and the restriction of export credits. Initially the Foreign Office aimed at a selective ban of imports from Argentina, but the British representative in Brussels correctly assumed that such a selective ban would be more difficult than a total trade ban to agree upon and to put into effect by the Ten. The latter had the advantage of being comprehensive and cutting short endless discussions as to which products were to be included in such a ban. Selective trade bans, as the EC's record on South Africa or even on Poland and the Soviet Union had shown, were frustrating, complicated and time-consuming exercises; these were pitfalls London wanted to avoid in the case of Argentina.

On 6 April 1982, the British deputy at COREPER, William Nichol, requested from his EC colleagues the adoption of a total trade ban by the EC. The initial reaction, especially from the French, Italian and German representatives, was not entirely encouraging, and so on the same day Prime Minister Thatcher addressed a personal letter to her colleagues in the EC. In the case of Greece the British Ambassador in Athens Sir Ian Sutherland, delivered the letter immediately to the Greek Prime Minister. Following this meeting Papandreou declared that 'the Greek Government is watching with profound concern developments [in the Falklands] and it condemns any resort to violence or any other form of action aiming at the conquest of territories by force. Greece's firm position is for the peaceful settlement of differences and for compliance with the Charter and the Resolutions of the UN.'[42]

41. *UN Doc. S/PV. 2364*, 24 May 1982, p. 9.
42. *To Vema*, 7 April 1982.

The effects of the Greek position on London's battle in Brussels were considerable. While most EC member states declared a ban on arms exports to Argentina, Greece stepped forward and announced a comprehensive ban on imports. Hence in an interesting twist of roles, Greece, the EC's *enfant terrible* which in recent months had earned a reputation for going it alone, especially on sanctions against the Soviet Union or Poland, appeared in a most communitarian role and as the champion of Community solidarity, thus driving traditional 'Europeanists' onto the defensive. After a stormy and somewhat unpleasant COREPER meeting on 9 April 1982, a Good Friday, the Ten finally agreed on a trade ban on Argentina, the details of which were to be finalized after Easter.[43] The following week the Greek Foreign Minister, after a meeting with the British Ambassador, endorsed the list of trade sanctions against Argentina drawn up by London, and reaffirmed Greece's opposition to armed invasion for territorial gains.[44] At the same time Greece, together with the other EC countries, refused to discuss at the UN a motion tabled by Argentina, the Soviet Union and the non-aligned countries, condemning the imposition of trade sanctions by the EC. Two weeks later, as Britain and Argentina were heading towards armed confrontation, Athens reaffirmed its stance on the issue.[45] Greece also supported Resolution 505 of 26 May 1982, which in essence was a reaffirmation of Resolution 502.

However, with the prospect of armed conflict in the South Atlantic nearing, the Greek position became a little more circumspect. In mid-May, while still lending its support to London in Brussels, unlike other EC members such as Italy and Ireland, Athens distanced itself from London in other international fora, such as the Non-Aligned Movement. Thus on 6 May 1982, Papandreou, at a state banquet for Nicolae Ceausescu, called on Britain to display the same sensitivity it showed towards the eighteen-hundred Falklanders to the plight of the Greek Cypriots. In a similar spirit the next day, following NATO's condemnation of Argentina's invasion, the Greek government again tried to keep a certain distance by stating that it viewed the escalation of the dispute over the Falklands as tragic. And while Athens still called for the implementation of Resolution 502, it now added the caveat that it favoured 'a peaceful solution to the problem, as the continuation of the undeclared war might have caused great suffering and unpredictable international complications'. For the above reasons, Greece appealed to the belligerents to suspend hostilities and to seek a peaceful settlement to the dispute.[46]

---

43. For the factual account of this episode we have drawn on *The Falklands War: The Full Story* by the Sunday Times Team, London: Sphere books, 1982, pp. 116-8.

44. *Kathemerini*, 14 April 1982.

45. *To Vema*, 27 April 1982; *Kathemerini*, 27 April 1982.

46. *Kathemerini*, 6 and 7 May 1982.

During the course of the armed conflict in the South Atlantic, the Greek government maintained this somewhat cautious stance of supporting London at the diplomatic level, particularly in Brussels, yet showing a growing affinity with the Non-Aligned Movement's views on the conflict. In time the latter line became more vocal, especially after the end of hostilities. The flaring up of the crisis in the Lebanon in June 1982 provided the opportunity for Athens to align itself closer with the 'radicals' in the Non-Aligned Movement; the evacuation by Greek ships of the besieged Yasser Arafat from Beirut in the summer of 1982 helped to re-establish Greek credentials among the radicals in the Middle East and in the Non-Aligned Movement. This was reflected in Greek voting on the Falklands in the UN since the end of hostilities. In any case the Falklands, as an issue, began to decline in importance after November 1982, when the UN General Assembly put it on its own agenda. It may be recalled that the General Assembly's agenda, as opposed to that of the Security Council, covers almost every international issue; this includes a lengthy general debate which is in effect a series of general speeches by national representatives. The Assembly can only make recommendations which do not place a formal legal obligation on the members of the UN.

In November 1982, twenty non-aligned countries tabled a draft resolution in the General Assembly asking the parties directly involved in the dispute, Argentina and the UK, to resume negotiations on the question of sovereignty in the Falklands. This resolution, by giving precedence to the principle of territorial integrity over the principle of self-determination, tilted towards Argentina's position, the more so as it called for negotiations between the two parties for the transfer of sovereignty of the Falklands to Argentina against the free will of the population. This draft Resolution 37/9 was adopted on 4 November 1982 by 90 votes to 12, with 52 abstentions. Greece was the only EC country to vote for the Resolution.[47]

Greece's vote for Resolution 37/9 was coupled to the caveat that 'the outcome of the negotiations between Argentina and the UK over the Falkland Islands (Malvinas) should not be prejudiced by any factor whatsoever'.[48] In 1983 and 1984, the Greek position in the UN shifted again and it fell in line with the majority of the EC countries who abstained from Resolutions 38/12 and 49/6, both sponsored by a non-aligned group. These, as did Resolution 37/9, urged Argentina and the UK to negotiate, this time on all their differences including the key issue of sovereignty.

---

47. The other Western country to deviate from the mainstream Western position and vote with the non-aligned countries was the United States.
48. General Assembly, *Official Records, A/37/PV. 55*, 4 November 1982, p. 961.

Conclusions

In June 1984 the first direct contact between UK and Argentine representatives since the Falklands War was held in Berne. This date could be taken as marking a new phase in the Falklands dispute in that bilateral contacts assumed a greater priority than scoring points at international fora, including the UN. Greece, especially since 1984, has like most other EC members adopted a low key position equidistant between the two sides. At the same time there has been a marked evolution in Greek attitudes to the dispute, from a pro-British line, at the time of the crisis in the spring of 1982, to a more even-handed attitude, which in its practical manifestation has remained mildly pro-Argentine. This evolution can be attributed to several reasons. First, Greece has always counted on the moral support of the General Assembly, especially when Cyprus was high on the agenda and following the declaration of secession by the Turkish sector of Cyprus in November 1983, there have been mounting Greek concerns over its possible recognition by the international community. Such recognition was feared more from the Islamic or non-aligned countries than from the Western or communist countries.

A second reason is related to the fact that with the fall of the military regime in Argentina the Greeks could sympathise with the new civilian government and draw certain parallels between their own plight under the colonels and that of the Argentine people under military rule. Moreover, as in the case of Cyprus in 1974, the military's adventure in the Falklands was seen as the folly of an unpopular regime for which the civilian population had to pay a high price. As a result, Greek sympathy for continuing British antagonism towards Buenos Aires diminished accordingly.

Third, with the deterioration in East-West relations, Greek perceptions moved further away from Mrs Thatcher's confrontational posturing. The onset of the 'Second Cold War' in the early 1980s was an anathema to Greece for a number of reasons, not least because it tilted the balance of power in the eastern Mediterranean in favour of Turkey. Greece's response to this neo-Cold War drift was the launching in 1984 of the 'Initiative of the Six', together with the Prime Ministers of Argentina, India, Mexico, Sweden and Tanzania, who tried to play a moderating role and to ease East-West tensions. In this context, Greece was bound to distance itself further from Britain's position on the Falklands.

The conflict in the South Atlantic remained a peripheral issue in Greek domestic politics; in fact it is questionable whether most Greeks were familiar with their government's precise position on the issue, all the more so as this involved international institutions and organizations like the EC or the UN, whose complicated procedures elude most Greeks. This explains the lack of a public debate on the subject. Throughout the conflict, there was not one single editorial in Greece's more serious newspapers on the subject. By contrast, the crisis in Beirut in the early summer of 1982 attracted a more lively interest in the media and the press. The same applies to the political parties; the Falklands did not become a subject of political controversy, apart from a plea to PASOK by New Democracy after the invasion to support Britain in the spirit of Community solidarity.[49]

To sum up, the Falklands crisis of 1982 provides an interesting case study of PASOK's 'multi-dimensional foreign policy', especially during its early period in office. The record suggests that PASOK showed more flexibility and greater imagination in exploiting opportunities than might have been expected given its rather simplistic rhetoric at the time. Its anti-NATO, and to a lesser extent anti-EC proclivities did not necessarily mean isolation from the West. Indeed, in the case of the Falklands PASOK was able to turn the tables and present itself in April 1982 as the champion of solidarity in the EC, to the embarrassment of some seasoned 'Europeanists'. Above all, PASOK's rejection of postwar Greece's unconditional adherence to Western structures is highly relevant in the present context of the 1990s, in which old structures have been crumbling with stunning speed, especially in the Balkans. In the new context, the room for a 'multi-dimensional foreign policy' is far greater than it was in the early 1980s. Perhaps the Falklands episode might be instructive in shedding light on PASOK's recent foreign policy escapades, not least the burial of its anti-Americanism which was almost an article of faith in the 1970s, in favour of a staunchly pro-American position by 1993. The new government in Athens attaches a higher priority to its 'excellent' relations with Washington than to the EU's putative Common Foreign and Security Policy, which, from the vantage point of the Balkans, appears to be a still-born exercise.

49. *Kathemerini*, 7 April 1982.

– 5 –

A Mixed Reaction: Denmark

Henrik Larsen

Introduction

The majority in the Folketing (the Danish Parliament) considered the Argentine invasion of the Falklands as illegitimate and gave the British almost immediate support, although it was made clear that Danish support did not necessarily mean that Denmark supported Britain's ownership of the islands. The Danish government objected to the Argentine means rather than the Argentine ends and the withdrawal of the latter was considered a precondition for a political solution.

The view of the government and a majority in the Folketing was that Article 113 in the Treaty of Rome could not and should not be used in relation to questions of foreign policy. Nevertheless, the Danish government allowed EC sanctions to be imposed for the period of one month following the Argentine invasion through the use primarily of Article 113, instead of Article 224 in the Treaty of Rome, because a fast response to the crisis was considered essential and because it did not want to destroy EPC solidarity. However, shortly after the EPC sanctions expired on 17 May 1982, the Folketing implemented national sanctions by passing legislation with reference to Article 224. Support for sanctions was undiminished following the implementation of national sanctions.

Before presenting an analysis of the Danish reaction to the Falklands conflict, this chapter describes the basic institutional structures of Danish foreign policy decision making and of Danish EC decision making. The decision-making structures go a long way to explain why the Danish reaction was different from that of other EC countries. The chapter concludes with a brief discussion of different theoretical approaches to the Danish reactions to the Falklands War.

Danish Foreign Policy: The Background

The Danish political system is based on coalition building. Elections to the Folketing take place on the basis of proportional representation. No single party has ever been able to gain an absolute majority in the Folketing; consequently the government has always consisted either of a coalition of parties or of a single party that needs to find majority support in parliament for its policies. This creates a situation in which the government can rarely ignore the wishes of other parties in the Folketing. Ensuring a majority in favour of government policy in the Folketing, or within the government in the case of a coalition, is a constant preoccupation. Although foreign affairs, as in other countries, have traditionally been an area in which parliament has had less control than in domestic politics, there is no doubt that special attention is given to the need for a majority in support of government foreign policy.

The post-1945 period has been characterized by greater involvement of the Folketing in foreign affairs. The constitution of 1953, under which the present system functions, gave a more important role to the Folketing in matters relating to surrendering sovereignty.[1] According to Article 2, relinquishing sovereignty, which must always be delimited in concrete terms, demands a five-sixths majority in the Folketing; if such a majority cannot be obtained, the law can be passed only by a majority of the voters in a referendum. It is this article in the constitution which was used in relation to Danish entry into the EC in 1972 and the Maastricht Treaty in 1992-3.[2]

While the government could never ignore the Folketing, it was the case that until the beginning of the 1980s there was a large degree of cross-party consensus on central elements of Danish foreign policy such as NATO membership, giving an important role to the UN and multilateral cooperation in general, and some kind of policy coordination with the other Nordic countries.[3] Particularly in relation to the Falklands issue, it is important to stress the high degree of legitimacy which the mainstream of the Danish political parties bestowed upon decisions by the UN. Membership of the EC, however, has always been controversial within large sections of the Social Democrats and the Radical Liberals and, to some extent, within the right-wing parties.[4] The Socialist Peoples Party (SF) and the Left

1. E. Bjøl, *Hvem Bestemmer – Studier i den Udenrigspolitiske Beslutningsproces*, Copenhagen: Jurist og Økonomforbundets forlag, 1983, p. 120.

2. The referendum about the Single European Act was a consultative referendum, and was not according to paragraph 20.

3 . The Socialist Peoples Party cannot be counted within this consensus.

4. The political parties in the Danish parliament, the Folketing, were at the time of the Falklands War:

*The Left Socialists (Venstresocialisterne, or VS). The most left-wing party (although not communist) in the Folketing, broke away from the SF in 1967 (see below).

Socialists (VS) were strong opponents of the EC and permanently on guard against any loss of sovereignty to the EC. In contrast to most of the other EC countries, opposition to the EC was more widespread on the left and in the centre of the political spectrum; divisions on the issue of EC membership were important for the Social Democrats and the Radical Liberals.

Danish European Policy (EC/EPC)

A key assumption on which mainstream support of Danish membership of the EC was based, at least until the late 1980s, was that the EC was an economic organization. Membership in 1972 was argued for in terms of the economic benefits which the country would obtain rather than in terms of potential wider political gains. Similarly, the debate in relation to the referendum on the Single European Act in 1986 was, for the proponents, a question of economic necessity, not political possibilities. The EC was seen in terms of economics, not politics, and it was only in the early 1990s that political arguments in favour of the EC appeared in the debate in the run up to Maastricht. This traditional distinction in Danish EC policy

---

*The Socialist Peoples Party (Socialistisk Folkeparti, or SF). A non-communist party to the left of the Social Democrats.

*Social Democrats (Socialdemocratiet, or SD). Minority government since 1979 as the only party, led by the Prime Minister Anker Jørgensen. Elections in December 1981 led to the creation of a new minority government also under the leadership of Anker Jørgensen. This government built on changing coalitions but the main supporters were the Radical Liberals and the Socialist Peoples Party, which were (and are) difficult to reconcile. This government resigned in September 1982 and the Conservative Poul Schlüter became the new Prime Minister and leader of a right-wing government.

*Radical Liberals (Radikale Venstre, or RV). A centre-right party which has always played an important role in Danish politics. A right-wing or a social democratic government always has to rely on the parliamentary support of RV which therefore holds the balance in the Folketing. The party is sceptical of the usefulness of military means in international politics.

*Christian Peoples party (Kristeligt Folkeparti). A centre-right-wing party with a Christian basis.

*Centre-Democrats (Centrum Demokraterne). A centre-right-wing party, the strongest proponent of the EC in the Folketing.

*Liberals (Venstre). A mainstream right-wing party committed to *laissez-faire* economics, with strong support amongst farmers, and strongly pro-EC

*Conservatives (Det konservative Folkeparti). A mainstream Conservative party; Pro-EC.

*Progress Party (Fremskridtspartiet, or FP). The Progress Party was founded in 1973 as a protest against the welfare state and in particular its taxation level. It defends a narrow concept of Danish national interests.

---

between politics and economics was reflected in the decision-making procedure in relation to the EC and EPC.

At the administrative level, EC policy was dealt with by the EC committee of high level civil servants (EF udvalget), whereas the EPC was dealt with in the foreign and security policy committee of high level civil servants (Det Udenrigs-og Sikkerhedspolitiske Udvalg). Furthermore, at the time of the EC referendum in 1972 the Social Democratic government divided the Ministry of Foreign Affairs between a Department of Foreign Affairs and a Department of Foreign Economic Affairs, to underline its basic argument that the EC was about economic matters and that politics and economics could be separated.[5] This dual administrative structure was still in place at the time of the Falklands conflict (it was abolished later by the right-wing government led by the Prime Minister, Poul Schlüter).

Within the government, EC policy was dealt with by the EC Committee of the government (Regeringens Fællesmarkedsudvalg), whereas matters relating to the EPC were dealt with by the government's Committee for Foreign Policy and Security (Regeringens Udenrigspolitiske Udvalg). In 1994 this governmental structure was modified and the government's EC Committee and the Committee for Foreign and Security Policy were merged to form the Foreign Policy Committee (Regeringens Udenrigspolitiske Udvalg). However, the agenda of this committee was divided according to the pillars emanating from the Maastricht treaty, and to a large extent the distinction between politics and economics remains.

Parliamentary control of government EC policy was exercised, and continues to be exercised, by the Common Market Select Committee (Markedsudvalget). The Markedsudvalget was created following the entry of Denmark into the EC, in order to scrutinize and control government EC policy. It is a powerful committee, as the government must seek a mandate for its day-to-day EC policy from it and government must consult it before taking important decisions on the EC. Parliamentary control of EPC policy is exercised by the Foreign Affairs Committee (Udenrigspolitisk Nævn).[6] Thus at this level the distinction between politics and economics was, and is, also maintained.[7]

The view of the EC as an economic community was thus central to the mainstream Danish approach to the EC, which underpinned the political procedures surrounding the EC and EPC decision-making procedures. This was the reason why sanctions carried out through the EC rather than

5. N. Haagerup and C. Thune, 'Denmark: the European Pragmatist' in C. Hill (ed.), *National Foreign Policies and European Political Cooperation*, London: Allen & Unwin, 1983, p. 108.

6. The Foreign Affairs Committee, however, does not give the government an actual mandate. The government is only constitutionally obliged to consult with the Foreign Affairs Committee, not to seek an actual mandate (Article 19 of the Constitution).

7. It should be noted that Markedsudvalget receives information about EPC issues.

through the national procedures became such a controversial point in relation to the Falklands issue; a central dogma underlying Danish EC policy was being challenged.

In legal terms, the fundamental reason why the distinction between the EPC and the EC was so crucial was that the Danish Constitution (Article 20) states that powers can only be transferred to supranational institutions in a 'clearly defined way' (*'i nærmere bestemt omfang'*). This article in the constitution made Denmark the most sensitive member state with regard to the legal basis of EC decisions.[8] Article 20 played a central role in the Danish debate over the Single European Act, when the issue was whether the SEA removed further powers from the Folketing or whether it only restructured powers which had already been surrendered by the Folketing.

The degree of controversy which surrounded Community membership, did not arise in the case of EPC. Debates about the EPC focused more on matters of procedure than of substance, and on the question of whether there was a blurring of the boundary between the EC and the EPC, the suspicion that the balance between economics and politics in the Community was shifting became central to the Danish debate on the Falklands issue. The relative popularity of the EPC was undoubtedly related to its intergovernmental nature. Moreover, Haagerup and Thune[9] have suggested that the fact that the EPC had often taken left-wing stances made it difficult for the left to challenge, while the EPC was difficult for the more pro-European right-wing parties to criticize.

Denmark's Reaction to the 1982 Conflict in the South Atlantic

There was no great Danish political interest in the Falklands issue prior to the Argentine invasion on 2 April 1982. Nor was there much public knowledge or interest, although the Danish newspapers did contain news on the Falklands issue in the days before the Argentine invasion. In the days following the invasion, some Danish newspapers carried headlines such as 'a Danish colony in the Falklands', but it was soon revealed that Denmark was only linked to the islands by a single Dane who had settled in the 1950s and a few Danish names in the phonebook of the islands.[10]

---

8. C. Gulmann, 'Danmarks og EFs sanktioner mod Sovjetunionen og Argentina', in C. Thune and N. Petersen (eds), *Dansk udenrigspolitisk årbog 1983*, Copenhagen: Jurist – og Økonomforbundets forlag, 1983, p. 118.

9. N. Haagerup and C. Thune, 'Denmark: The European Pragmatist', pp. 107-8.

10. *Politiken*, 10-11 April 1982.

Throughout the conflict, the approach of the Danish media was very much that of a detached observer watching a television show.

At the time of the Falklands conflict, the government was a Social Democrat minority government under the leadership of Prime Minister Anker Jørgensen and with Kjeld Olesen as Foreign Minister. The government relied for parliamentary support on the Socialist Peoples Party (SF), a party to the left of the Social Democrats in the political spectrum, and the Radical Liberals (Det Radikale Venstre, RV) a centre-right party to the right of the Social Democrats. On the Falklands issue, some adaptation to SF and RV was necessary on the part of the government, in spite of the government gaining support from the mainstream right-wing parties (the Liberals and the Conservatives).

The reaction of the Danish government was to condemn the Argentine invasion in strong terms.[11] Drawing on Resolution 502, the government stance was that a political problem should not be solved by military means. However, it made clear at the same time that opposition to the invasion did not imply a stance on the rightful ownership of the islands. The Foreign Minister, Kjeld Olesen, said: 'The Danish government refers to the resolution of the Security Council and we do not desire to engage ourselves in a complicated constitutional problem. But it must be clear that no country can obtain a right by use of military means. Therefore the Security Council demands as the first thing that Argentina withdraws before negotiations can start.'[12]

The initial UN resolution became a crucial point of reference; indeed, it formed the basis for government support for discussions on sanctions within the EPC.[13] As the conflict continued, the legitimacy of the UN as a forum for its resolution was constantly repeated, and when hostilities broke out the role of the UN was emphasised again.[14] It was stressed that the EC was not the only forum in which the reactions to the war were formulated; this was not least for domestic political reasons, as the UN occupied the moral highground in the Danish political debate.

The Danish government willingly accepted the British wish for immediate sanctions against Argentina[15]and consulted the political parties in the Markedsudvalg (Parliament's Common Market Select Committee) on the question on 14 April 1982.[16] The majority accepted the imposition of

11. See, for example, radio interview with Foreign Minister Kjeld Olesen on 6 April 1982 quoted in *Berlingske Tidende*, 7 April 1982.

12. Kjeld Olesen quoted in *Information*, 17-18 April 1982 - (author's translation).

13. Foreign Minister Kjeld Olesen's account of the motives behind the Danish imposition of sanctions in *Information*, 16 April 1982.

14. Foreign Minister Kjeld Olesen, *Information*, 27 April 1982.

15. Sources in the Cabinet office have disclosed that the Prime Minister, Anker Jørgensen, was initially very sceptical about helping Mrs Thatcher, with whom he had had clashes over the EC. However, he was persuaded to change his view.

16. *Information*, 16 April 1982. See also *Berlingske Tidende*, 10 April 1982, which

sanctions and the procedure by which the EC would implement them during the first month (see below). Only the Socialist Peoples Party (SF), the Left Socialists (VS) and the right-wing Progress Party (FP) expressed criticism of the procedure used, claiming that the EC, through Article 113, was being used for political purposes. They were adamant in their opposition to the use of Article 113 to implement sanctions. For the government, the implementation of sanctions by Article 113 in the Treaty of Rome was based on pragmatism and political necessity rather than desire. The government's view thus deviated from the EPC consensus on the issue of the procedure for sanctions; its view, widely shared by the other political parties and the press, was that sanctions should be organized at the national level rather than at the EC level, raising the question of whether Article 113 or Article 224 in the Treaty of Rome should be used. The government justified the Danish decision to allow Article 113 to be used in terms of the necessity of urgent action and the willingness not to block an EC decision. The Foreign Minister, Kjeld Olesen, argued that other countries had lengthier procedures for national implementation and so the use of Article 113 speeded up the process, a necessary move in order to signal a quick political reaction.[17] The government was willing to support a position which would gain broad support within the EC.[18]

In spite of the use of Article 113, the government argued that the decision-making procedure had been in line with the spirit of Article 224 on the national implementation of sanctions. Article 224, Kjeld Olesen claimed, had indirectly been the foundation for Danish action during the whole period. The Danish government's view was accommodated in the EC Regulation 877/82 of 16 April 1982, imposing economic sanctions on Argentina for one month; the preamble began with a reference to the consultations with the member states under Article 224, and then went on to say that within the framework of these consultations it had become clear that the countries had to adopt similar measures. Only then came the reference to Article 113.[19] Denmark also sent out a declaration saying that it would have preferred to use Article 224.[20]

The government was under political pressure, not least during the debate in the Folketing on 12 May 1982, to make it clear that the Danish view was that sanctions should be national, and should be implemented using Article 224. Under the influence of this pressure, the government

suggests that the parties were consulted beforehand.

---

17. *Information*, 16 April 1982.
18. Foreign Minister Olesen, *Berlingske Tidende*, 11 April 1982.
19. C. Gulmann, 'Danmarks og EFs sanktioner mod Sovjetunionen og Argentina', p. 121.
20. Foreign Minister Kjeld Olesen, *Folketingets Forhandlinger*, 19 May 1982, p. 7903, *Dansk Udenrigspolitisk Årbog* 1982, p. 252.

prepared for national legislation under Article 224 to be made the only basis of the Danish sanctions. When the EC sanctions under Article 113 were extended by one week on 16 May 1982, the Danish government only supported the decision on the condition that the new regulation under Article 113 would only be applicable to Denmark until Danish national legislation establishing a trade embargo against Argentina had come into place.

On 25 May 1982, national legislation banning trade with Argentina was voted through in the Folketing. Three parties, the SF, the VS and the FP, voted against the legislation, the first two because they felt that the Danish position in the conflict was too pro-British and the right-wing Progress Party because it felt that sanctions threatened Danish interests. On 21 June 1982 Danish national sanctions were lifted, simultaneously with the lifting of EC Regulation 1577/82 by the seven members of the EC who had chosen the use of Article 113 following the termination of the month of EPC sanctions on 17 May 1982. Therefore the consequences of the Danish implementation of sanctions on a national basis from 25 May to 21 June were not materially different from the consequences of the use of Article 113 by the other EC countries. The Danish government had supported the condemnation in the EC of the Argentine invasion, the reference to the UN resolution and coordination of sanctions in the EC; the only difference lay in the view on the correct sanctions procedure and the resulting implementation of national sanctions by Denmark following the end of the first month of EPC sanctions.

The difference between the Danish stance and that of the majority of the EC states appeared to have little impact on the Argentines themselves. The Danish ambassador to Buenos Aires received the same protest against the imposition of sanctions as the other EC ambassadors,[21] although the Argentines later tried to use the Danish case to suggest the existence of splits in the EC camp.[22]

A key question is whether there was a change in the Danish stance when the UK started to reconquer the islands, beginning with the recapture of South Georgia on 25 April 1982. The position of the government, and the great majority of the parties in the Folketing, was that the start of battle did not change the assumptions behind the EC sanctions against Argentina and that sanctions should therefore be maintained. Although British military action was not given explicit support, the policy line remained the same after the outbreak of armed hostilities. At the height of the fighting on 24 May the Social Democrat, Kelm Hansen, said in the Folketing:

---

21. *Politiken*, 13 April 1982.
22. It is interesting that the Scandinavian countries did not share the same position on the issue of sanctions. Norway decided not to introduce sanctions on 12 April 1982, *Berlingske Tidende*, 13 April 1982.

When debating the present bill [about national implementation of sanctions] it may be difficult to ignore the last days' bloody developments in and around the Falkland Islands. However, it would be regrettable if the debate focuses on this rather than on the deeply serious principles which have been violated in this case and which represent the point of departure for the government presenting its bill.[23]

A special meeting in the Markedsudvalg was called by SF who felt that the situation was now different from when sanctions were originally imposed,[24] but the policy was not altered. The majority in the Markedsudvalg supported the government's policy.[25] No links were made between the debate about the start of military confrontation and the debate on whether sanctions had been imposed according to the right procedures, that is, the debate about Article 113 versus Article 224.

It should be stressed that the Danish view on the function which sanctions should perform was special. It was stated repeatedly that sanctions were not imposed as a step on the way towards the military recapturing of the islands by the British; rather, sanctions were a means of signalling to the Argentines that negotiation and withdrawal were necessary. It was stressed that a solution should be found at the negotiation table, not on the battlefield.[26] The Danish government did not openly oppose the British recapture of the islands by military means,[27] but took a reticent stance.[28]

Explaining the Danish Reaction

The generally positive Danish policy in support of UN Resolution 502 and the positive Danish stance towards sanctions against Argentina can be accounted for by several factors.

First, Danish relations with the UK were more important than the relationship with Argentina. Danish relations with the UK have historically been very important for Denmark, and a considerable proportion of agri-

23. Kelm-Hansen (SD), *Folketingets Forhandlinger*, 24 May 1982, col. 8203.

24. *Information*, 29 April 1982.

25. However, the left-wing newspaper *Information* which had previously refused to take a stance in relation to sanctions now declared that sanctions had to be lifted in order to ease tension. See editorial in *Information*, 27 April 1982.

26. Foreign Minister Olesen, *Information*, 27 April 1982.

27. This was also the case of the press, although the right-wing *Berlingske Tidende* came closer to defending the use of military power while the fighting was taking place (see the editorial of *Berlingske Tidende* on 8 April 1982, and *Politiken*'s editorial on 26 April, which stressed that the EC countries had given support only to sanctions, not to military reconquest).

28. See for example the interview with Foreign Minister Olesen in *Information*, 17-18 April 1982, where he does not answer the question of whether Britain would be right to reconquer the islands militarily but only refers to the UN resolutions which appeal to both parties not to use military power.

cultural exports go to Britain. The Danish policy in relation to entry into the European Community was influenced very much by the policy of the UK, not least because of the importance of Britain as a market for agricultural products. Within the EC, the Danes and the British generally took similar stances on the institutional development of the Community and the structure of the EPC. While there are differences between the Danish left and right on this issue, it is possible to say that the Danes are, in general terms, rather positively disposed towards Britain, partly owing to the role of the latter as liberators in the Second World War. It is probably not an exaggeration to say that Denmark is an Anglophile country. An opinion poll on 19 April 1982 showed that 56 per cent sympathised with the British in the conflict over the Islands whereas only 9 per cent sympathised with Argentina.[29]

Although it would be wrong to characterize the Danish relationship with Argentina as special, there were clearly elements which made the relationship distinctive, particularly in a Latin American context. There are not many Danish immigrant communities overseas; however, one of the most important ones in terms of numbers and cultural identification with Denmark is to be found in Argentina. Moreover, Argentina was Denmark's second biggest trade partner in South America,[30] although Danish exports to Argentina represented less than 0.5 per cent of total Danish exports. Interestingly, these elements were not present at all in the political debate in relation to the crisis and few people declared their sympathy for Argentina in conflict in an opinion poll (see above). The emotional and political/economic links to Britain clearly weighed more heavily.

Second, expression of support for a UN resolution gave additional legitimacy to the opposition to the Argentine invasion. Denmark has always attributed an important role to the UN and, in the internal political debate, support for a UN resolution was much more uncontroversial than was an independent EPC stance. The central role of the UN and its diplomacy were repeatedly stressed.

Third, pressures against breaking ranks with the EPC consensus were undoubtedly present. The Danish goverment agreed on the principle of sanctions; therefore, the pressures only applied to the issue of the way in which the sanctions were to be carried out (through Article 113). However, when the Irish and the Italians later broke ranks, the Danish government did not follow them although they had a political opportunity to do so. During the debate on the implementation of national sanctions, the

29. Opinion poll by the Observa Institute for *Jyllands Posten*, published on 24 April 1982, and in C. Thune and N. Petersen (eds), *Dansk Udenrigspolitisk Årbog*, p. 425; 22 per cent did not sympathise with either country.

30. Danish imports from Argentina in 1981 were worth 696 million crowns and exports 256 million crowns, *Politiken*, 13 April 1982.

mainstream parties and the government never considered withdrawing their support from Britain.

The problem for the Danish government lay in the procedure rather than in the substance. It did not emanate from a different interpretation of the conflict. It was a function of Danish policy towards the EC rather than of their specific view on the Falklands conflict. The dominant position in Denmark was that economics and foreign policy should not be mixed procedurally in relation to the EC. When sanctions were at first implemented for a month according to Article 113 on 16 April 1982, the government admitted that this was not its preferred procedure, but it still argued that the procedure was in line with the spirit of national implementation. It was criticized by SF and VS on the left for smuggling foreign policy into the remit of the EC. In addition, the centre right (Radical Liberals) and the right-wing newspaper *Berlingske Tidende*[31] also voiced scepticism. The right-wing parties (the Conservatives and the Liberals), on the other hand, both supported the government's initial adaptation to the EC line and applauded the introduction on 25 May of national sanctions.[32]

From the outset of the conflict, the role of the EC in sanctions against Argentina was a sensitive question in Danish domestic politics. By fitting Article 224 into EC Regulation 877/82, the government attempted to avoid the criticism it had borne in relation to the trade sanctions against the Soviet Union. The EC had introduced sanctions against the USSR in March 1982 in response to the situation in Poland. On this occasion, Article 113 had been used, the government argued that it had tried to use Article 224 but that this had not been possible due to the opposition of their EPC partners. The government bore much criticism for this both before and after the Falklands War as the sanctions against the Soviet Union continued. In the debate in the Folketing on 12 May 1982, the government suggested that Denmark had been accommodated on the Falklands issue to a greater degree than in the case of Poland.[33]

It is interesting that some of the political parties that were the most outspoken in opposition to sanctions against Argentina in the EC context (SF, VS and the Radical Liberals) did not oppose sanctions *per se* as long as they would be implemented within the appropriate institutional framework. Whereas UN (and, for that matter, national) sanctions were seen as legitimate, the framework of the Treaty of Rome was not deemed to be so.

It is important to add that different parts of the Danish political spectrum viewed the Falklands conflict and the various possible solutions in

---

31. Editorial of *Berlingske Tidende*, 8 April 1982.
32. Only the very European Centre Democrats (CD) supported the use of Article 113 without ambiguity - they even saw it as progress.
33. *Folketingets Forhandlinger*, 12 May 1982, col. 7225.

quite different ways. Across the spectrum, it was widely accepted that Argentina had violated international law by using force to acquire new territory and that this ought to be condemned. But, for the left wing (SF, VS and the daily broadsheet newspaper, *Information*), it was not obvious that the islands belonged rightfully to Britain; and for the Danish left wing, Mrs Thatcher was like a red rag to a bull. What complicated the issue for the left, of course, was that the Argentine government was an extreme right-wing military dictatorship and that the Falklanders themselves wanted the islands to belong to Britain. The newspaper *Information* expressed the left's problem well by declaring that it was a conflict between a decadent military dictatorship and a declining empire and that, at a deeper level, it was a question of the peoples' right to self-determination versus the results of an unjust empire.[34] The more radical left-wing (VS) also reflected the dilemma, but they resolved it by seeing the support the British were given by most of the Western countries as a case of the north ganging up against the Third World.[35] SF and VS pointed to the inconsistency of applying sanctions against Argentina but not against other aggressors. For SF and VS, the problem was not the concept of sanctions per se, but their target and the framework within which they took place;[36] both SF and VS voted against the law in the Folketing on 25 May on implementing national Danish sanctions. Their arguments were that sanctions would only intensify tension and that sanctions, whether national or within the EC framework, would signal unambiguous support for Britain. Finally, they argued that sanctions *de facto* would be coordinated by the EC. The very right-wing Progress Party argued against sanctions on the grounds that they would be detrimental to the Danish economy and that economic interaction was a basis for peace, and because of the British stance on the issue of the EC budget.[37]

For the mainstream right – the Conservatives, the Liberals, the Centre Democrats and the Christian People's Party - the Argentine invasion was seen much more unambiguously as a violation of British sovereignty. This was linked to an emotional attachment to Britain. The Conservative, Ole Bernt Henriksen, said that 'nobody in this House...can allow themselves to support a police state, where law and order does not exist, against the world's oldest democracy, which this house has very strong family links with, both as far as traditions and outlook are concerned.'[38] Henning

---

34. Editorial in *Information*, 3–4 April 1982. See also the editorial in the same paper, 27 April 1982, which has a slightly different emphasis: here the argument is that both governments need the war for internal political reasons and what should really count is the view of the Falklanders themselves – based, that is, on the people's right to self-determination – who would probably not choose Argentinian citizenship.

35. S. Riishøj (SF), *Folketingets Forhandlinger*, 25 May 1982, col. 8225.

36. S. Folke (VS), *Folketingets Forhandlinger*, 12 May 1982, col. 7243.

37. M. Glistrup (SF), *Folketingets Forhandlinger*, 12 May 1982, col. 7237-8.

38 . O. B. Henriksen (Cons.), *Folketingets Forhandlinger*, 12 May 1982, col. 7232.

Christophersen (later to become a European Commissioner), from the right-wing, pro-European Liberal Party (Venstre), said: 'There must not be any doubt that we support this democratic member of the European family in the immensely complicated and dangerous situation which has arisen following the Argentinian invasion',[39] and that Denmark was not a neutral country but an ally of Britain and the West.[40] These elements were so important that the institutional question of sanctions was treated as secondary.

But on the right as well as in the middle and on the left of the political spectrum, including in the right-wing broadsheet newspaper *Berlingske Tidende*,[41] there was a refusal to reveal to whom it was thought that the islands should rightfully belong. The Social Democratic government also followed this line, but expressed it by use of a less mythical vocabulary in relation to Britain than was used by people like Christophersen (quoted above). The Social Democratic government, and to a lesser extent the right, were both silent on the question of the legitimacy or not of British military action. The declared rationale for sanctions was that they would prevent military action since the Argentines would succumb to the political and economic pressure. Of course, very few governments would stress the value of armed force; nevertheless it is surprising that there was almost no discussion about whether military action could be legitimate under some circumstances (for example, if the Argentines did not withdraw). It is striking that the left-wing SF and VS, as parties which accepted that sanctions might in other circumstances be acceptable, did not mention the situations in which use of military power would be legitimate. This was an expression of traditional small-state thinking (that military solutions set a bad precedent for conflict resolution in the international system).

After the War

Shortly after the war ended, Denmark assumed the Presidency of the European Council (July – December 1982). Under a new government consisting of a coalition of centre-right and right-wing parties, the Danish Presidency tried to restore the relationship with Latin America.[42] The new Foreign Minister, the leader of the right-wing Liberal Party, Uffe Elleman-Jensen, said on behalf of the Ten in the General Assembly of the UN:

39. H. Christophersen (Liberals), *Folketingets Forhandlinger*, 12 May 1982, col. 7234.
40. Ibid., col. 7235.
41. Editorial of 8 April 1982.
42. E. Jørgensen, 'Den internationale situation og Danmarks udenrigspolitik 1982' in C. Thune and N. Petersen (eds), *Dansk Udenrigspolitisk Årbog* 1982, p. 25.

'The Ten wish again to confirm the importance they attribute to good relations with all the countries in Latin America.'[43]

The Danish stance towards the Falklands question in the aftermath of the war remained close to the view of the mainstream in the EC. In the resolution put forward every year in the UN General Assembly (co-sponsored by Argentina until 1989 when the UK and Argentina resumed diplomatic relations at the general consulate level), which urged the UK and Argentina to resume talks on the future of the islands, Denmark abstained while the UK voted against. The official reason given by Denmark was that the resolution did not mention the basic principle of the people's right to self-determination, that is, the view of the Falklanders. When in 1985 countries including France, Spain, Greece, Italy, Sweden and the USA supported the 'Argentinian' resolution, Denmark continued to abstain, and continued still when the Netherlands and Norway turned to support the resolution in 1986. When Britain put forward its own amendment to the preamble and the operational part of the resolution in 1985 containing references to the principle of the people's right to self-determination, Denmark supported the British amendment. This voting behaviour in the UN underlines the point that the particular Danish stance during the Falklands conflict was a question of European policy rather than a divergent view on the Falklands issue. Denmark was clearly amongst the staunch supporters of the UK when it came to the substance of the conflict.[44]

An important long-term consequence of the Falklands War for Denmark was the intensification of the debate about the use of sanctions within the EPC framework. The EC sanctions against the USSR became the subject of heated discussion. The sanctions which had been decided in the EC on the basis of Article 113 in March 1982 were extended for one year in December 1982, but the Folketing objected to the decision by the government to agree to the use of Article 113,[45] and, in early March 1983, the government presented a bill on sanctions against the Soviet Union according to Article 224 in the Treaty. The government did not, however, succeed in passing this bill and Denmark consequently broke with the EC consensus and lifted sanctions against the USSR. The Folketing passed a motion on 14 April 1983 saying that Article 113 could not be used in the future for political purposes.[46] Uffe Ellemann-Jensen argued that the sanctions against Argentina showed that a country could choose when to use

43. Foreign Minister Uffe Elleman-Jensen on behalf of the Ten in the General Assembly of the UN on 28 September 1982, ibid., p. 200.

44. See annual *Beretning fra FNs Generalforsamling* from the Danish Ministry of Foreign Affairs.

45 . This led to a debate on the nature of the mandate of Foreign Minister Uffe Elleman Jensen in the Markedsudvalg.

46. C. Gulmann, 'Danmarks og EFs sanktioner mod Sovjetunionen og Argentina', pp. 123-8.

Articles 113 and 224.[47] However, the discussions about the possible use of Articles 113 and 224 did not cease.

Conclusions

The central finding in relation to the Danish reactions to the Falklands War was that Denmark differed with the majority of EC countries in its view on the procedures of the EC rather than on the interpretation of the conflict. The question of which EC procedures should be used to carry out sanctions (Article 224 rather than Article 113) remained a key issue - if not the key issue – in references to the conflict in the Danish political debate in the years following 1982. This illustrates the more general point that Danish discussions about the EPC have often been about procedures rather than about the substance of the decisions. The Falklands conflict as such did not continue to receive broad political attention.

In terms of theoretical approaches, the main element which distinguished Denmark from the other EC countries – the wish for national implementation of sanctions – was a result of political considerations at the most general level. It was an expression of one of the basic premises of Danish EC policy: that the EC should deal with economics and not politics. This was a view which cut across most sections of Danish society, including the political parties, the media and public opinion, and it stemmed from a broadly based Danish belief-system in relation to the EC (or, if we leave the terms of traditional foreign policy analysis, a discourse). It was this belief-system which constituted the underlying framework for the Danish stance and which led to rising pressures towards national implementation of sanctions soon after the EPC had decided on sanctions. Middle-range theory, therefore, is not central to explaining the Danish deviation from the EC mainstream in relation to the conflict. The decision-making procedure was not placed in a vacuum but touched upon the politicized area of Danish EC policy. It can even be argued that the agencies which constitute the central elements in middle-range theory were themselves carriers of the Danish EC discourse.

The other internal structural factor of importance for the Danish deviation was the Danish parliamentary system. This system, which means that the government often cannot take a parliamentary majority for granted, meant that discursive pressures were easily translated into parliamentary pressures.

As far as an analysis of open sources can show, the impact of bureaucratic politics on concrete aspects of the decision-making procedure was

47. Ibid., p. 126.

small. Faurby has argued that the modest impact of bureaucratic politics is a general feature of Scandinavian decision making.[48] However, the Ministry of Foreign Affairs was a strong supporter of EPC and this was definitely a factor behind joining the EPC consensus immediately after the Argentine invasion. There were signs that, from the point of view of the Ministry of Foreign Affairs, the special Danish position on sanctions was an administrative problem to be circumvented rather than a political issue.[49] This can, at least in part, explain the Danish acceptance of the Article 113 procedure in the first place. The EPC consensus was crucial. But the Falkland issue was special in that it involved the invasion of the territory of a member state. If EPC solidarity were to have any meaning, there were undoubtedly pressures on all member states to support Britain at the outset of the conflict.

48. Faurby notes that in Scandinavia 'bureaucratic battles, however energetically fought, are not the main determinants of policy'. See Faurby in W. Wallace and W. Paterson (eds), *Foreign Policy Making in Western Europe*, Farnborough, Hants : Saxon House, 1978, p. 124, quoted in M. Clarke and S. Smith (eds), *Understanding Foreign Policy – the Policy Systems Approach*, Southampton: Edward Elgar, 1989, p. 122.
49. 'Diplomatic sources' quoted in *Politiken*, 11 April 1982.

– 6 –

The Internal Dissenter (I): Italy[1]

Domitilla Savignoni

Introduction

The Falklands crisis of 1982 presented Italy with a very sensitive political dilemma for its foreign and internal policies. Unlike the other European Community (EC) and NATO countries, Italy had close links both with Britain and with Argentina, a country with a strong Italian ethnic population. The crisis was also a test for the EC which revealed the difficulty of taking a common political stance. It showed also that even one of the most pro-European countries (such as Italy) could break, if deemed necessary, the fragile EC solidarity.

By the middle of April 1982, the EC had adopted economic sanctions against Argentina for one month. This was a major demonstration of the European spirit, which occurred during an intra-EC crisis as a result of a strong British position over agricultural price negotiations. The decision made by the European countries was helped by the fact that the Argentine military *junta* had flagrantly violated international law in an attempt to overcome internal economic and social difficulties. The European governments, especially Italy, were conscious of the political and economical costs of sanctions. Italy was the country that, due to its traditional bonds with Argentina (economic, political, ethnic and cultural), was going to bear the highest burden in order to reconfirm its loyalty to Europe.

The Italian government, in a climate of serious internal difficulties due in particular to a new wave of violence induced by the Mafia and to trade union unrest, decided to follow the path set by the Italian parliament and

1. The author would like to express her sincere thanks to Gen. Luigi Caligaris for his suggestions and support. Her thanks extend to Luis Ruzzi and Luis Troisi (Argentine Embassy, Rome), Andrew Jones (British Embassy, Rome), Counsellor Giulio Cesare Piccirilli (Political Affairs Department, Italian Ministry of Foreign Affairs, Rome). She would also like to thank Peter Glendening, Gianfrancesco Peretti, and Andrea Signori for their help with the translation from Italian.

dissociated itself from the EC decision to extend sanctions against Argentina on 17 May. Almost all the political parties of the country agreed with that decision, especially the Socialist party, which had at the time a strong influence on the coalition in power. 'This taking of a stand – which once more identified us as timorous and untrustworthy allies - was legitimized through its serious purpose.'[2] Almost half the Argentine population had Italian names and Italian blood. Furthermore, and even more concretely influential, certain economic situations forced the Foreign Ministry to be cautious: Italy had important interests in Argentina and the representatives of those interests had various political contacts in Rome. But, above all, however, the most important factor that played a role in the Italian volte-face, was the need to maintain the internal political balance of the coalition government at the time in order to avoid the real possibility of a political crisis.

Italian Foreign Policy

Italy's Role on the International Scene

After the end of the Second World War Italy, although one of the founder members of NATO (1949) and the host of the foundation of the EC in Rome (1957), did not play an active role in international politics. Italy pursued one ambition alone, to join the circle of the great powers and be invited to participate in Western political and economic summit meetings. Hence the dubious fame earned by the country, of practising what was ironically described as 'the foreign policy of sitting down'.[3]

Italy, defeated during the war, needed to have new allies and to be trusted. The country chose its allies in relation to its economic needs and had to modify its governmental system following the dictates of its major ally (the United States). Each change in the Italian political balance[4] had to receive international approval; furthermore, each new balance had some influence on foreign policy so as to modify its style and its reliability.[5] During the 1950s Italy had an unsteady, hesitant foreign policy, to which the instability of the government contributed. Its foreign affairs were con-

2. I. Montanelli, M. Cervi, 'In bilico tra Reagan e Arafat', *il Giornale*, 30 August 1993.

3. A term coined by an Italian ambassador to indicate Italy's constant concern to be present (hence 'sitting' rather than participating actively) at important meetings.

4. The 'left-centre side' during the 1960s, the governments of 'national solidarity' (alliance between DC and PCI) during the 1970s.

5. S. Romano, *Guida alla Politica Estera Italiana*, Milano: Rizzoli, 1993, pp. 1–2.

tinually under pressure from two opposing directions, its Atlantic and EC undertakings, signed in the previous years, and Third World demands, which were tantamount to permanent blackmail of the government.[6]

During the 1960s and the 1970s, Italian foreign policy was overshadowed by the importance of the internal political debate which meant that the country adopted a rather low profile in international affairs. The summit meeting of the seven leading industrialized countries in Venice in 1980 marked a renewed activism of the Italian political class in foreign policy. The problems of internal policy in the 1970s were assuredly not resolved, but terrorism looked defeated, at least at the political level, and the economy started to show fresh vitality.[7] A number of important international events, which were well beyond Italy's control, (including the debates on the European Monetary System, the retaliatory measures to be adopted against the USSR following the invasion of Afghanistan, and NATO's decision to install new nuclear weapons in Europe), involved it in various new initiatives which forced politicians to face up to difficult political choices. Nonetheless, Italy was not yet considered on a par with the other major Western powers, even if it did participate in the official summit meetings.

By the 1980's the Italian political class had started to develop policy lines which, while remaining true to the main trends of the alliance, had some degree of autonomy and originality. Italy, no longer content to be merely towed along by NATO's foreign policy, refused the role of the 'Bulgaria of NATO' it had been assigned and sought new international responsibilities, both in the military and economic fields. New themes such as pacifism, conscientious objection and relations with the Third World countries involved increasingly broader sectors of public opinion. The question of the Euro missiles (in the summer of 1981), the participation of an Italian contingent in the UN multinational peace force in Sinai (in the autumn of 1981), and the events in the Falklands (in the spring of 1982) were the subjects of debates in Parliament. Due to the greater activism of the politicians, foreign policy became for the first time a matter of internal debate.

The Actors in the Decision-Making Process

In Italy, the government, as the main representative of the executive power, has the major responsibility in the decision-making process of foreign policy. Within it, the prime minister has greater influence than the foreign minister. During the 1970s, in addition to the foreign minister, (whose influence varies according to the political importance of the person who assumes

6. Ibid., pp. 133-4.
7. P. Garimberti and M. Carnovale, 'La politica estera nella stampa italiana', in M. Carnovale (ed.), *Sicurezza e Informazione*, Milan: Il Sole 24 Ore, 1988, p. 35.

the job), the Ministries of Commerce and Industry became very impor-tant and, thanks to their choices regarding export and energy policies, increased their clout in the international scene. Occasionally, the president of the republic can play a major role.

There are also other places and organizations involved in the conception and execution of foreign policy. A privileged forum, at least as far as debate over foreign policy is concerned, is the parliament; in addition to controlling government's decisions, the parliament acts as provider of general guidance in foreign policy. Other important actors are the political parties and the big enterprises which deal with external economic and financial relations.

It can therefore be said that the 'maker' of government policy is not one calculating decision maker but rather a conglomerate of large organizations and political actors. The traditional assumption – that foreign policy should be moulded by the minister of foreign affairs – seems to have proved increasingly inadequate. It would appear that the old formula can no longer cope either with new international challenges, or with the domestic distribution of power among key agencies involved in promoting national security and foreign policy decisions.

The Players in the Crisis

Italy's Ties with Argentina

The Spanish Governor of Buenos Aires, who drove the British out of the Falklands in 1770, had an Italian surname, Buccarelli, as did Galtieri, the Argentine President of Calabrian origin who invaded the islands on 2 April 1982. This is not a bizarre joke of destiny; 52 per cent of all surnames in Argentina are of Italian origin. There are numerous ethnic and cultural ties with Argentina; about 1,300,000 Italian citizens live there, while 10 million of the 28 million population are of Italian origin. At the turn of the century, the possibility of introducing bilingual (Italian and Spanish) instruction in the schools was debated in the Argentine Congress. Thanks to the law on dual nationality,[8] the necessity of doing military ser-

8. The law on Italian citizenship is based on the principle of *jus sanguinis*, i.e. a son of an Italian wherever he is born is Italian. By contrast, in Argentina the law on citizenship is based on *jus soli*: anyone born in Argentina, even of foreign parents, is automatically an Argentine citizen. The coexistence of these two laws has made it possible for those born in Argentina (and therefore Argentine citizens) to be also considered as Italians if their father is Italian.

vice in one of the two countries does not in itself entail loss of citizenship of the other country.

However, the ties between Argentina and Italy go far beyond ethnic and cultural questions. Of Argentina's trading partners in 1982, Italy occupied fourth position (second in Europe) for both imports and exports, and the volume of Italian investments in Argentina ($341 million in 1982) was second only to that of the United States. In the period 1970–81, Italian imports from Argentina doubled in value,[9] reaching a peak in 1979. Italian exports to Argentina also increased after 1978[10] thanks to the policy of cooperation begun the previous year by the Argentine government and the preference given to Italian products.[11] Economic relations between Italy and Argentina are managed mainly through Argentine associates of the leading Italian companies.[12] Among the chief firms of Italian origin with a noteworthy presence in Argentina are Fiat-Concorde, a holding company with 8,000 employees, Techint, which carries out public works, Impregilo, which builds dams, gas pipelines and nuclear power stations and Olivetti.[13] ENI (National Hydrocarbons Agency) has operated in Argentina since 1958; the Italian state corporation designed and built the first important Argentine gas pipeline in 1963–4, stretching from Patagonia to Buenos Aires. There are also thousands of small and medium-size enterprises in Argentina, set up by Italians whose activities support those of the big names in Italian industry. In this positive context of Italo-Argentine trade, the dispute over the Falklands introduced a disruption of the established balance, arousing considerable concern among the political forces and the Italian construction firms working in the Argentine market.

9. Italy imports mostly agricultural produce, such as maize and soya seeds, but also meat, wool, hides, machine tools, and chemical-pharmaceutical products; C. Dini, 'I Rapporti economici con l'Argentina', *Politica Internazionale*, La Nuova Italia editrice, no. 6, June 1982, p. 121.

10. Italian exports went up from 181 billion lire in 1977 to 303 billion lire in 1978. Exports include non-electrical machines and equipment, manufactures, aircraft and their spare parts, etc. Since 1979, they also include consumer goods; Ibid.

11. Among all the cooperation agreements signed between the two countries, special attention is given to the 'economic, industrial and financial outline agreement' signed on 12 June 1979.

12. There are about 500 Italian associations in Argentina.The most powerful one is Mutulita' e istruzione della capitale, which owns real estate in the centre of Buenos Aires (there are also sports amenities attached to its branches); it is similar to a multinational called Unione e benevolenza.

13. Other firms of Italian origin operating in Argentina include Pirelli, Telettra, Dalmine, Siderca, Agipgas and Italimpianti.

Italy's Relationship with the United Kingdom

In the years following the end of the Second World War, relations between Italy and the UK were poor. The British wanted to teach Italy a lesson by reducing its role in the Mediterranean and linking it closely to the interests of British policy. With the establishment of the Atlantic Alliance, it was France that strove to bring in Italy so as to broaden the Alliance to the Mediterranean; to the majority of the participants in the Atlantic Pact, and primarily the UK, Italian membership was not desirable. But Italy did become a member of NATO, the EEC and the WEU, and very soon the UK began to regard Italy as being on the same footing as the countries that had won the war.

An example of this unbalanced relationship which predated the war in the South Atlantic is the supposedly secret initiative by the British Foreign Secretary, Lord Carrington, who, on 5 July 1981, convened his German and French colleagues (excluding Italy) for a final consultation before going to Moscow to present the European plan for a solution to the Afghanistan situation. The Italian government was offended, as the initiative was reminiscent of the mini-summit meeting held six months earlier just after Ronald Reagan's entrance to the White House,[14] again without Italy's presence. When the Falklands crisis occurred, relations between Italy and the UK were good, especially in the NATO context, but it remains true that the UK has never been convinced that Italy should form part of the community of great powers in Europe. Italy's admission to the Group of Seven was authoritatively suggested by the United States and not by its European partners.

Italy's Position During the Crisis

The Question of Sanctions: A Difficult Decision

The day following Argentina's invasion of the Falklands, the EC unreservedly condemned this act of aggression by the Argentine government and adopted an embargo on arms exports to Argentina and the suspension of all Argentine imports into the Community. These sanctions, initially envisaged to last for one month, were also adhered to, albeit reluctantly, by Italy. A Foreign Ministry official note stated that Italy was 'displeased'

---

14. On that occasion the three governments did not even await Colombo's return from the USA, where he had gone for a first talk with the new American President.

that it had to have recourse to economic measures against a nation with which it has profound ties of solidarity.[15]

Italy's stance began to emerge as a major problem for Britain when the Socialist Party, a member of the governing coalition, came out strongly against any renewal of economic sanctions while military action continued. Some Europeans saw this as a major embarrassment for Italian Prime Minister Giovanni Spadolini, who was known for his pro-European attitudes and thus had supported EC solidarity. The British press, however, guessed that Spadolini would win this domestic debate and that Italy would be unwilling to drop sanctions if West Germany and France called for their renewal.[16]

During the EC foreign ministers' meeting, which took place as scheduled in Luxembourg on 16 May, the most vociferous opposition to sanctions came from Italy. Emilio Colombo, the Italian Minister for Foreign Affairs, argued that he could not approve continued sanctions due to domestic opposition, despite a personal visit from Secretary of State Haig urging him to support renewal. Italy's decision was very difficult: to refuse solidarity with Britain would mean that Italy's prestige in Europe would be lost, but at the same time the government could not possibly ignore the will of the Italian parliament, where a majority was against renewing sanctions. Italy, followed by Ireland, invoked the Luxembourg Compromise, which allowed EC members to veto actions that affected their 'vital national interests', to allow for its abstention.[17] Both countries agreed to continue the arms embargo against Argentina but refused to extend the economic sanctions. Italy's government declared that its choice had been taken with an awareness of the deep-rooted historical and cultural ties between Italy and Argentina, and on the basis of a clear guideline expressed by the parliament.

Prime Minister Spadolini, found his government's decision difficult, but his coalition partners had vowed to bring down the government if he went ahead with sanctions, even for seven days.[18] On this occasion Spadolini stressed that Italy had warned 'President Reagan and the European allies in good time of the insuperable constraints on Italian support for London.'[19] According to him, European unity had not been affected by Italy's decision, above all because Italians maintained their absolute solidarity with Britain in condemning Argentina's aggression and continued to uphold the arms embargo.

15. Italy had earlier adopted restrictive measures against Iran and the Soviet Union (in the latter case over Afghanistan and Poland).

16. J. Wyles, 'EEC States Withhold Renewal of Sanctions', *Financial Times*, 10 May 1982.

17. P. Calvert, *The Falklands Crisis: The Rights and Wrongs*, New York: St Martin, 1982, p. 125.

18. J. Buxton, 'Britain asks Rome to Explain', *Financial Times*, 19 May 1982.

19. P. Garimberti, 'Non è stato tradimento', *La Stampa*, 19 May 1982.

Italian Diplomatic Efforts for a Peaceful Resolution to the Conflict

Although from the very outset Italy had found itself in a particularly delicate predicament, the government had not hesitated to condemn the violation suffered by Britain and to approve economic sanctions, 'adopted as an act of solidarity towards a European partner which had suffered a clearcut abuse of its rights; and also as a means of pressure to induce the Argentine government to return to the sphere of international legality.'[20] The government asked for moderation from Argentina and Britain, seeking a negotiated solution in every possible forum: it backed the mediation efforts by the US Secretary of State Haig and those of the Secretary General of the UN, it maintained close contacts with its Community partners and in particular with Paris and Bonn, and it started consultations with Brazil, Venezuela and Peru.

In the talks in Rome on 16 April between Colombo and the German Foreign Minister, Genscher, it was decided that both governments would instruct their ambassadors in Washington to make a joint approach to the US government to express their full support for Haig's peace efforts. At the same time instructions were given to the respective ambassadors in London and Buenos Aires to outline the Italian and German positions, aimed at urging the maximum goodwill from the parties concerned towards the proposals of the American Secretary of State.

Following Haig's decision to give up his role as mediator, the Italian government decided to appeal to the UN. In a political speech on 4 May, the Italian Foreign Minister stated the need to sustain the way of negotiations, and called upon the UN Secretary General to undertake the burden of a peace initiative; simultaneously the Italian representatives in London and Buenos Aires requested greater flexibility from the British and Argentines and an open attitude towards Pérez de Cuellar's initiative. As a solution to the Falklands crisis, Italy's government proposed to 'freeze' the whole question of sovereignty over the archipelago, to secure the withdrawal of the opposed military forces, to ensure that negotiations of the archipelago's future should commence with no prejudicial conditions, and to implement in the meantime an administration of the islands guaranteed by the UN.[21]

Internal Balances

When the Falklands crisis erupted, a five-party coalition was in power in Italy formed by the Christian Democrats (DC), the Socialist Party (PSI),

---

20. E. Colombo, *Atti Parlamentari*, Camera, 'Resoconti', pp. 8-11, 11 May 1982.
21. Ibid.

the Liberal Party (PLI), the Republican Party (PRI) and the Social Democrats (PSDI). During the crisis two opposing fronts were formed. These gathered very heterogeneous forces, ranging from the far right to the far left of the political spectrum. On the one hand, were the parties which, while condemning the Argentine act of force, wanted a negotiated solution, criticized Britain's 'exaggerated' reaction and declared their opposition to economic sanctions. These parties were the DC, the PSI, the Communist Party (PCI), the Party of Proletarian Unity for Communism (PDUP), the Radical Party (PR) and the Social Movement (MSI). On the other hand, were the parties which considered that Argentina was guilty of a grave breach of international law and also that Italy had the obligation to follow what had been decided at EC level, even if the real effectiveness of sanctions could be questioned. These parties were the PSDI, the PLI and, to some extent, the PRI.

In the decision not to renew the sanctions the PSI's conflictual attitude towards the DC carried a great deal of weight. The accusation made on many sides against the DC was that of having yielded to a sort of political blackmail by the Socialists. Due to its pivotal role in the government, the PSI, which favoured an end to economic measures, made veiled threats that it would leave the government coalition. The threats worked, because both politically and numerically support was decisive for the life and action of the government.[22] The PSI emphasised the 'absurd character' of this war of 'false pride, anachronistic national passion, and cultural intolerance', criticized the government's behaviour over sanctions (arguing that the Socialist group had not been previously informed) and hinted at a possible split from the government coalition if sanctions had to be renewed.[23] The PSI is a party with a strong ideological imprint on international political issues that has maintained within itself diverse positions, from the pro-Atlantic position of the autonomous wing, to the neutralistic pro-Third World positions of the left wing. With the rise of Bettino Craxi to the leadership of the party in 1976, the PSI's approach to international politics was modified, becoming less fragmented and less pro-Third World, and more Western and European. But in the case of the Falklands crisis, unreserved support for the UK and the choices of the EC could engender serious economic damage to corporations under Socialist influence such as ENI, which was carrying out large business transactions in Argentina. In addition, the PSI could not

22. In the 1980 administrative elections the PSI managed to obtain 12.75 per cent of the vote, making realistic the political design of Secretary Bettino Craxi whose aim was to take the place of the DC as the pivotal party of the Italian political system.
23. 'Appreciation of the government's action will be closely tied to the political choice that the government makes on the question of sanctions', A. Labriola, *Atti Parlamentari*, Camera, 'Resoconti', 11 May 1982, p. 56.

forget the millions of Italian citizens that had economic or family ties with Argentina, who could vote for the socialists in the coming administrative elections.

The DC condemned the Argentine invasion but at the same time recognized strong historical, legal, and geographic reasons for claiming sovereignty over the Falklands.[24] The fear of the Christian Democrats was that communism would spread: the Soviet Union, which remained dangerously neutral, and was even showing a certain sympathy for the Argentine attack, could have expanded its influence in South America. For this reason the DC was very cautious and hoped for a negotiated solution that would put an end to the use of force by both parties as soon as possible and as a result, would eliminate the threat of Soviet interference.

The PCI, at that time Italy's second political group and the main opposition party of the left, condemned both the Argentine act of force and the 'imperialistic' British reaction. These actions were exercised, according to the communists, with the same goal, to distract the attention of the public opinion of those countries from the internal political crisis. The PCI, criticizing the 'pseudo-democratic whining in favour of Britain' and the 'Tory bloody-mindedness' of the British government, supported the government's decision not to renew the sanctions.

According to the MSI, which considered Argentina as a part of Italy, the invasion of Falklands was not an act of piracy, but an exercise of the right to self-protection and self-defence.[25] For the Social Movement, the entire Italian and EC approach was wrong, because it divided the unity of the Atlantic interests, indirectly helping the Soviet Union.[26] The PDUP followed the same line, stating that Argentina had the right to claim its sovereignty over the Falklands. In addition, the Proletarian Communists claimed that Britain had shown an intransigence that could not justify the solidarity shown by Italy.

The PSDI, PLI and the PRI considered Argentina guilty of violating international law and believed that Italy should comply with what had been decided at the EC level. But while the PSDI and the PLI justified the British reaction, even though it was deemed exaggerated, the republicans condemned both Argentina's act of force and the British reaction.

According to the PR (radicals), the Argentine act was the nationalist adventure of a military regime in search of a distraction from internal failures. The British government, however, was guilty of not applying to the international organizations, and of replying in a military manner suggestive of a punishing intent. The radical deputy Cicciomessere took a dis-

24. M. Gilmozzi, 'Lo Scandalo della guerra', *Il Popolo*, 5 May 1982.
25. U. Del Donno, *Atti Parlementari*, Camera, 'Resoconti', 11 May 1982, p.112.
26. A. Greggi, O. Del Donno, A. Tripodi, *Atti Parlementari*, Camera, 'Resoconti', 11 May 1982, p. 121.

cordant stand in favour of sanctions in order to respect international agreements; he put a Parliamentary question regarding military supplies, which were, according to him, still being sent by Italy to Argentina. Cicciomessere asked the government about the arms systems that should have been exported, or were on the point of being exported, to Argentina.[27] Cicciomessere suspected that certain members of political parties were not indifferent to the desire of some sectors of Italian society to continue in this profitable activity; he asked the government about the role of one Mr Fabri, probably a 'mediator' in arms traffic,[28] and about the value of the consulting fees (apparently running in tens of billions of lire) authorized by the ministry committee constituted within the Foreign Trade Ministry in favour of Mr Fabri, who was resident at Buenos Aires. Despite numerous requests by Cicciomessere, the government never answered this *interpellanza.*

The maintenance of internal balances within the governmental coalition had great influence on the Italian decision not to renew the sanctions. The party with the most weight in the government, namely the PSI, was able to take advantage of the situation of weakness in the party of relative majority, the DC. The fact that this was a time of campaigning (for the administrative elections scheduled in June) certainly influenced the opinions and the choices of those parties which feared that taking the side of the UK would lose the votes of the 1,300,000 people with Italian passports residing in Argentina.

The Role of the Vatican

During the Falklands' crisis, Pope John Paul II several times requested an 'immediate ceasefire',[29] obtaining polite but negative answers from Galtieri and Mrs Thatcher. The British Prime Minister wrote to the Pope that an essential condition for a ceasefire was the withdrawal of the Argentine army from the Falklands, while Galtieri was ready for a ceasefire if Britain renounced its 'colonial offensive'.

Among the actions taken by the Pope to stop the war was the unusual step of calling a meeting in Rome of Argentine and English bishops, during the very hours when their respective governments were taking the most

27. R. Cicciomessere, *Atti Parlamentari*, Camera, 'Resoconti', 11 May 1982. The radical deputy had found his information about the export of armament in *Almanacco navale 1981*, edited by the Italian Navy.

28. Cicciomessere explained to the parliament that the mediators usually gain high percentages (in this case, 15 per cent) for the conclusion of these kinds of contracts. These payments represent enormous funds that some firms could call upon abroad. These funds, according to Cicciomessere, were used in part to pay the mediator and in part to pay political parties which facilitated commerce.

29. L. Accattoli, 'Il Papa deciso ad andare in Gran Bretagna', *Corriere della Sera*, 24 May 1982.

serious decisions. This was the first time that the Pope succeeded in directly involving in his peace appeal the representatives of the two Catholic communities fighting against each other. The Church leaders signed a common document in which they undertook 'to be witnesses of peace and reconciliation'.[30]

The decision of the Pope to confirm his trip to London, due on 28 May, was hotly contested; His presence in England, although he had cancelled all meetings with government officials, could have given the impression to Argentine and Latin American Catholics that he had failed in his duty of neutrality. But it also might have been risky to cancel a visit defined as 'historic' by the Italian press, and cancellation would have disappointed the English Catholic minority which was awaiting this visit as a sign of emancipation, and cooled the dialogue with the Anglican community.

Pressure Groups, Public Opinion and the Media

The close ties existing between Italy and Argentina meant that the Falklands crisis was felt strongly in many sectors of Italian society. The industrial groups with important business in Argentina put pressure on the politicians not to compromise their interests; the Italo-Argentine community pressed, with all the means at its disposal, the political parties, the Church and members of the government to contribute towards immediate negotiations; representatives of Argentine parties came to Rome to meet the secretaries of the government parties to set forth their position on the Falklands, and several committees, associations and movements of varied origin and nature attempted to inform public opinion and political forces about the crisis.

Pressure Groups (I): The Large Italian Industrial Groups

It has been said that 'the art of lobbying is as old as lawmaking and that pressure groups are as old as politics.'[31] Certainly lobbying activity is widespread in every country of the world, especially in Italy were business and politics are carried out not only in the halls of Parliament but also often in the 'antechambers', either the high society salons or discreet restaurants.[32]

30. Ibid.
31. K. Schriftgiesser, *The Lobbyists: Art and Business of Influencing Lawmakers*, Boston: Little Brown, 1951, cited in M. Franco, Lobby. *Il Parlamento Invisibile*, Milano: Il Sole 24 Ore ed., 1988, p. 32.
32. J. La Palombara, *Politics Within Nations*, New Jersey, 1974, cited in L. Caligaris and C. M. Santoro, *Obiettivo Difesa*, Bologna: Il Mulino, 1986, p. 235 (note 180).

During the crisis, the economic lobby was the most powerful one. There were many Italian firms, even state-owned ones, which felt the pinch from the trade embargo on Argentina. SACE, the organization that provides insurance for export credits, had $460 billion worth of credits insured with Argentina which it would have to pay back gradually to Italian firms and banks if its counterpart blocked payments. One of the trickiest cases was the one concerning the Italian company of Condotte, where at first Argentina blocked payments for the construction of the Cerro Pelado hydroelectric plant on the Rio Grande (worth $350 million). The situation was partly settled when Argentina resumed payments into an account held with a New York bank.

Italian groups taking part in tenders for large scale projects also felt the negative effects of the sanctions. These included Impregilo, the leader of a consortium with Argentine firms bidding for part of a 'maxi contract' (about $2 billion) to construct a dam on the River Yaciretà, and Italtel, which had been awarded the supply of electronic systems for $22 million, suffered delays and stoppages in its payments. SAIPEM, part of a consortium in the construction of a gas pipeline from Santa Fé to Buenos Aires (worth $50 million), was excluded from the pre-qualification bid. The sanctions particularly risked harming the negotiations in which certain state corporations, such as ENI (controlled by PSI) and ENEL were engaged, the former to obtain authorization to conduct oil prospection and the latter to negotiate the purchase of one million tonnes per year of coal from the Rio Turbio mines. FINSIDER (another state corporation) was discussing an important supply of pipes intended for the construction of a water conveyance line.[33]

The major Italian private automobile maker, FIAT, and companies in the defence sector such as Oto Melara, Agusta and Beretta had ongoing contracts for about $150 million, which were then frozen. According to the Radical Party, FIAT and the Italian military firms exerted pressure on the government and on certain coalition political forces to avert the threatened nationalization of Italian companies announced by the Argentine military *junta*, and the breaking of contracts for the purchase of Italian arms systems.[34]

---

33. *Atti Parlamentari*, Camera, Interpellanza, 18 May 1982, p. 23.
34. Ibid., p. 24.

Pressure Groups (II): The Italo-Argentine Community and Pacifist Movements

News of the decision taken by the Italian government to dissociate itself from the renewal of economic sanctions against Argentina brought immediate satisfaction within the Italian community in Latin America. Nor could the fact that half the population of Argentina is of Italian origin, and that consequently not only young men of Italian origin but ones of Italian nationality were fighting on the Falklands front, be underestimated.

During the Falklands War the Committee of Argentinian Italians for a Just Peace was set up in Italy to represent groups of various origin and inspiration. Its members included Italo-Argentine industrialists, members of the PSI, the DC and the PCI, as well as representatives of the traditional committees of assistance and mutual aid. The Committee sought solidarity and sympathy for Argentina, but without being tied to the initiatives of the military *junta*; its goal was to secure the end of Europe's sanctions against Argentina. In Rome for a series of contact meetings, the members of the Committee were able to meet the President of the Republic, the Prime Minister, the Foreign Minister, other state personalities and various political groups and trade unions. The Committee found a fairly favourable audience, and enthusiastically set forth its position using every channel available to gain a voice. It is not unreasonable to suppose that in the Italian government's decision not to associate itself with the renewal of European sanctions, no small part was played by the Committee during its visit to Rome.[35]

Of the various associations which developed during the crisis, the Movement for Life (a pacifist association), expressed in a note its 'censure of both protagonists in the absurd, anachronistic war'.[36] The Rome Committee for Peace organized a sit-in in Rome on 7 May outside the British and Argentine embassies, and was joined by, among others, members of the PDUP and the PCI. The demonstrators, each with a placard round their necks, called for 'the immediate cessation of hostilities and a return to mediation by the UN.'[37] On the same day, in Naples, the Radical party organized a protest meeting against the Falklands War and against hunger in the world, outside the Argentine and British consulates.

---

35. D.Vecchioni, *Le Falkland-Malvine*, Milan: Eura Press, 1987, p. 76.
36. *Dea* (Archivio Ansa), Rome, 6 May 1982, 'Falkland: Movimento per la vita', 194/1.
37. *Dea* (Archivio Ansa), Rome, 7 May 1982, 'Falkland: Manifestazione per la pace a Roma', 228/3.

The Media and Public Opinion

In the early 1980s, after years of taking a back seat, foreign policy once more made the front pages of the newspapers and absorbed the energies of the best Italian correspondents. For the previous decade between 1969 and 1980, dramatic domestic events such as the spread of terrorism, had compelled the press to reduce the attention it had paid to foreign policy since 1950.

The Argentine 'little coup' in the Falklands was not treated lightly by the majority of Italian newspapers. Foreign policy commentators condemned Argentina's colonial coup and defined it as 'an imperialistic and geopolitical fraud', a 'pretext for a nationalistic outburst in a country in revolt', 'an insult to the UN' and 'an act of international piracy'. However, almost all of the leading independent Italian newspapers, both those representing the right-wing Catholic forces, such as *Il Tempo*, and those representing the lay left, such as *la Repubblica*, while recognizing that Argentina's action had violated the principles of international law, regarded from the very outset the question of sovereignty over the Falklands as debatable. *La Repubblica*, one of the country's largest circulation newspapers, accused the UK of not having tried to resolve the long dispute over the possession of the islands at the appropriate international level (the UN). Furthermore, the British military reaction was deemed 'hasty' and 'disproportionate'. *The Corriere della Sera*, an establishment newspaper, considered Thatcher's response 'the most female of reactions', while *La Stampa*, a conservative newspaper owned by the FIAT group, viewed the British premier as 'overly intransigent'.

But the most heated moment of the debate came with the Italian government's decision not to renew economic sanctions against Argentina, and Italy went from being a mere spectator to a protagonist in the crisis. The independent press harshly criticized the choice to break from the Community common front, accusing the government of earning for Italy the definition of a partner who is ' 'untrustworthy', capable of 'deviating' at any moment and on any grounds.[38] The government's decision was presented as Italy's 'U-turn' and the refusal to renew sanctions was called an 'absurd, inexplicable' action, an 'historic blunder' of Italian diplomacy. According to some commentators, the Italian government was now isolated in the international field and had severed the fragile thread of solidarity among the countries of the EC.[39] The twofold tie with the UK (through the Community and NATO), apart from historical reasons, ought to have urged the government to renew the solidarity expressed to the British in early April. These standpoints reflected the European-oriented outlook of

38. *La Repubblica*, 18 May 1982.
39. *Corriere della Sera*, 18 May 1982.

a large part of the independent Italian press, who were more inclined to support the decision of their European partners than to back a choice that created a break within the EC.

The Anglo-Argentine crisis disturbed Italian public opinion, split between the traditional blood ties uniting it with Argentina and the need to respect and restore the rule of international law on behalf of the UK. Associations of varied origin and inspiration sprang up, pacifist movements attacked both the British military expedition and the Argentine dictator, and the question of the *desaparecidos* also became a centre of attention. Lacking any opinion polls on the matter, the real position of the majority of Italian citizens remains uncertain. What seems clear is that the profound ethnic, cultural, economic and political ties with Argentina, not forgetting the natural sympathy for another Latin people, constituted a solid cordon that not even Galtieri's 'little coup' appeared to have dented.

Italy's Role in the Post-Falklands War Period

The particularly moderating activity performed by Italy during the most critical phases of the controversy enabled it to play an active and appreciated role in the attempt to 're-attach' Latin America to the EC. Among the many efforts made by Italian diplomacy to mend Euro-Argentine relations after the crisis, the Italian Foreign Minister Colombo's visit to Buenos Aires (8–9 August 1982) is particularly important. Taking place a few days after the Argentine political parties (with whose leaders Colombo had talks) were legalized, the purpose of the Foreign Minister's visit was to sound out the possibilities of a compromise between the military *junta* and Western countries. The latter were prepared to assist the ravaged Argentine economy only if given the guarantees of a democratic shift of the regime. To Colombo the situation was still 'dramatic', and Western countries had to ponder a great deal on their responsibilities.

Italy did not lose the opportunity, both in the UN and in the EC, to try to reconcile the two parties, supporting the resolutions which it considered helpful towards settling the lengthy dispute. At the UN General Assembly, after having abstained for three years (1982–4),[40] Italy decided in 1985 to vote in favour of the pro-Argentine resolution on the grounds that, contrary to before, Resolution 40/21 called for a 'global' solution

---

40. In all resolutions nos. 37/9, 38/12, 39/6, the text reads: 'Request the government of Argentina and the United Kingdom of Great Britain and Northern Ireland, to resume negotiations in order to find as soon as possible a peaceful solution to the sovereignty dispute relating to the question of the Falkland Islands (Malvinas).' In 1983, Italy declared that 'it abstained to keep alive the possibility of pursuing its efforts to re-establish a dialogue between the parties', in *ONU Yearbook*, New York, 1982-4, respectively p. 987 and p. 667, p. 89.

including the Falklands dispute. This explains why in the same year Italy refused to back two British amendments on the rights of people to self-determination; the Italians claimed that these amendments were not clear enough about the wider issues at stake.[41]

With regard to Italian-British relations, the rift caused by Italy's decision to disassociate itself from the Community's sanctions against Argentina was soon resolved. Margaret Thatcher came to Italy on an official visit at the invitation of Prime Minister Spadolini on 7 July 1982, preceded by one day by her Foreign Minister Francis Pym. Then, at the end of his trip to South America, Colombo met the British ambassador in Rome (12 August) to inform him of the outcome of his visit to Argentina. On 26 January 1984, Mrs Thatcher again visited Rome; on that occasion, the Italian Prime Minister Bettino Craxi proposed that Italy should play an active role in the Falklands dispute, but this offer was turned down by Mrs Thatcher who stated that it was a British problem. However, Italy did not renounce its role as an intermediary between the two countries, with which it had and still has profound ties of friendship. The election of the new President, Carlos Menem, enabled Argentina to emerge from this impasse; it also helped to make the UK more ready for a dialogue. Italian-Argentine relations have became closer with the end of the dictatorship.

Conclusions

The Falklands crisis exemplified certain characteristics of Italian foreign policy, amongst which, as highlighted by the journalist and writer Sergio Romano, was 'the reluctance to accept rules and undertakings, even though taken within the EC, which might endanger the domestic political equilibrium'.[42]

The need to maintain a balance in the government coalition may have been the decisive factor in Italy's decision to dissociate itself from the EC's choices, but it was certainly not the only one. The pressure groups, which possessed a capacity of influence by being the bearers or the expression of vested interests, contributed towards determining the Italian foreign policy line. Also the country's national attributes, and its 'historical constants' (in this case the ethnic, cultural and economic ties with Argentina) exercised influence on Italy's important decision not to renew the sanctions.

According to Rosenau's theory,[43] no foreign policy is made without regard for domestic consequences, and vice versa. Indeed, foreign and domestic

41. *ONU Yearbook*, New York, 1985, p. 543.

42. S. Romano, *Guida alla Politica Estera Italiana*, Milano: Rizzoli, 1993, p. 41.

43. J. N. Rosenau, *The Scientific Study of Foreign Policy*, New York: Free Press, 1971, pp. 95-150.

policies are intimately linked. In Italy, foreign policy decisions have often been subservient to the requirements of domestic policy, or rather to the precarious balances keeping a given government in power: precarious by being based on temporary alliances and, at times, targeted on a specific goal. When that alliance collapses, the whole government falls. What has often appeared as a tendency in Italy's foreign policy to change its position has in reality been the consequence of the fragile balances of power both between government and opposition and within the coalition governments themselves.

In Italy the link between foreign policy and domestic policy has dominated the country for the last forty-five years and has had a strong effect on the political life and its external image. Hemmed in between two overriding necessities – the exigencies of the Cold War and those of associative democracy, the calls to order of the leading ally and the progressive push of the left-wing forces – Italian diplomacy has adopted an ambiguous, wavering style of action. The Cold War allowed Italy to be at the same time an ally and 'neutral'.

Today, it is more difficult to use diplomacy in a world that has emerged from its fear of a great war to the explosion of many minor but dangerous regional conflicts. It is hard to make forecasts about the future role of foreign policy in Italy. The country today is living through a time of great internal political turbulence in which everything is being questioned; the 'discovery' by Italian public opinion that the ruling class which has governed it for the last forty years was dishonest and corrupt is causing an unprecedented political and social 'earthquake'. While the internal system is weakening, overcome by an almost general crisis, Italy's external military presence is being extended and built up. Italy is increasingly and actively engaged in the UN peacekeeping missions in crisis areas, most recently Somalia and Mozambique, but also the Lebanon, Bosnia and Albania. Italy is facing the conclusion of a phase of its foreign policy corresponding to the death of the First Republic. Once again, therefore, foreign policy and domestic policy are closely linked and bound to mutually affect each other.

– 7 –

The Internal Dissenter (II): Ireland[1]

Ben Tonra

Introduction

Ireland's[2] response to the Falklands conflict should be understood in the context of the structure of its foreign policy process and the substantive background in which that policy was framed. This background includes the historical framework of Irish foreign policy – revealing the unique nature of Irish neutrality and the centrality of Anglo-Irish relations – and the key contemporary features which impinged on Irish policy. The latter included Ireland's concurrent domestic political crisis, the management of Anglo-Irish relations, the institutional tension between the Department of the Taoiseach[3] and the Department of Foreign Affairs, Ireland's unusual international profile at the United Nations, the reappearance of neutrality as a major domestic political issue, and Ireland's distinctive relationship with Argentina.

Structure of the Policy Process

Ireland's foreign policy process may be characterized as closed, elite-formulated and executive-driven.[4] As in the Westminster model, ultimate collective responsibility for Irish foreign policy is vested in a cabinet government enjoying the confidence of an elected parliament. The Minister for For-

1. Sincere thanks go to Patrick Keatinge for his incisive and constructive comments on earlier drafts of this chapter. All errors of omission and commission remain my responsibility.
2. 'Ireland' is taken to refer to the Republic of Ireland.
3. Prime Minister.
4. See P. Keatinge, *The Formulation of Irish Foreign Policy*, Dublin: Institute of Public Administration, 1973.

eign Affairs – a member of the legislature – is appointed by the President on the nomination of the Taoiseach and is charged with responsibility for the department's administration and political direction. The department is staffed by policy generalists while recruitment is separate from that of the general civil service.[5]

Policy making occurs in a very limited setting. The input of Parliament, for example, is weak: in theory the Oireachtas supervises government policy,[6] but in practice, Parliament's only weapon is a constitutional blunderbuss, a vote of no confidence and the subsequent resignation of the entire government. A strong party system also mitigates against interventionism; party loyalty and the whip system ensures that a government majority will normally last throughout a parliamentary term with little or no likelihood of a backbench revolt. Until 1993 neither Dáil nor Seanad possessed a parliamentary committee to monitor foreign policy. Limited sittings of Parliament preclude close surveillance of policy, as the Dáil sits for an average of just ninety days per year. Supervision is restricted to annual policy debates surrounding the budgetary estimates, government statements, special debates, votes on international treaties or agreements and parliamentary questions to the Minister for Foreign Affairs or the Taoiseach. Government control over the business of Parliament ensures that the latter's influence is tightly circumscribed.

The participation of other groups is even more marginal. Party discipline within Parliament is matched by that outside; foreign policy discussions within political parties are sporadic and usually limited to set-piece debates at annual party conferences. The government's social partners – trade unions, employers organizations and farming representatives – while regularly and formally consulted on issues of economic welfare, have neither sought nor been given input to foreign policy (outside the sphere of the EC's socio-economic policies). Single-issue interest groups, churches and the media have no direct line of communication with the government on issues of foreign policy and rely almost exclusively upon mobilizing public opinion. Irish public opinion in turn rarely mobilizes on a foreign policy issue.[7]

---

5. D. Keogh, 'Ireland: The Department of Foreign Affairs', in Zara Steiner (ed.), *The Times' Survey of Foreign Ministries of the World*, London: Times Books,1982, pp. 275-97.

6. The Irish Parliament (Oireachtas) comprises the Presidency, an indirectly elected upper Chamber (Seanad) and a directly elected lower Chamber (Dáil). Both the Presidency and the upper Chamber have limited constitutional functions. The primary role of supervising government policy is the preserve of the Dáil.

7. For example, the 1985 Live Aid concert for African famine relief galvanized the Irish public, raising over £7 million from a population of 3 million. Despite efforts, this did not translate into any serious political pressure to increase Ireland's Overseas Development Assistance (ODA) commitment, which was among the lowest of the OECD countries and remains so.

Background to the Policy Process

At almost every stage of its development Irish foreign policy has been set against its relationship with Britain. This dates back to the foundation of the state in 1921 when the right to issue passports, the right to fly the Irish flag at sea and the right to establish diplomatic missions abroad were all contested by the former colonial power.[8] Irish governments responded on two fronts: they worked assiduously in the League of Nations to establish Ireland's international *bona fides* and within the British Empire they successfully sought to re-define imperial relationships.[9] For twenty-seven years consecutive Irish governments adjusted and readjusted the constitutional position vis-à-vis the United Kingdom. This was finally resolved in 1949 when the state cut all ties with the British Commonwealth and formally became a republic; nonetheless, the issue of the partition of the island of Ireland remained a bone of contention between Dublin and London.

During the Second World War neutrality was partly seen as the ultimate affirmation of Irish independence and sovereignty.[10] Irish sovereignty was again invoked in 1949 when Ireland refused an invitation to become a founding member of the Atlantic Alliance. The government argued that membership of a defence pact with the United Kingdom would have signified *de jure* recognition of partition.[11] In much the same way, however, that Britain was 'of Europe yet not in Europe,' Ireland was of the Western Alliance yet not in the Western Alliance. One principle guiding Ireland's UN policy was the commitment to defend Christian civilization from 'the spread of communist power and influence'.[12] Irish neutrality was not ideologically-based nor was it built upon a strict interpretation of

8. *Dáil Debates*, vol. 3, pp. 2388-2400, 25 June 1923.

9. On Irish participation in the League of Nations see P. Keatinge 'Ireland and the League of Nations', in *Studies*, vol. 59, no. 234, 1970, pp. 67-82; C. C. O'Brien, 'Ireland in International Affairs', in O. D. Edwards (ed.), *Conor Cruise O'Brien Introduces Ireland*, London: Andre Deutsch, 1969, pp. 104-35; D. W. Harkness, *The Restless Dominion: The Irish Free State and the British Commonwealth of Nations*, London: Macmillan, 1969. On Ireland in the Commonwealth see D. W. Harkness, The Restless Dominion; N. Mansergh, *Survey of British Commonwealth Affairs: Problems of External Policy, 1931–1939*, Oxford: Oxford University Press, 1952; D. McMahon, *Republicans and Imperialists: Anglo-Irish Relations in the 1930s*, New Haven: Yale University Press, 1984.

10. Perhaps the best analysis of Irish war-time neutrality is to be found in R. Fisk's, *In Time of War: Ireland, Ulster and the Price of Neutrality*, London: Andre Deutsch, 1983; see also T. Ryle Dwyer, *Irish Neutrality and the USA 1939-1947*, Dublin: Gill & Macmillan, 1977, and J. T. Carroll, *Ireland in The War Years*, Newton Abbott: David & Charles, 1975.

11. Comprehensive coverage of Irish attitudes towards the formation and membership of NATO may be found in R. Fanning, 'The United States and Irish Participation in NATO: The debate of 1950', *Irish Studies in International Affairs*, vol. 1, no. 1, 1979, pp. 38–48; and W. Fitzgerald, Irish Unification and NATO, Dublin: Dublin University Press, 1982.

12. *Dáil Debates*, vol. 159, p. 144, 3–4 July 1956.

international law; it was essentially rooted in Ireland's relationship with the United Kingdom.[13]

The Falklands crisis occurred during a uniquely inauspicious period in this relationship. The Taoiseach, Charles J. Haughey, had based much of his political career upon a trenchant approach to Northern Ireland. He had to reconstruct his political base within Fianna Fáil after his forced resignation from government in 1970 over allegations that he had conspired to supply arms to the nationalist minority in Northern Ireland. Following the surprise resignation of the party leader and Taoiseach, Jack Lynch, in 1979, Haughey's bitterly-fought leadership battle sowed the seeds of continuing division. Major party figures gave only grudging support to Haughey's leadership, with some drawing jesuitical distinctions between Haughey as Taoiseach – who commanded their constitutional backing – and Haughey as party leader – against whom they continued to canvass.

When he first became Taoiseach in 1979 Haughey used his reputation as an ardent nationalist as capital for a new Anglo-Irish initiative. At their December 1980 summit in Dublin, he and British Prime Minister Margaret Thatcher agreed to initiate a series of studies examining the 'totality of relationships' between the two islands. Soon afterwards, however, in March 1981 a new wave of IRA-sponsored hunger strikes in Northern Ireland by republican prisoners seeking 'special category' status strained relations. Haughey's relationship with Mrs Thatcher did not sway her vehement rejection of the prisoners demands.

Haughey called an election for June 1981 in the midst of these hunger strikes and following the death of several of the prisoners. Nine prisoners were nominated for Dáil seats and two won in traditional Fianna Fáil constituencies; the others siphoned off crucial republican and nationalist votes from Fianna Fáil candidates. This cost Haughey his first election success as party leader.

Following a brief Fine Gael-Labour coalition *interregnum*, Haughey returned to office in March 1982, having beaten off a leadership challenge from within his own party. His new cabinet was built around figures from the nationalist core of the party. In April, already poor bilateral relations deteriorated even further when Haughey denounced the published outline of a British government plan to establish a new constituent assembly for Northern Ireland. Anglo-Irish relations were probably at their lowest ebb for a decade.

This was also a period of unprecedented domestic political fragility. Parliamentary stability and a conservative political culture are character-

13. For a vigorous exposition of this argument see T. Salmon, *Unneutral Ireland: An Ambivalent and Unique Security Policy*, Oxford: Clarendon, 1989.

istic of Irish government and are reflected in the party political structure.[14] The two largest parties, Fianna Fáil and Fine Gael, originated from a bitter civil war split in the nationalist movement at the state's foundation. Thus, despite the existence of a smaller trade union-based Labour Party, Irish politics was divided on issues of nationalist identification rather than socio-economic cleavage. The diminished saliency of nationalist issues over the years produced a political system largely dominated by two competing non-ideological catch-all parties.

The period 1981–2, however, was marked by an extraordinarily weak and unstable parliamentary situation. A four-year old Fianna Fáil administration was replaced in 1981 by a minority Fine Gael-Labour coalition; but in February 1982 this government fell after only eight months in office. Subsequent elections were again indecisive. On 3 March 1982 Charles Haughey succeeded in crafting a Fianna Fáil minority administration which relied upon the votes of two independent TDs (parliamentary deputies) and the three deputies of the Marxist Workers' Party. In an attempt to strengthen his parliamentary position, Haughey also offered to return a former Irish EC Commissioner Richard Burke to the Berlaymont. As a Fine Gael opposition TD, Burke's subsequent resignation from the Dáil immediately reduced the opposition's parliamentary voting strength; it also opened the possibility of a Fianna Fail by-election victory in Burke's former Dublin West constituency. The by-election writ was moved on 5 May with polling set for 25 May.

The government's political weakness and the precarious state of Anglo-Irish relations were also reflected in administrative conflict during Haughey's second administration. The Department of Foreign Affairs, according to political intimates of Mr Haughey, was not 'sound' on issues of Irish nationalism. The Department was understood to be overly anxious to maintain good Anglo-Irish relations at the expense of promoting the cause of Irish unity. Furthermore, Haughey had been embarrassed in 1980 over his attempt to remove Ireland's Ambassador in Washington, Sean Donlon.[15] Haughey had been concerned that Donlon's success at building up a moderate and well connected Irish-American constituency was splitting nationalist opinion in North America. The very determined intervention of senior Irish-American politicians had forced Haughey to back away from his proposed diplomatic reshuffle, and during the intervening Fine Gael-Labour coalition Donlon had been promoted to Secretary of the Department. Partly as a consequence of this mistrust, Haughey had built up his own kitchen cabinet on foreign policy and Northern Ireland, headed by Dr Martin Mansergh who was a former official with the Department

---

14. J. Coakley, 'Society and Political Culture', in J. Coakley and M. Gallagher (eds), *Politics in the Republic of Ireland*, Dublin: PSAI Press, 1992, pp. 23-40.
15. J. Joyce and P. Murtagh, *The Boss*, Dublin: Poolbeg Press, 1983, pp. 154–5.

of Foreign Affairs and who was now a full-time researcher, advisor and speechwriter for Mr Haughey. Mansergh also became a special advisor to the Taoiseach's Department.

An exceptional domestic situation was matched by an atypical external environment. First, a renewed freeze in superpower relations had politicized Irish neutrality. This new Cold War had emerged in the early 1980s; in Ireland, the resulting international tension shattered the dormant consensus which had surrounded the largely undefined policy of neutrality.[16] The Haughey-Thatcher Anglo-Irish summit of 8 December 1980 prompted extensive speculation that Irish concessions on defence had been proposed in return for a British compromise on constitutional issues. It also exposed wide political differences on the definition and application of neutrality which were reflected in a bad-tempered Dáil debate on neutrality in March 1981: the first of its kind to be held on the subject.[17]

The short-lived Fine Gael-Labour coalition of June 1981 to February 1982 faced a similar controversy. Ireland's response to proposals to strengthen EC foreign policy cooperation had been initially ambiguous.[18] In a bitter Dáil debate following the publication in October 1981 of the London Report on EPC, the Fine Gael Taoiseach, Dr Garret FitzGerald, traded allegations with former Foreign Minister Mr Brian Lenihan of Fianna Fáil as to which of them had undermined Irish neutrality first.[19] The discordant nature of that debate also raised the political stakes on neutrality.

Within the hothouse debate surrounding Irish neutrality, the Falklands crisis also touched a rather unusual nerve in Irish foreign policy. The focus of the crisis, Argentina, held a special place in Irish policy. In 1920, even before the establishment of the state, the first Dáil had established a roving mission to Buenos Aires seeking diplomatic recognition for the underground Irish government and making contacts with the significant expatriate community there. An embassy was established in 1947, and remains the only resident Irish mission in Latin America. The Irish-Argentine community is the third largest in the Western hemisphere with over 300,000 Argentines claiming Irish ancestry. Indeed, the town of Foxford, County Mayo, proudly boasts that it is the birthplace of the father of the Argentine navy, Admiral Guillermo (William) Brown, who was born there in 1777.

From 1965 to the mid-1970s Ireland's position on the disputed sovereignty of the remote Falkland Islands had been one in favour of negotia-

16. For a review of Irish neutrality in the 1980s see P. Keatinge, *A Singular Stance: Irish Neutrality in the 1980s*, Dublin: Institute of Public Administration,1984, and D. Driscoll, 'Is Ireland Really Neutral', *Irish Studies in International Affairs*, vol. 1, no. 3, 1982, pp. 55-61.

17. *Dáil Debates*, vol. 327, pp. 1392-1490 and pp. 1562–9, 11 March 1981.

18. See T. Salmon, *Unneutral Ireland: An Ambivalent and Unique Security Policy*, p. 252.

19. *Dáil Debates*, vol. 330, pp. 124-34 and pp. 305-18, 15 October 1981.

tions but neutral on the substantive issue, in effect a pro-Argentine position. At the UN General Assembly in 1965, Ireland voted in favour of sovereignty negotiations at a time when the UK government refused to concede the principle of talks. Subsequently in 1973, Ireland supported calls for an acceleration in the talks process: again in the teeth of forceful British opposition. By 1976, however, Argentina's poor human rights record became an issue and under a Fine Gael-Labour coalition Ireland's position was modified. In that year's General Assembly resolution and subsequently, Ireland abstained on calls for sovereignty talks.

The novelty of a vigorous political debate on neutrality and an international crisis affecting an exceptional inter-state relationship would probably have been just a matter of domestic controversy, were it not for Ireland's unusual position at the United Nations. Ireland's role in the Falklands crisis was significantly heightened by the fact that it held a seat on the United Nations Security Council, having been elected in 1980 for a two-year term beginning in 1981.[20] This position meant that from the very start of the crisis Ireland was involved at a singularly high level of the multilateral UN process. The United Kingdom and France's permanent seats on the Security Council entailed a special dispensation from the obligations of consultation and coordination of policy under European Political Cooperation (EPC). Ireland's later performance raises the question as to whether this qualification applied to a member state holding a temporary seat on the Council.

The 1982 Falklands Crisis and Irish Policy

On 2 April 1982 Ireland's permanent representative to the United Nations, Ambassador Noel Dorr, joined his Security Council colleagues in their denunciation of the Argentine invasion. This was followed by Irish support for UN Security Council Resolution 502, demanding a cessation of hostilities, Argentine withdrawal and negotiations on the islands' status. Dorr went to great lengths, however, to draw a line between Ireland's principled stand on the use of force and its insistence that it took no stand on the islands' sovereignty. Dorr also signalled Irish concerns at a possible escalation of conflict following the British launch of the Royal Navy task force to the South Atlantic.

Dorr's denunciation of the Argentine intervention reflected that of Irish Foreign Minister Gerry Collins, also on 2 April. An agreed statement on

---

20. Ireland's Falklands' policy at the United Nations and in the European Community is explored in N. MacQueen, 'The Expedience of Tradition: Ireland, International Organization and the Falklands Crisis', *Political Studies*, vol. 33, January 1985, pp. 38-55.

behalf of the Ten denounced the invasion and insisted that Argentina refrain from using force to press her sovereignty claims. Both statements were based firmly upon established precedents of Irish foreign policy.

On 6 April the UK sought European Community (EC) economic sanctions against Argentina. This request met resistence in Dublin; according to a spokesperson in the Taoiseach's office the government was reluctant to support sanctions believing them to be counter-productive.[21] A Cabinet meeting the next day discussed the sanctions request but came to no conclusion. Mr Haughey was described as being 'in particular' opposed to sanctions.[22] Ireland's economic interests were minimal. Irish trade with Argentina amounted to less that 10 million Irish pounds a year and studies by the Department of Industry and Commerce could identify no Irish factory in which jobs might be threatened by sanctions.[23] Coras Trachtala (the Irish Export Board) could see no serious adverse consequences of sanctions for Irish industry, and in fact identified potential opportunities for Irish firms to pick up Argentine business in the UK. The Confederation of Irish Industry (CII) made known its principled opposition to sanctions, but did so with little passion.[24]

EC sanctions were agreed on 10 April but the Irish government had already begun to distance itself from the political implications of its support. The Taoiseach in particular was especially uncomfortable in being seen to support the jingoistic British military response which was emerging. First came the rumour that Ambassador Dorr had acted with undue haste and with insufficient consultation in supporting UN Resolution 502. In a widely read – and usually authoritative – political column in the mass-circulation *Sunday Independent* newspaper, it was stated that government sources were insisting that Ambassador Dorr had not consulted the Department of Foreign Affairs before his vote and statement on UN Resolution 502. Ambassador Dorr was described as being in 'hot water' with the government and, the article continued: 'The Taoiseach considers that by Mr Dorr's ready support of the British claim to overlordship of the Falklands the Irish government may in future be inhibited in their dealings with the British in their government to government drive for Irish unity.'[25] The *Irish Press* newspaper, a daily with strong political and historical links to the Fianna Fáil party, also asked whether the Ambassador had acted in accordance with the government's political judgement: 'in the case of the Security Council vote, did we have to vote as it were against Argentina and for Great Britain... Did someone in Foreign Affairs simply authorise the vote

21. *The Irish Times*, 7 April 1982.
22. Ibid.
23. *The Irish Times*, 12 April 1982.
24. *Irish Press*, 8 April 1982.
25. *Sunday Independent*, 11 April 1982.

without considering the political implications – it certainly doesn't look as though an opportunity for full political consideration at the highest political level was afforded.'[26]

These suggestions provoked anger within the Department of Foreign Affairs.[27] Senior officials present at the time insist that the Taoiseach personally authorized the UN vote and was kept fully informed at all stages.[28] In the case of the *Sunday Independent* article, legal action was threatened and a full retraction published.[29]

As it became clear that political dissociation from the government's own decision was not feasible, suggestions soon emerged from cabinet that Irish support for EC sanctions was contingent on or at least linked to other issues. In return for solidarity on sanctions, the argument went, the Irish government sought a more helpful UK position on Common Agricultural Policy (CAP) farm price increases, worth over £100 million.[30] Articles such as 'Hopes of Farm Deal as we back British' and 'A Secret Deal' made a clear linkage between the two issues; these were supported by ministerial statements to the effect that EC solidarity was a two-way street.[31] Later, Mr Haughey himself noted in a broadcast interview that any 'sensible person' knew that the two issues were linked by their appearance on the same political agenda.[32]

While the Dáil was in recess for the Easter holidays, Irish members of the European Parliament (EP) contributed to the emerging sanctions debate and reflected changes in Irish opinion. On 22 April and on 12 May the EP debated motions on sanctions.[33] In the first vote three Irish Members, Clinton (Fine Gael), Treacy (Labour) and Davern (Fianna Fail), supported the motion for sanctions; while no Irish MEP formally opposed sanctions on this occasion, five Irish members (two Fianna Fail, two Fine Gael and one independent) joined a total of just four other MEPs in abstaining.[34] By the time of the second vote, however, just three weeks later, only Tom O'Donnell (Fine Gael) supported continuing sanctions while two Fianna Fail MEPs (Lalor and Davern) were now opposed. Only Maher (independent) registered his abstention – the balance of Irish members were absent.[35] Earlier, T. J. Maher, MEP had expressed his 'amazement at the meekness of the Irish government' in agreeing to sanctions while the UK held up agree-

26. *Irish Press*, 16 April 1982.
27. *The Irish Times*, 13 April 1982.
28. Author's interview with senior Irish official, 1992.
29. *Irish Independent*, 18 April 1982.
30. *Sunday Independent*, 11 April 1982; Irish Press, 19 April 1982.
31. *Irish Independent*, 21 April 1982.
32. *The Irish Times*, 14 May 1982.
33. *EC-Bulletin*, vol. 15, no. 4, pp. 51-3, April 1982; Ibid., vol. 15, no. 5, p. 73, May 1982.
34. *Official Journal of the European Communities*, C125, 17 May 1982.
35. *Official Journal of the European Communities*, C149, 14 June 1982.

ment on a new agriculture budget.[36] On 19 April, Neil Blaney, TD and MEP – one of the independents upon whom Mr Haughey's government still depended for its parliamentary survival – had pressed the government to support Argentina in the dispute and drew parallels with the situation in Northern Ireland.[37]

Opposition to sanctions from Haughey's own nationalist wing of Fianna Fáil was articulated publicly for the first time during the the EP debate by Sile de Valera, MEP and granddaughter of the party's revered founder. De Valera accused the government of compromising Irish neutrality by giving support to the UK, and complained that 'the influence of Britain and her supporters among the other member states [in the EC] has affected our objectivity in the Falklands matter and eroded our neutral stance'.[38]

The Irish government's dilemma over sanctions was exacerbated by British military action to retake the South Georgia Islands on 25–26 April. Newspaper reports indicated that Irish support for sanctions was limited and that Ireland would unilaterally reassess its position in the event of further armed conflict.[39] Officials described as 'close to Foreign Minister Collins' contended that the attack on South Georgia represented a 'whole new ballgame' for Irish policy.[40] Collins publicly acknowledged this new emphasis in Irish policy with a speech to the Council of Europe's Committee of Ministers on 29 April. A special government meeting was convened for Sunday 2 May at which the cabinet reviewed Irish policy on the crisis.[41] The outline of a statement was agreed which would shift Irish policy into a more independent and neutral path. It noted that: 'From the outset of the Falklands crisis the policy of the Irish government, both at the United Nations and within the EEC has been directed at preventing a wider conflict and promoting a negotiated honorable settlement by diplomatic means ... The government wish to reaffirm Ireland's traditional role of neutrality in relation to armed conflicts.'[42] Late that same evening, at about 8.00 p.m., reports began to circulate of a British attack on the Argentine cruiser the *General Belgrano*. Reports were unclear as to scale of the loss of life.

Into this political maelstrom came Paddy Power, TD and Minister for Defence. Speaking that Sunday night at a local constituency Fianna Fáil meeting, the Minister gave a speech which explicitly linked British actions in the South Atlantic to the situation in Northern Ireland.[43] The Minister spoke movingly about the occupation of small islands by great powers

---

36. *The Irish Times*, 15 April 1982.
37. *The Irish Times*, 20 April 1982.
38. *The Irish Times*, 23 April 1982
39. *Irish Independent*, 26 April 1982.
40. *The Irish Times*, 30 April 1982.
41. *Irish Independent*, 30 April 1982.
42. *The Irish Times*, 3 May 1982.
43. *Irish Press*, 4 May 1982.

and the methods employed to keep control over them. He also noted that the British Ambassador had only that very weekend admitted that fourteen days previously a British submarine had sunk an Irish fishing trawler and failed to come to the assistance of its five-man crew. At sea, the Minister alleged, Britain behaved like 'a hit and run driver'. The Minister went on to argue that the attack on the *Belgrano* now made Britain 'very much the aggressor' in the Falklands crisis. He assured his listeners that the Irish government would soon formally assert its neutrality in the conflict.

Reports of Power's remarks were being extensively reported in Ireland and the UK on Tuesday 4 May when the *HMS Sheffield* was reported attacked by Argentine jets. Just hours before reports on the *HMS Sheffield* began to come through, the government had responded to the huge loss of life in the *Belgrano* incident; in its statement the Irish government called for an immediate cessation of hostilities, an immediate meeting of the UN Security Council and the end of EC sanctions. British outrage with the statement was matched by irritation at UN headquarters in New York and confusion in EC capitals.

British wrath was directed at both the timing and the substance of the Irish statement and at the tone and content of Power's remarks. Both were framed in the context of the loss of *HMS Sheffield* and the deaths of over thirty of her crew. The Taoiseach's disavowal of Minster Power's statement as being 'personal...understandable...spontaneous' made little headway in London. The *Irish Times* later noted that 'It is not possible to explain to the Englishman that many regard Mr Power as a Dunderhead; a dunderhead of a peculiar Fianna Fáil species.'[44] However, the government's call for an immediate cessation of hostilities could only be seen as undermining the UK's position. Such a ceasefire, with no mention of an Argentine withdrawal, would leave Argentina in control of the islands and the British task force literally bobbing at sea.

In New York, there was irritation at the Irish call for an 'immediate meeting' of the UN Security Council. The latest diplomatic efforts by the Secretary General had just reached a critical juncture; within hours he expected formal British and Argentine responses to his latest set of proposals. A full meeting of the Security Council would have sent both parties scurrying back to their original positions as the world focussed on a public confrontation.

In the EC the Irish manoeuvre created confusion. No prior consultation with Ireland's EPC partners had occurred before the 4 May statement was issued, even though a Political Committee meeting was scheduled for that same evening to discuss the Falklands' situation. Several EC leaders had expressed similar reservations about the UK's seemingly anxious rush

44. *The Irish Times*, 2 June 1982.

to military confrontation, including Chancellor Schmidt.[45] The Irish move, however, immediately put these governments under pressure to affirm their solidarity lest it be perceived that the UK's allies were abandoning her. Such assurances were swiftly sought and received by Whitehall.

The Irish government found itself forced to reassess its position. Within hours in the Dáil the opposition parties, through Private Notice Questions, demanded clarification of the government's position and condemned its handling of the affair. The Taoiseach was prompted by the Leader of the Opposition, Garret FitzGerald, into restating Ireland's support for UN Resolution 502, its condemnation of Argentine aggression and insistence upon Argentine withdrawal as the basis for any solution to the conflict. The Taoiseach was also taken to task by the Fine Gael Deputy Leader, Peter Barry on the question of EC sanctions; Barry pointed out that by virtue of the fact that sanctions had been enacted by an EC Regulation 877/82 – which was binding on all EC states – Ireland would breach EC law if it attempted to unilaterally break sanctions. The Taoiseach did not address himself to the legal issues posed but agreed that Ireland would not suspend the operation of EC sanctions without its partners' agreement.

Later that same day, it emerged that the government had also agreed, following communication with the UN Secretary General's office, to revise its request for an 'immediate meeting' of the Security Council.[46] Instead, Ireland made an 'immediate call' for such a meeting. In a television interview on the national network RTE that evening, the Taoiseach was reduced to extemporizing as to the possible shape of a new Security Council resolution.

The 4 May statement was clearly a disaster of foreign policy management. The worsening of already poor Anglo-Irish relations, the lack of consultation with EC partners and the UN debacle indicate either that officials in the Department of Foreign Affairs were not consulted or their advice disregarded. Policy making had clearly shifted to the Department of the Taoiseach. The 4 May statement was, however, a domestic political success.

Outside the Dáil, most major newspapers enthusiastically supported the government's position. The weekly mass circulation *Sunday Independent* was perhaps typical:

> Participation in the embargo has seriously compromised our neutrality and, thankfully, Mr Haughey has recognized that danger. His remarks on the matter late this week were well considered and must be supported by all irrespective of their political persuasion. So too should our peace efforts at the United Nations. Peacemaking is never popular. We should not be afraid to take some

45. *The Irish Times*, 5-6 May 1982; Dáil Debates, vol. 334, pp. 806-14, 11 May 1982.
46. *The Irish Times*, 5 May 1982.

stick from across the water [reference to the United Kingdom] because of it. Whether they know it or not we are acting in their best interest. [47]

The new Irish stance was also welcomed by various peace groups and political lobbies such as the Irish Campaign for Nuclear Disarmament and the Irish Sovereignty Movement, the latter two groups being established critics of EC foreign policy cooperation. Little domestic support existed for maintaining sanctions. Criticism of the government's initiative was largely restricted to the Dáil and complaints against the government's handling of the situation. The Leader of the Opposition's attack, for example, was not loudly echoed even within his own party; even its youth wing supported the government's move.[48] In the media, only the *Irish Independent* newspaper came close to defending Ireland's initial position: 'The government itself is floundering around, trying, it appears, to find a formula which meets two requirements: to please the green [nationalist] wing of the Fianna Fáil party which wants Britain to be found guilty no matter what the dispute is about; the second is to adopt a position which recognizes the realities of the current crisis.'[49]

This domestic policy success was built upon the exploitation of the highly malleable character of Irish neutrality. Neutrality, however, was not the policy objective (as its redefinition during the conflict seemed to suggest); the main objective was to distance the Irish government from British policy. The prospect of supporting British military action designed to forcibly restore colonial control over a group of small, distant islands with a settler population was politically repugnant to a fragile Fianna Fáil administration led by Mr Haughey. Haughey's precarious position both as head of government and party leader demanded adherence to, and cultivation of, the nationalist orthodoxies. Neutrality was the ideal tool and the UN the ideal forum to pursue that objective.

On 11 May a full Dáil debate on the Falklands crisis became the crucible for parliamentary criticism. In his statement, the Taoiseach responded forcefully to allegations that government policy had been misdirected and poorly handled, and he emphasised the consistency of its approach. Referring to criticism that the government's UN initiative was mistimed he argued that: 'It seemed important to us that an initiative should be taken which would restore diplomacy and the search for a peaceful solution to the centre of the stage... The non-implementation of Resolution 502 seemed to us to render a new UN initiative necessary to secure the cessation of hostilities.'[50]

47. *Sunday Independent*, 9 May 1982.
48. *Irish Independent*, 8 May 1982.
49. *Irish Independent*, 5 May 1982.
50. *Dáil Reports*, vol. 334, pp. 798-819, 11 May 1982.

On EC sanctions, the Taoiseach argued that government policy was again entirely consistent and in an aside directed at those who emphasised the duty of EC member states to maintain mutual solidarity during the crisis, the Taoiseach was direct:

> It would help unity and solidarity if the Community and all its institutions were more conscious of the limitations of Community action imposed by the true nature and the ideals of the Community... The Community has no role in the military sphere, and it would be better for European unity and solidarity if it were not seen to take actions supportive of or complementary to military action.[51]

Finally the Taoiseach replied to attacks that Irish policy had been driven by anti-British hysteria: 'It is of importance that I make it clear that we have not acted in any spirit of animosity towards our closest neighbour but rather in a desire to help... We have not allowed ourselves to be influenced by feelings which we may legitimately have on other issues and happenings both inside and outside the Community.'[52]

In his reply to the Taoiseach's statement the Leader of the Opposition, Garret FitzGerald, repeated his allegations that the government had badly mishandled the situation and damaged Ireland's relations, not only with Britain but with its European partners and its friends at the United Nations. Both FitzGerald and the Labour Party leader, Michael O'Leary, highlighted the apparent tensions within the executive and consequent policy inconsistencies. FitzGerald stressed the debacle at the UN where the Irish government appeared uninformed of the Secretary General's negotiations; Similarly, O'Leary was critical of the government's handling of the crisis and used as his example the apparent lack of coordination between the Taoiseach's advisors and the Department of Foreign Affairs. [53]

Ireland's request to drop sanctions was not formally tabled at the EC Council meeting in Liège of 8–9 May, as preliminary discussions revealed that no support existed for their premature cancellation. The government did, however, welcome the statement which emerged from the meeting that linked sanctions with a diplomatic resolution of the conflict; in line with the Taoiseach's assurances to the Dáil, Ireland continued to apply sanctions. This adherence by Ireland to agreed sanctions, rather than the pursuit of a unilateral policy, suggests that Ireland's interest in EC solidarity outweighed the clearly expressed preference of the Irish government and public opinion. While it may be argued that Ireland was bound by EC law, it is probably more useful to suggest that the inevitable loss

---

51. Ibid.
52. Ibid.
53. *Dáil Reports*, vol. 334, pp.814–9, 11 May 1982.

of goodwill from EC partners in the ongoing CAP negotiations was probably more persuasive.

In the run-up to the 17 May sanctions renewal deadline, a cabinet meeting on 14 May signalled no definitive Irish position before the scheduled EPC officials meeting of the 15th which failed to resolve the issue.[54] At the subsequent foreign ministers' meeting the next day Collins let the Italian minister, Emilio Colombo, illustrate how critical the issue was for Rome and followed suit when Colombo invoked Italian national interests as precluding Italy's further participation in sanctions.[55] In the face of technical difficulties, sanctions were renewed for one week and later renewed until 24 May. Ireland and Italy, however, were excluded from their operation.[56]

In the government's subsequent Dáil statement of Tuesday 18 May, the Taoiseach was again at pains to justify policy on the grounds of consistency in the government's approach and international support for Ireland's position.[57] The Leader of the Opposition addressed himself to government claims that sanctions in support of military actions were inconsistent with Irish neutrality. Drawing on previous Irish support for sanctions against belligerents, FitzGerald insisted that using neutrality as a justification for the Irish position was a chimera He pointed to domestic political considerations as the rationale for the government's 'ham-fisted handling of the affair [which was] motivated by a desire to achieve temporary popularity at home, at the expense of our international credibility.'[58] Labour Party leader Michael O'Leary argued that the issue had been poorly handled by the government, but that in defence of Irish neutrality this was an acceptable risk.[59]

The failure of Secretary General Javier Pérez de Cuellar's peace efforts on 21 May – the same day that British troops landed on the Falklands proper – prompted the Taoiseach and Minister for Foreign Affairs to seek a reactivation of the government's call for a meeting of the Security Council. Ambassador Dorr's contribution to the debate, which was formally initiated by Panama,[60] was to restate the Irish government's position and to emphasise that the new military situation needed to be addressed by the

54. *The Irish Times*, 15 May 1982.
55. N. MacQueen, 'The Expedience of Tradition: Ireland, International Organization and the Falklands Crisis', pp. 49–50; *The Irish Times*, 18 May 1982.
56. For a discussion of the legal issues involved in both enforcing sanctions and the Irish and Italian 'opt out' see P.J. Kuyper, 'Community Sanctions against Argentina: Lawfulness under EC and International Law', in D. O'Keefe and H. Schermers (eds), Essays in European Law and Integration 1983, Deventer: Kluwer, 1983, pp. 113-47.
57. *Dáil Reports*, vol. 334, pp. 1424-34, 18 May 1982.
58. Ibid.
59. Ibid.
60. N. MacQueen, 'The Expedience of Tradition: Ireland, International Organization and the Falklands Crisis', p. 50.

Council in order to 'avert greater tragedy'.[61] In press interviews, the Ambassador refused to characterize his speech as a call for a ceasefire but rather as part of an overall diplomatic offensive. A new Irish initiative sought to give a formal Security Council mandate to the Secretary General to pursue another round of negotiations. A first draft of the Irish resolution, drawn up in consultation with the Council's non-aligned members (Jordan, Zaire, Uganda, Panama, Togo and Guyana) had devised a three point approach; a seventy-two hour ceasefire, UN-sponsored negotiations and a report to the Security Council at the end of the ceasefire period.

The British reaction to the proposal was swift. The *New York Times* quoted a 'senior British UN official' – identified in newspaper reports as the British UN Ambassador's deputy – as saying that the Irish draft was: 'a wolf in sheep's clothing [and the] unacceptable consequences of the sloppiest thinking seen around here in a long time.'[62] More formally, the British let it be known that any resolution on the above lines would be vetoed. Discussions ensued with the Foreign Office's Assistant Under-Secretary for Western Europe, Alan Goodison, at the Irish Department of Foreign Affairs' headquarters at Iveagh House on Tuesday 25 May. Goodison, who later became ambassador to Ireland, made it clear that the UK would not countenance any resolution which effectively left Argentina in control of the islands. The final Irish proposal was tabled on Wednesday 26 May; this draft dropped the seventy-two hour ceasefire and simply mandated the Secretary General to enter into a new round of talks with the Security Council's formal endorsement and report after seven days on his progress. It was accepted unanimously. The Secretary General, however, complained that the absence of a ceasefire made negotiations extraordinarily difficult. He noted caustically that he was faced with 'a real challenge... It seems I am being given seven days to solve the problem. What can I do in seven days?... I would prefer not to say it was absurd. I can assure you that I will try my best.' [63]

Even Ambassador Dorr appeared somewhat fatalistic in his presentation of this proposal:

> If the parties do not now accept it (UNR 505), so be it. If they want to fight to a finish, so be it. If this council, for whatever reason, cannot or does not wish to adopt our proposal, so be it. If a better formula can be found then so be it... Whatever happens in face of this tragic conflict, Ireland will continue to believe that it was at least right to have tried. Whatever the outcome it will not be said

61. *The Irish Times*, 22 May 1982.
62. *New York Times*, 25 May 1982.
63. *The Irish Times*, 28 May 1982.

at the end of our short term of membership of this Council that we did not even try.[64]

In the event the Secretary General's efforts were in vain, and he reported the failure of talks on 2 June. An Argentine request to Ireland to sponsor a ceasefire resolution was declined.[65] However, a subsequent proposal sponsored by Panama and Spain demanding an immediate ceasefire did have Irish support. A later draft of this proposal, revised by the non-aligned states, included provisions for an Argentine withdrawal. This was vetoed by the UK and the United States.

The military campaign moved inexorably to its final conclusion, and the Argentine armed forces on the main islands surrendered on 14 June. Renewed EC sanctions, with the exception of the arms embargo, were lifted on 21 June. The issue of sovereignty over the islands returned to the United Nations soon after the war and the fall of General Galtieri's military *junta*. In November 1982 a Latin American co-sponsored resolution called for resumed negotiations over the islands' future. Ireland abstained on this proposal, arguing that to support negotiations now was to favour one party (Argentina) over the other. Initially characterized as an exercise in Anglo-Irish fence-mending, this stance has been maintained by Ireland in all subsequent UN votes calling for renewed sovereignty talks.

Conclusions

Many theories and models which are applied more or less successfully to explain the decision-making process of major powers (such as Allison's Organizational Process and Bureaucratic Politics) are of limited utility, or indeed are inappropriate for minor powers such as Ireland.[66] In this case we are not dealing with a complex bureaucratic structure with extensively differentiated interests, objectives and strategies; the Irish administrative system is small, generalist and hierarchical. However, the applicable elements of the above models centre on the automatic bureaucratic response to external stimuli. The prompt Irish denunciation of the Argentine invasion, for example, is illustrative. The condemnation of the use of force and the demand for an Argentine withdrawal was an archetypal Irish response which was based upon well established precedents.

For their part, the theoretical approaches which engage theories of bounded rationality, implementation and non decisions are of minimal util-

---

64. *The Irish Times*, 26 May 1982.
65. J. Joyce and P. Murtagh, *The Boss*, p. 165.
66. The models considered here are outlined in J. Greenaway, S. Smith and J. Street, *Deciding Factors in British Politics – A Case-Studies Approach*, London: Routledge, 1992.

ity. Both emphasise the role of intermediary groups and agencies which either delimit the choices available to the policy maker or impede their application. The centralization and hierarchical organization of Irish foreign policy making thwarts the influence of such intermediaries - and in the specific case of the Falklands' conflict – even orthodox actors within the civil service were intentionally marginalized.

Finally, Sabatier's model suffers a similar fate in this exercise. The sophistication of its analysis as applied to less politicized issue areas becomes superfluous where policy circles, advocacy coalitions and policy learning are effectively absent. The model does, however, usefully re-emphasise the importance of core beliefs and ideological filters which are so important in the Irish case.

The centre of any explanatory theory or model in this case must be the role played by Mr Haughey. As outlined in some detail above, his domestic political position was difficult in the extreme. Assailed from within and without, Mr Haughey's attention was clearly and obviously focussed on his own political survival; indeed, his situation was so vulnerable that his government eventually succumbed in October 1982. In such a context an intriguing analysis arises. If we operate on the not unlikely assumption that Haughey's focus was on his own political survival, then the case quickly emerges for arguing that his Falkland's policy was determined by how best he could use the situation to support his domestic political position. In such a scenario the application of a rational actor model becomes especially useful.

Employment of the rational actor model, however, must be qualified. Greenaway, Smith and Street correctly highlight at least one central flaw, that the theory effectively excises politics from decision making. The evidence that Mr Haughey and other policy makers made an empirically-based assessment of options and marginal utility cannot be established. Instead, the effect of core political beliefs (nationalism and anti-imperialism), the impact of ideological filters and the misperception of issues are all conspicuous. Thus, it appears clear that the belief system of key Irish policy makers is a crucial theoretical adjunct.

The launch of the British task force to retake the islands witnessed the re-awakening of fervid British patriotism. The combination of military adventurism, ardent British nationalism and a whiff of old-style imperialism was a potent cocktail in domestic British politics. It was also a heady brew in an Irish context but for very different reasons. Mr Haughey, acting to maximize his domestic political gains, operated within three crucial parameters. First, Fianna Fáil, as a populist party, had to reflect the strong currents of anti-imperialism which, normally quiescent, had been aroused by the political carnival which surrounded the launch of the British fleet. Second, the Fianna Fáil party and Mr Haughey's leadership of it, was based upon a trenchant representation of Irish nationalism. Third, while the exploitation of anti-imperialist sentiment and nationalist passion might normally have been problematic for a governing party, the poor state of Anglo-Irish relations actually appears to have freed Mr Haughey's hand. The refusal of the British government to compromise over the hunger strikes, and its rejection of Irish demands on new constitutional structures in Northern Ireland, led Mr Haughey to conclude that nothing could be gained from forbearance. Domestically, however, much more might be achieved from an explicit and high profile manipulation of traditional values.

Thus the stage was set for a juxtaposition of established policy-making routines and a newly ideologized political leadership, capable of and willing to annex policy formation. The contradictions between the two led inevitably to disjointed and incremental policy making. The incidents at the United Nations and within European Political Cooperation are illustrative.

Similarly, the decision-making model which best represents the Irish case is one which highlights the centrality of the Taoiseach and a supporting role for the cabinet. Other major policy actors were either absent or marginalized. The lack of any significant commercial or economic interest meant that there was only peripheral interdepartmental input to the crisis. The activity of advocacy groups was limited to the publication of declaratory statements. The weakness of Irish parliamentary structures frustrated the ability of the Oireachtas and the opposition parties to effectively monitor government policy, although later they highlighted policy inconsistencies which the government had to address. Finally, the diplomatic service was deliberately detached from policy at a critical moment. Were it not for the enhanced role of the Taoiseach and a lack of collegiality, the cabinet government model would come nearest to providing a paradigm of decision making. The cabinet, while consulted on major shifts in policy, did not act collectively; the Taoiseach directed policy formulation from an ad hoc group established within his own department.

This case study emphasises that students of international relations ignore the domestic scene at their peril. As a minor state on the international scene, Ireland rarely plays a significant global role. During the Falkland's crisis, however, Ireland's position was inimical to the interests of her largest trading partner and neighbour and a significant middle-ranking power; it also contributed to frustrating the efforts of Ireland's major European partners to construct a unified policy. Ireland exercised an independent and sovereign policy in the teeth of significant external pressure. The reasons for this extraordinary policy are to be found in the domestic political environment, and underline the importance of understanding and integrating domestic factors into theoretical constructs of states' international behaviour.

– 8 –

The External Dissenter: Spain

Esther Barbé

Introduction

This chapter examines the Spanish position on the dispute over the Falkland Islands (Malvinas)[1] between Argentina and the UK, from the war in 1982 until the Second Latin American Summit held in Madrid in July 1992. As we shall see, Spain's position during the war was a special one when compared to other countries of its geopolitical area, the European Community countries and Portugal. However, we must begin by pointing out that in 1982 Spain was in itself a special case for three reasons.

First, the absolute priority of domestic policy over foreign policy should be stressed. In 1982 Spain was in the final stages of political transition from the Francoist dictatorship to democracy. In fact, the elections of 28 October 1982 which the Partido Socialista Obrero Español (PSOE), the Spanish Workers' Socialist Party, won with an absolute majority meant the consolidation of the democratic system that was installed with the 1978 Constitution.[2] During the Falklands War the attention of Spanish politicians was centered on the squabbles dividing the governing Party (Unión de Centro Democrático, UCD) which paralysed the activities of the executive, on the sentences against the Coup leaders of the 23–F[3] which were about to be passed and, obviously, on the elections being prepared for the month of October.

---

1. The term Falkland Islands (Malvinas) corresponds to the official term used in English texts of the United Nations. Throughout this chapter the reduced form 'Falklands' will be used in order to facilitate its reading. This is done for purely practical reasons, to reduce the length of the text and make the book homogeneous. However, the term Malvinas or Islas Malvinas is maintained when making literal quotations from other authors.

2. R. Morodo, *La transición política*, Madrid: Tecnos, 1984.

3. This refers to members of the army who participated in the abortive coup attempt of 23 February 1981.

Second, when the Falklands War began, the diplomatic agenda of the Spanish government was focussed on the entry of Spain into the Atlantic Alliance, and the ratification of Spain's adhesion by the fifteen members of NATO, which was to be finalized on 30 May. This entry was yet another of the international consequences of the political transition in Spain; in fact, the transition meant the re-definition of Spain's role in international relations. In April 1982, this meant that the government of Calvo Sotelo was expecting its incorporation into NATO as well as the beginning of negotiations with the UK on the future of Gibraltar (scheduled to start on 20 April) and the renewing of the bilateral agreements with the United States (due to begin in May, although they were not signed until 2 July, after arduous negotiations).[4]

Third, Spain maintained a policy toward Latin America that differed from that of the other European countries. Post-Francoist diplomacy defined Spain's relations with the said countries in terms of 'brotherhood' or of 'family relations'.[5] This, from the point of view of European diplomacy, was a Spanish peculiarity.

The Spanish reaction to the Falklands War was characterized, as will be seen, by ambiguity. This reaction was due to a combination of the factors which have just been described, but at the same time it reflected one of the basic dilemmas of democratic Spain's foreign policy: how to create a coherent structure between on the one hand, its relations with Latin America, and on the other hand, its relations with the European Community. In fact, it was this structure which was the determining factor in Hispano-Argentine relations from 1982 until 1992 (including the Falklands issue).

Foreign Policy Making in Democratic Spain

The period under study (1982-92) coincides with the creation of a style of foreign policy making by democratic Spain. In reality, after the promulgation of the Constitution in 1978, we can refer to the existence of a democratic institutional framework for the elaboration of a foreign policy. However, it was with the coming to power of the PSOE in 1982 and, more specifically, under the political leadership of Prime Minister González, that the new practice and working habits in international issues began to take shape in democratic Spain.

4. A. Marquina Barrio, *España en la Política de Seguridad Occidental*, Madrid: Ejército, 1986, pp. 909-31.
5. M. Oreja, 'Discurso de Marcelino Oreja en la XXI Asamblea General de Naciones Unidas (27-9-1976)', in J.F. Tezanos et al. (eds), *La Transición Democrática Española*, Madrid: Sistema, 1989, p. 17.

The Spanish Constitution of 1978 received negative criticism from Spanish analysts.[6] It was qualified as being barely innovative and limited with regard to the more democratic character of foreign policy and the introduction of internationalist principles. The shaping of foreign policy according to the Constitution, is shared by the king, who is in charge of representing the Spanish state in international relations (Article 56); the government, in charge of directing foreign policy (Article 97); and the parliament, in its generic role as controller of the government (Article 66). The representative figure of the King of Spain in international relations has become an important tool for Spanish diplomacy, so much so that through Juan Carlos I the image of the country has grown in prestige. The role of the king is particularly significant in Spain's relations with the Arab and Latin American world.

The directing of foreign policy by the government as a collectivity implies in fact that the said policy is directed by the prime minister.[7] The Constitution implicitly made the prime minister the director of foreign policy, and later practice and working habits strengthened the latent 'presidentialism' of the Constitution. Thus, the personality and leadership, first of Adolfo Suarez (1976–80), and later, in a more decisive and important manner, of Felipe González (1982–) mean that it is possible to speak of a 'presidentialist system'[8] in relation to the elaboration of foreign policy. Felipe González has clearly demonstrated his wish to take on the direction of foreign policy; hence the creation by the Prime Minister of his own team of advisors in international relations, considered by Roberto Mesa[9] as a parallel Ministry of Foreign Affairs. The Constitution, which introduced 'limited democratization' in foreign policy matters,[10] affords the parliament a role that is similar to those granted by the majority of the constitutions of Western Europe to their respective parliaments. Thus the parliament is involved in the ratification of certain international treaties, and authorizes the king to declare war and peace; hence, the criticism of the elitist and not very democratic nature of the Constitution in external affairs. Remiro Brotons[11] reminds us in this regard of the more progressive proposals that arose during the period in which the Constitution was drafted – to increase

6. A. Remiro Brotons, *La Acción Exterior del Estado*, Madrid: Tecnos, 1984; R. Mesa, 'El Proceso de Toma de Decisiones en Política Exterior', in *Documentación Administrativa*, no. 205, 1985, pp. 143-63.

7. In Spain the prime minister is called the 'President of the Government', hence the use of the term 'presidentialisation' of Spanish foreign policy.

8. K. Saba, 'The Spanish Foreign Policy Decision-Making Process', in *The International Spectator*, vol. 21, no. 4, 1986, p. 28.

9. R. Mesa, 'El Proceso de Toma de Decisiones en Política exterior', in *Documentación Administrativa*, no. 205, 1985, p. 158.

10. R. Brotons, *La Acción Exterior del Estado*, p. 23. The Cortes, or the Spanish Parliament, is made up of two Chambers: the Congress and the Senate.

11. Ibid., p. 23.

the role of parliament, to generously regulate the use of the referendum, and to introduce public initiative – which were finally abandoned in favour of a more traditional and conservative approach.

The control of governmental foreign policy by members of parliament – basically in the framework of the committees for foreign affairs in both chambers – was reduced in more than internal policy matters. In the first instance, this was because a consensus was reached between the political parties in foreign policy matters in order to facilitate the internal political transition;[12] later, during the socialist decade (after the October 1982 elections), the absolute majority of the PSOE in parliament, on the one hand, and the support of the opposition on the other on decisive matters (EEC policy, participation in the Gulf War), led the legislature to maintain a policy clearly convergent with that of Felipe González's government on international issues. Thus, we can speak of a state policy regarding Spain's foreign policy for the period 1982–92, to a certain degree, with the exception of the confusing issue of Spain's membership of NATO.

Spain's Position in the Falklands War: The Question of Decolonization and the Condemnation of the Use of Force

The Falklands War (2 April–15 June 1982) coincided with a sensitive time in Spanish politics, at both internal and international levels. Internally, Spain was going through a decisive phase in the consolidation of its democratic transition (the failed coup attempt leaders were being sentenced and the governing party was being dissolved). Externally, the government was busy with the most sensitive issues on its agenda (NATO, Gibraltar and relations with the United States). This led Mujal León to say that the government of Calvo Sotelo 'centered its attention on domestic issues, and this was a perspective that dominated even Calvo Sotelo's NATO decision. Consequently, Spain lost interest in Latin America, a trend reinforced by events in Nicaragua after 1979 and by the Malvinas/Falklands War in 1982.'[13]

One might consider that the war was 'inopportune' from the point of view of the Spanish government's interest. Indeed, the description and the retrospective analysis of the Spanish position during the Falklands War enables us to confirm the 'inopportuneness' of the war for Spanish interests in 1982, as well as to draw lessons of a general nature about Spanish options in international relations. This section considers first the govern-

12. E. Barbé, 'La Transición Española: Cambio y Continuidad en la Política Exterior y de Seguridad', *Papers*, no. 33, 1990, pp. 103–20.
13. E. Mujal León, 'Spain and Latin America: The Quest for Partnership', in H.J. Wiarda (ed.), *The Iberian-Latin American Connection. Implications for U.S. Foreign Policy*, Boulder: Westview Press, 1986, p. 378.

ment's reaction to the war, before going on to examine that of the King and finally, the reactions of political parties and other social groups.

With Argentina's occupation of the islands, the reaction of the Spanish government was rapid; on 2 April itself the Council of Ministers issued an official note stating the government's position containing four basic ideas: first, the defence of the decolonization of the islands in favour of Argentinian territorial integrity; second, the view that prolonging a colonial situation leads to tension and conflict; third, the opposition to the use of force; and fourth the peaceful resolution of conflicts through the United Nations and its Secretary General.

The main principles defended in the note of 2 April (decolonization and condemning the use of force) formed the basis of the Spanish position throughout the war. Consequently, the Spanish representative[14] in the Security Council of the United Nations abstained during the vote on 3 April on Resolution 502 which 'required an immediate end to hostilities..., the withdrawal of Argentina's forces...and the search for a diplomatic solution.' The Spanish representative, Jaime de Piniés, stated that his country was opposed to the use of force. However, he justified his abstention on the grounds that the resolution did not mention the underlying problem (decolonization), and by recalling the Spanish government's support for Argentina's territorial claims.[15]

Spain's Foreign Minister reiterated Spanish support for Argentina's territorial claims over the Falkland Islands, recalling the continuity of Spanish policy in this matter,[16] since Spain had traditionally voted in favour of decolonization of the islands in the General Assembly of the United Nations (December 1965, December 1973, December 1976).[17] The decolonization principle thus became the differentiating factor of Spanish policy when compared to the policy adopted by other countries of its geopolitical area on the Falklands issue. Spain's attitude regarding the position of the Council of Europe, the EC and NATO illustrates this point. The Committee of Ministers of the Council of Europe drafted a resolution (7 April) on the basis of terms taken from Resolution 502 of the Security Council. Spain was the only country to abstain from the vote, on the basis of the same argument used in the United Nations.[18]

14. In 1982 Spain was a non-permanent member of the Security Council.
15. P. A. Fernández Sánchez, 'La crisis de las Malvinas ante las Naciones Unidas', *Revista de Estudios Internacionales*, vol. 5, no. 4, 1984, p. 933.
16. P. Pérez Llorca, 'Intervención del Ministro de Asuntos Exteriores ante la Comisión de Asuntos Exteriores del Congreso sobre el problema de las Malvinas', *Actividades, Textos y Documentos de la Política Exterior Española* 1982, Madrid: Oficina de Información Diplomática, 1982, p. 125.
17. S.Stavridis, *The Constraints of an International "Double Vocation": The Reaction in Spain to the Falklands War of 1982*, University of Bristol: CMS Occasional Paper no.5, November 1992, p. 2.
18. The Spanish minister did not attend the said meeting in order to avoid an encounter

On April 14 the European Community agreed to an economic embargo against Argentina. Once the Spanish government was informed it refused to participate in the embargo because, as the Spanish minister said, 'it was a serious political error of the Community not to have sufficiently assessed the full depth of Argentina's national claims.'[19] In fact, during a GATT meeting on 8 May, the Spanish government joined a proposal of the Latin American group to revoke the embargo imposed on Argentina by the Community, the United States and Australia on the grounds that it infringed GATT rules.

Spain's entry into NATO in June provided yet another Western forum in which it pointed out its difference of opinion. The unanimous support of the fifteen NATO members for Britain in its clash with Argentina was brought to an end with the first official statements of the minister Pérez Llorca on 4 June in defence of Argentina's territorial integrity.[20] During the Atlantic Council held in Bonn on 10 June, Prime Minister Calvo Sotelo took advantage of the occasion to mention 'the serious crack' that was being opened by the conflict and reminded them of Spain's 'Latin American vocation', without directly referring to the support of his government for the decolonization of the islands.

The position of the Spanish government, which placed it on ambiguous ground and, in a position different from that of the other countries of its geopolitical area,[21] showed signs of becoming more active from the moment when the conflict escalated with bombardments, the sinking of warships and a spectacular increase in the number of casualties. Thus from 1 May, when the British bombing of the islands began, the Spanish government showed signs of greater activity. This activity could be seen first in Spanish offers to mediate: on 3 May Calvo Sotelo announced that he would act as mediator and on the same day Pérez Llorca once again offered Pérez de Cuellar Spain's mediation. Second, there was Spanish support for Latin American actions including Belaunde Terry's offer to mediate[22]

with his British counterpart.

19. P. Pérez Llorca, 'Intervención del Ministro de Asuntos Exteriores ante la Comisión de Asuntos Exteriores del Congreso sobre el problema de las Malvinas', p. 126.

20. Pérez Llorca excused himself on the grounds of work in order not to attend, as an observer, a preparatory meeting of the Atlantic Council, held in Luxembourg on 17 May. In this way the minister avoided broaching the Falklands issue, hoping for a quick solution to the conflict before Spain's entry into NATO came into effect.

21. Leo Tindemans, then President of the Council of Foreign Ministers, said on 3 May that the Spanish position was 'special and delicate', in *El País*, 4 May 1982. The Irish and Italian positions, unwilling to continue sanctions against Argentina, satisfied Spain, thereby making the Spanish position less special.

22. D. B. Bendahmane and J. W. Mc Donald, 'Mediation Attempts in the Falklands/Malvinas Crisis', in D. B. Bendahmane and J. W. Mc Donald (eds), *Perspectives on Negotiation: Four Case Studies and Interpretations*, Washington: Foreign Service Institute, 1986, pp. 51-98.

and the presentation to the Security Council, together with Panama, of a draft resolution on 2 June which called for a ceasefire, vetoed two days later by the British. Third, Spanish bilateral deals were proposed; on his visit to Washington on 5 May, Pérez Llorca asked Haig to negotiate a bilateral arrangement in which the United States would act in favour of a ceasefire. Finally, Spain continued to support the negotiations of the Secretary General of the United Nations.

Once the war had actually begun, the position adopted by the Spanish government and the efforts it had made revealed, in the words of Pérez Llorca, two essential objectives: 'I think that Spain, by always maintaining, correctly in my view, an independent position, clear and unequivocal, albeit serene, has contributed to a large extent to the avoidance of a tragic break between its European and Latin American links.'[23] In other words, on the one hand, the Spanish government wished to behave independently when elaborating its foreign policy and, on the other hand, it wished to act as a bridge between Europe and Latin America.

With the general lines of the government's position dealt with, it is necessary to mention the activities of the King of Spain with regard to the war, particularly if we bear in mind that this war concerned a Latin American country, and also that according to the Spanish Constitution of 1978, the king 'assumes the highest representation of the Spanish State in international relations, especially with nations belonging to its historical community' (Article 56). The latter refers to Spanish-speaking American countries. The historical argument of Spain's link with Latin America was included in the letter sent by the King of Spain to the Secretary General of the United Nations on 5 May requesting a ceasefire, the King himself offering 'to contribute to achieving peace and justice'. The monarch's mediation offer, which passed unnoticed in Europe, was well received in Latin America. The Spanish monarch sent a further message to President Reagan on 20 May requesting that he should intervene diplomatically.

The action of the King, diplomatically limited to the above-mentioned messages, is important with regard to his own image on the domestic scene, and his prestige as defender of the democratic system, as well as to his image in Latin America. In fact, the king's action, approved unanimously by all political and social groups, must be placed within the internal context of the consolidation of democracy and not within the general debate on Spain's role in the war.

---

23. P. Pérez Llorca, 'Intervención del Ministro de Asuntos Exteriores ante la Comisión de Asuntos Exteriores del Congreso sobre el problema de las Malvinas', p. 129.

The Main Political Issues Debated During the War

The government's position and the actions of the King throughout the war are part of a general debate that will be described in detail within references made to the position of the political parties and in a more specific manner, the references made to other social forces, the press and public opinion. The most important role was that of the political parties, which found an opportune pretext in the Falklands War to make the foreign policy of the government a matter of debate. It must not be forgotten that in April 1982 the parliamentary forces were no longer committed to a policy of consensus in foreign affairs; this had been broken by the government's decision to enter into NATO, a decision which the socialists and the communists had voted against. This explains why the South Atlantic became a unique occasion on which to discuss all the foreign issues of the state in a heavily charged agenda, including negotiations on Gibraltar, the entry into NATO, the renewing of agreements with the United States and, as a backdrop, the entry of the country into the European Community.

The opposition tried, without success, to force the calling of a plenary session of Congress to vote on a resolution. The government agreed to hold a debate on the subject, but only in the Foreign Affairs Committee and without a vote. The meeting took place on 11 May when the different groups expressed their opinions on the government's behaviour with regard to the war and its consequences for the external relations of Spain as a whole. The interventions during the session touched on all the subjects that the press had dealt with. Five main subjects can be identified: the Falklands War as an independent variable, or as a subject that affects the entire Spanish diplomatic agenda; the approach to the war mainly in terms of the principle of decolonization and the condemnation of the use of force; the approach to the war mainly in terms of the dictatorial style of the Argentinian regime, or else, setting aside all reference to the dictatorial/democratic pattern in the conflict; the war demonstrating the capability, or, inversely the incapability of the Spanish government to elaborate an independent foreign policy; and the war broaching the subject of the point to which relations with Latin America were a priority option for Spain in the international framework. Without aiming to be exhaustive, these cleavages will be reviewed in order to assess the positions of the major political parties, and occasionally other social forces and the media.

As far as the first of the points outlined above is concerned, the UCD, as the governing party, was in charge of defending governmental orthodoxy in the sense that the war was an independent issue set apart from the global agenda of Spanish foreign policy. In contrast with the position of the UCD, mention must be made that all the political parties and social forces upheld the idea that the war directly affected Spanish interests, starting with the issue of Gibraltar, a subject that unites all opinions in Spain.[24] It must be remembered that in Spanish public opinion the question of Gibraltar was a highly sensitive one;[25] if the link between the Falklands and Gibraltar can be defined as a minimum linkage approach, which was widely accepted, then we can also speak of a maximum linkage approach. This is what the PSOE had achieved when it linked the war with all the sensitive issues on the Spanish agenda:

> The Falklands crisis as it is currently approached and in its possible evolution can have an effect on: a) the feasibility and the procedural pace chosen to obtain the reintegration of Gibraltar; b) important aspects of the hypothetical plan of the government with regard to the manner of integration in NATO; c) the climate prevailing in Spain's negotiations to become a member of the European Community; d) the absolute need to harmonize our European interests and our vocation, links and understanding of Latin America.[26]

On the second of the points raised above, the UCD defended the government's position which consisted of simultaneously defending the principle of decolonization and condemning the use of force. The other political parties held positions that were totally opposed. On the one hand, the Alianza Popular (AP) considered the right to decolonization as the primary reason for supporting Argentina. The leaders of the AP harshly criticized the nineteenth-century colonialism of the UK and recalled the end of the colonial era. By contrast, the PSOE (together with the communists (PC), the Basque Nationalist Party (PNV) and the Catalan minority), condemned from the very outset the use of force, identifying Argentina as the aggressor country, however, this did not prevent them, especially the ranks of the communists, from severely criticizing 'British brutality', as Santiago Carrillo put it. In any case, the PSOE condemned the government's attitude in the United Nations when they abstained from voting on Resolution 502. The socialists considered that the Spanish attitude was dangerous on an internal level (Spanish patriotism that might lead to armed action

24. S. Stavridis, *The Constraints of an International "Double Vocation": The Reaction in Spain to the Falklands War of 1982*, p. 14.

25. Public opinion polls illustrate the interest the subject of Gibraltar has for the Spanish. In December 1979 the Center of Sociological Research carried out a study in which 2,022 persons were asked to indicate in a list of nine areas of Spanish foreign policy the three they considered most important. The global results show that the most important was the entry into the Common Market (50 per cent), followed by the recovery of Gibraltar and relations with Latin America, (32 per cent in both cases). The answer with regard to the recovery of Gibraltar is very homogeneous, irrespective of the ideology of the interviewee; left (36 per cent), center (37 per cent), right (39 per cent) and extreme right (37 per cent), with the exception of the extreme left (13 per cent). See Banco de Datos del CIS, 'La opinión española ante la OTAN', in *Revista Española de Investigaciones Sociológicas*, vol. 22, 1983, pp. 208-9.

26. F. Morán, *Una política exterior para España*, Barcelona: Planeta, 1980, p. 13.

in the case of Gibraltar) and also with regard to Morocco (not fully condemning the use of force opened the door to future Moroccan actions in Ceuta and Melilla).[27] The socialists also criticized the fact that the government did not maintain equidistant positions since it had criticized the use of force by the British more harshly than it did the Argentinians. Referring to the communiqué of the diplomatic information office (1 May) that condemned the escalation of the conflict by the British, the socialists perceived that this attitude disqualified Spain as a possible mediator.

The third main point (the dictatorial nature of the Argentinian regime) also became another differentiating aspect between the political parties and Spanish society. The government had not assessed the dictatorial nature of the Argentine regime as an outstanding factor in the conflict. According to the Foreign Affairs Minister: 'The problem of the Falklands is no longer a local conflict, with the possibility of becoming a generalized confrontation between two peoples. Two peoples who, independently of their political systems, belong to the same world.'[28] In fact, the position that played down the dictatorship/democracy aspect with regard to the war was the one which dominated in the ranks of the UCD.

This view was directly opposed by several political parties. At one extreme, the AP considered that the nature of the political regime was not relevant when a genuine national claim existed, and some AP leaders pointed out that even the Montonero guerrilla group were on the side of the military *junta* on the issue regarding the recovery of the islands. In contrast to the nationalist attitude of the AP, the PSOE, the PC and the PNV stressed the dictatorial nature of the regime, and the extent to which the invasion of the islands represented a *fuite en avant* for the military *junta*. This matter directly related to the Spanish situation, given the process of the consolidation of democracy in the country. Some newspapers and magazines, such as *El País* and *Cambio 16*, stressed in their analyses the dictatorial nature of Argentina and the democratic nature of Britain. However, the majority of the Spanish press ignored or paid little attention to the factor of Argentine dictatorship in their analyses.

Mention must also be made here of the creation in Madrid of the Movement Against the War in the South Atlantic, formed by five hundred Argentinians exiled in Spain. This movement based its campaign on the fundamental idea that only the fall of the military dictatorship could restore full sovereignty.

Fourth, the capacity of the Spanish government to elaborate an independent foreign policy was a central issue of the debate. As we have seen, the government insisted on stating its independent stance, and this posi-

---

27. Ceuta and Melilla are two Spanish cities, situated on the African coast in Morocco.
28. P. Pérez Llorca, 'Intervención del Ministro de Asuntos Exteriores ante la Comisión de Asuntos Exteriores del Congreso sobre el problema de las Malvinas', p. 124.

tion was backed by the UCD. Javier Rupérez, spokesman of the UCD in the Foreign Affairs Committee, stated during a session of the committee on 11 May that the attitude of the government of Calvo Sotelo during the war was neither pro-Argentine nor pro-British, but pro-Spanish. Contrary to the UCD, the PSOE, the PC and the Mixed Group[29] unanimously considered that the government's position was ambiguous and of a low profile due to the little room for autonomy left to Spain once it had decided to enter NATO. The war made it possible for the debate on NATO membership to be reopened in Parliament, against the wishes of the government which had already calmed down the debate.

Fifth, Spain's relations with Latin America was considered in all the different perspectives broached so far. No political party, nor Spanish society as a whole, denied the existence of special relations between Spain and the Latin American countries; on public television, this came across clearly as pro-Argentinian propaganda,[30] criticized by other media (an editorial in *El País* on 16 June accused Spanish television of manipulating reality throughout the war in favour of Argentina). These relations in some cases were commented upon using a rhetoric that was typical of the Franco period. The Alianza Popular or the Andalusian Party,[31] for example, referred to the relations in terms of family, 'our Argentinian brothers' and honour, 'treason'. A declaration of 'the Federation of Hispanic Societies' (formed by regional centres) even informed the nation that sixty Spanish officials were offering their services to the Argentinian Embassy in Madrid to fight in the South Atlantic.

The UCD wished to defend the government's desire to increase the special historical dimension between Spain and the Latin American countries by serving as a bridge between the latter and Europe. This latter role, which was not enacted by the Spanish government during the war, led to the creation in Madrid of an 'Hispano-American Association for Integration, Development and Advanced Democracy' made up of Spanish and Latin American intellectuals, whose aim was to reinvigorate relations between Europe and Latin America.

However, within the UCD, there were differences in this regard between the followers of the former Prime Minister Adolfo Suarez and the gov-

---

29. The Mixed Group is made up of political groups that do not have sufficient seats to create their own parliamentary group. In 1982, Francisco Fernández Ordóñez (former minister of the UCD and from 1985 until his death in June 1992, Foreign Affairs Minister with the PSOE) was a member of this group.

30. S. Stavridis, *The Constraints of an International "Double Vocation": The Reaction in Spain to the Falklands War of 1982*, pp. 12-3.

31. The attitude to relations with Latin America is not homogeneous throughout Spain. While in Andalucia 32 per cent of the population believe that these relations are one of the most important areas of Spanish foreign policy, in Catalonia only 11 per cent agree, 'Study on Foreign Relations. December 1979'. See Banco de Datos del CIS, 'La opinión española ante la OTAN', *Revista Española de Investigaciones Sociológicas*, vol. 22, 1983.

ernment of Calvo Sotelo. This is not surprising if we bear in mind that the Suarez premiership was characterized in international matters by a certain 'Third-Worldism', which stressed relations with Latin America,[32] in contrast with Prime Minister Calvo Sotelo who had opted for Spain's complete integration into the Western European world. The Latin American option of the socialists and the communists was within a less historical and more political context that combined various elements, both from the recent past (anti-Americanism,[33] Third-Worldism) and from the present (the defence of an autonomous space for democratic Spain's foreign policy in the European framework and the defence of democracy in the American continent).

The Triangle of Spanish Diplomacy (1982)

Some analysts have judged the attitude of the Spanish government during the war to have been ambivalent;[34] its attempt to mete out Solomon's justice instead led to paralysis.[35] In reality, the war between the UK and Argentina was inopportune because as a result, the Spanish government had to face an upsetting fact: its agenda of priorities in international affairs could not be fully carried out. It is not surprising therefore that the protagonists of the time, such as Calvo Sotelo or his Home Minister, Rodolfo Martin Villa, have avoided any reference to the war in their memoirs, or, as in the case of the UCD member of Parliament and Spain's ambassador to NATO, Javier Rupérez, referred to it only indirectly as a disturbing element in the Gibraltar question.[36]

The diplomatic agenda of the Spanish government in 1982 can be described in metaphorical terms as an equilateral triangle, whose three vertices have the same distance (importance) between them. The three vertices are occupied by the decolonization of Gibraltar, Spain's entry in the European Community (the subject of NATO will not be dealt with here because from the point of view of multilateral negotiations it was already

32. J. M. Armero, *Política exterior de España en democracia*, Madrid: Espasa Calpe, 1989, p. 125.

33. In 1980, 12 per cent of Spaniards believed that national security was threatened. Among them, 29 per cent felt that the most important threat came from the United States compared with 20 per cent from the Soviet Union and 11 per cent from Morocco. See *Estudios CIS, Centro de Investigaciones Sociológicas*, E. 1207, June 1980.

34. S.Stavridis, *The Constraints of an International "Double Vocation" : The Reaction in Spain to the Falklands War of 1982*, p. 1.

35. E. Mujal León, 'Spain and Latin America: The Quest for Partnership', p. 360.

36. L. Calvo Sotelo, *Memoria viva de la transición*, Barcelona: Plaza Janés, 1990; R. Martín Villa, Al servicio del estado, Barcelona: Planeta, 1984; J. Rupérez, España en la OTAN, Barcelona: Plaza y Janés, 1986, p. 203.

finalized), and Spain's maintenance of privileged relations with Latin America.

The first vertex is the claim for Gibraltar, vigorously defended in the United Nations by Fernando M. Castiella, Minister of Foreign Affairs during the Franco regime and author of a famous book on the subject (1941). It occupied a major place in the agenda of Francoist diplomacy. The transition to democracy did not reduce the importance of the subject; Roberto Mesa noted that 'Gibraltar is not a Francoist claim, nor a Quixotic endeavour of the minister Castiella: All the Spanish people demand the recovery of Gibraltar to thus finalize the process of territorial integrity.'[37] There were important advances on this issue after April 1980 when the governments of Madrid and London decided to start negotiations in Lisbon to overcome their differences on Gibraltar. The Lisbon agreement moved a further step forward on 8 January 1982 when Calvo Sotelo paid Margaret Thatcher a visit; during this visit, it was decided that negotiations would begin on 20 April 1982 and that the Spanish government would at the same time open the border to the Gibraltar population which had been closed from the 1960s. For her part, Mrs Thatcher showed her country's support for the entry of Spain into both the EC and NATO.

The Falklands War broke out a few days before the Hispano-British negotiations on Gibraltar were due to start. It is not surprising that Calvo Sotelo's first reaction on 3 April, in an attempt to save the Hispano-British negotiations, was to consider the case of the islands as distinct and separate from that of Gibraltar. The decision to abstain from voting on Resolution 502 of the Security Council was interpreted by some analysts as a way of trying to save the negotiations on Gibraltar.[38] However, on 9 April it was decided to postpone the negotiations till 25 June. This was requested by the Spanish government because it was clear that it was not the right moment; in reality the opinion that prevailed in Spain was that the war in the South Atlantic had delayed the solution to the Gibraltar issue.

Fernando Morán, the then new Minister of Foreign Affairs and a diplomat influenced by the ideas of Fernando M. Castiella, was in charge of initiating conversations with the British that would lead to the Brussels communiqué of November 1984, in which for the first time London declared itself willing to negotiate the question of sovereignty. However, Spain's actions regarding Gibraltar were also conditioned by the second

37. R. Mesa, *Democracia y política exterior en España*, Madrid: Eudema,1988, p. 46. According to a survey carried out in 1991 (1,000 persons interviewed), 64.2 per cent of the Spanish considered that Gibraltar was an obstacle to Hispano-British relations. Regarding the best solution for Gibraltar, 93.6 per cent of the Spanish felt that it should be returned to Spain. See S. del Campo, *Informe Incipe 1991. La Opinión Pública Española y la Política Internacional*, Madrid: Tecnos, 1991 pp. 62-3.
38. D. S. Morris and R. H. Haigh, *Britain, Spain and Gibraltar 1945-90*, London: Routledge, 1992, p. 110.

vertex of its foreign policy: entry into the European Community. The Spanish government had to choose in 1982 between cooperating with the UK in order to gain entry into the European Community, or focussing on the claim for Spanish sovereignty over Gibraltar and thus entering into conflict. With regard to the Community, it was clear that in 1982 Spain needed British support, especially given the French attitude;[39] President Giscard d'Estaing had frozen negotiations on Spain's adhesion in 1980[40] and Mitterrand, during his visit to Spain on 22 June, a few days after the Falklands War, had expressed several reservations about Spain's entry into the EC.

The link between entry into the EC and the claim on Gibraltar is clear, and the war in the South Atlantic complicated matters for Spanish interests. An editorial of *El País* on 22 June reported the dominant opinion that the subject of Gibraltar would be more easily resolved within the framework of the EC; this idea, along with the negative momentum generated by the war – the exacerbation of British nationalism with regard to its colonies – made entry into the EC a priority objective. Thus the first vertex of the Spanish diplomatic triangle (the claim on Gibraltar) was subordinated to the second vertex (the entry in the EC): a vertex which, in the words of Fernando Morán,[41] has *per se* a metapolitical value. More important even than the economic advantages, Spain's entry in the European Community was a decisive psychological factor for the society of democratic Spain. For the Spaniard of 1982, the element that would differentiate him from his Francoist past, was European-ness.

However, the rupture with the past is not always easy, and even less so in foreign policy, which is generally characterized by its continuity. This brings us to the third vertex of Spanish diplomacy in 1982, the privileged relations with Latin America and the continuity in Spain's international dimension. In the nineteenth century the Hispanists defended the existence of a trans-Atlantic race based on a common culture and spirit; Franco's Spain, based on the ideas of being Hispanic, Catholic and anti-democratic, achieved the creation of a network of relations in Latin America – which substituted for relations with Europe[42]– that was managed very pragmatically over the years.[43]

39. J. R. Groom, 'L'évolution de la Question de Gibraltar' in M. Rousset (ed.), *La Méditerranée Occidentale, Espace de Coopération*, Grenoble: CEDSI, 1991, p. 61.

40. P. Preston and D. Smyth, *España ante la CEE y la OTAN*, Barcelona: Grijalbo, 1985, p. 150.

41. F. Morán, *Una Política Exterior para España*, p. 289.

42. Ibid., p. 18.

43. B. Pollack, *The Paradox of Spanish Foreign Policy. Spain's International Relations from Franco to Democracy*, London: Pinter Publishers, 1987, p. 82; L. C. Wilson and J. T. Perfit, 'Spain and Latin America: Diplomatic and Military Ties', in H. J. Wiarda, (ed.), *The Iberian-Latin American Connection. Implications for U.S. Foreign Policy*, 1986, p. 171.

Power and purpose explain Spain's policy towards Latin America, both during the Franco period and when the Falklands War broke out. Spain used its relations with its former colonies as a way of increasing its influence at an international level,[44] and the Spanish 'mission' in Latin America is a constant feature found under different ideologies both in Franco's Spain and in the Spain of 1982. Thus according to the traditional conservative the common links between the two shores of the Atlantic focus on the Catholic religion, whereas according to the democrat they focus on the common language and democratization, while according to the Third-World leftist they focus on the resistance against the hegemony of the United States, or the will to be different from the Anglo-Saxon world.[45]

The authors of the Constitution of democratic Spain referred to the special character of the above; the first chapter of the Constitution of 1978 mentions the Spanish, the Latin Americans, and foreigners. The possibility of having dual nationality (included in Article 11.3) resulted in three million Latin Americans gaining Spanish nationality in 1982. At the same time, and because of the dictatorial regimes in the southern Latin American countries, there were 50,000 Argentinians, 15,000 Chileans and 10,000 Uruguayans in Spain who had been granted political asylum. These elements served to reaffirm the continuity of democratic Spain as a reality expressed in human terms.

During the negotiations for entry into the EC, Spain presented its privileged relations with Latin America as a positive factor and an element of prestige. Pérez Llorca's speech on the role of Spain as a bridge between Europe and Latin America is illustrative of this point. However, the Falklands War placed the Spanish government in a difficult position by revealing its inability to act as a bridge between the two regions.[46] The reality is that the double dimension of its interest – Europe and Latin America – paralysed the government's actions, ensuring that the positive became negative. The need to choose made it impossible to maintain the equidistant relation between the second vertex (the European Community) and the third (Latin America).

The lesson to be drawn from the war and from the later relations between Spain and the two opponents is to be found in the confirmation of the subordinate role of the third vertex (Spanish relations with Latin America) with respect to the second vertex (the relations with the European Community). The Spanish diplomatic agenda did not have the shape of an equilateral triangle, with three vertices separated by identical sides, but that of

44. E. Mujal León, 'Spain and Latin America: The Quest for Partnership', p. 378.

45. H. J. Wiarda, 'The Relations of Iberia and Latin-America and Some Implications for the United States', in H. J. Wiarda, (ed.), *The Iberian-Latin American Connection. Implications for U.S. Foreign Policy*, 1986, p. 446.

46. C. del Arenal, *España e Iberoamérica, de la Hispanidad a la Comunidad Iberoamericana de Naciones*, Madrid: Cedeal, 1989, p. 45.

an isosceles triangle in which the Community vertex is clearly above the other two (Gibraltar and Latin America).

The Lessons to be Learned from Spain's Behaviour (1982 – 92)

Once the war in the South Atlantic ended, the Falklands did not disappear from the Spanish diplomatic agenda; on the contrary, with the establishment of democracy in Argentina in December 1983, the subject reappeared. Statements made by Morán in the General Assembly of the United Nations in 1983 and 1984 included some sentences dedicated to the decolonization of the islands. However, it was the Hispano-Argentine declaration signed in June 1984, during President Alfonsín's first visit to Madrid, that best illustrated the position of the two countries. Point 6 of the declaration reads: 'Spain and Argentina, victims of an anachronic colonial situation, support their respective claims of sovereignty on the Falkland Islands and Gibraltar in order to restore the integrity of their national territories through peaceful means, conforming with the pertinent resolutions of the United Nations.' This declaration, which Margaret Thatcher condemned in the House of Commons on 14 June, was the product of a very specific moment in Hispano-Argentine relations. President González found the ideal partner in democratic Argentina to initiate his own international career, and together with the historical/sentimental factors which united Spain and Argentina, González and Alfonsín introduced an image of democracy and human rights which was favourable for both the leaders and their respective international images. In fact, Felipe González's first government (1982–5) carried out a 'presidentialist' policy in Latin America which led to frequent visits to the region.

The logic that identified Gibraltar with the Falkland Islands disappeared from the agenda of the Spanish government from the moment when Spain and the UK reached the Brussels agreement in December 1984. Fernando Morán himself said that the Brussels agreement on Gibraltar did not serve as a precedent for the Falkland Islands. This did not mean that Spain modified its attitude on decolonization of the Falklands, as was seen from its vote in the General Assembly of Nations until 1988 (the last year in which the subject was put to the vote), and it in no way affected the importance that King Juan Carlos I gave the subject during his first visit to a democratic Argentina in 1985. However, from 1985 onwards the Spanish government separated the issue of the Falklands from that of Gibraltar, which was treated in bilateral or European Community frameworks. From being an explicit and important subject in Hispano-Argentine relations, the Falklands became merely a focus of symbolic gesture at the United Nations.

From 1986 onwards, Hispano-Argentine relations evolved in a different atmosphere, given Spain's entry into the European Community. It is clear – and the discourse of the Spanish government on 'the bridging role' during the 1982 war was evidence of this – that Spain's entry into the EC would have consequences for its relations with Latin America. Both the former Francoist right and the ideologists of socialist diplomacy approached the EEC-Spain-Latin America relationship in terms of a lobby;[47] in other words, they defined the role of Spain as a representative or a transmitter of Latin American interests to the EC. It is in this context that, in October 1986, Spain reacted against the British decision to create a 150-mile exclusion zone around the Falkland Islands, on the basis (according to a note from the Diplomatic Information Office) of the Spanish position on sovereignty of the islands. However, Spain's condemnation was not reflected in any subsequent actions in the framework of the fishing policy of the EC; when the UK began to issue fishing licences in the area, Spain raised no objections. It must be remembered that in 1986 Spain was the EC country with the greatest fishing interests in the South Atlantic, along with the Soviet Union, Japan, Taiwan, Poland and South Korea.

The above illustrates the change that took place in Hispano-Argentine relations from the time of Spain's entry in the Community. Two broad features characterized this change: first, the policy of shared ideologies (democratization, territorial claims) led to a policy of economic interests which were divergent in many cases, and second, González's 'presidentialist' policy in Latin America was substituted by a bureaucratic policy[48] which was more appropriate for the new type of relations centred on economic cooperation, while González himself showed a greater personal interest in his relations with countries of the European Community.

The period 1982–7 in Hispano-Argentine relations is described by the analysts as a period rich in political links, but poor in 'business'.[49] This corresponds to a constant feature in Hispano-Argentine relations (and by extension relations with all Latin America), the asymmetry between the political and the economic fields which shows that Spain has more influence than actual power in Latin America. In fact, the economic weight of Spain is small: in 1980, the Spanish market represented 3 per cent of total

47. Respectively, M. Fraga Iribarne, *España, Entre dos Modelos de Sociedad*, Barcelona: Planeta, 1982, p. 47; and, J.A. Yáñez Barnuevo, 'Relaciones entre Europa e Iberoamérica en el Marco de las Relaciones Norte-Sur y Este-Oeste', in *Encuentros en la Democracia: Europa-Iberoamérica*, Madrid: ICI, 1986, p. 249.

48. C. del Arenal, *España e Iberoamérica*, de la Hispanidad a la Comunidad Iberoamericana de Naciones, p. 34.

49. R. Russel, *Las Relacions de Argentina con Europa Occidental*, Madrid: Irela, 1991, p. 13.

trade exchanges of Latin America and 3 per cent of Latin American debt was contracted with Spanish banks.

The interests of Spain and Argentina increasingly diverged after Spain's entry into the EC and the negative impact this had on the Argentine economy. The traditional Argentine trade surplus with Spain disappeared between 1984 and 1987 ($200 million in 1984) and Spanish investments were reduced by one-half between 1985 and 1986. This corresponds to what is Spain's growing economic orientation towards Europe, which was evident even before entry into the EC; in 1991, 65 per cent of Spanish imports came from the EC-EFTA compared with 4.5 per cent from Latin America, and 75 per cent of Spanish exports went to the EC-EFTA compared with 3.5 per cent to Latin America.

The more non-ideological and pragmatic nature of Hispano-Argentine relations was strengthened by the election in Argentina of Carlos Menem, who adopted a more realistic attitude than the radical government in international matters. This led in the case of the Falklands, to the re-establishment of diplomatic relations between Argentina and the UK in 1990, after negotiations in Madrid which had begun in 1989.[50]

Conclusions

The evolution of Spain's position between 1982 and 1992 on the Falklands issue represents a reflection of the wider changes that took place in Spanish foreign policy making. The decade of the 1980s coincided with the period in which democratic Spain's foreign policy was being defined both in content and in form. Hence an analysis of the war and the follow up of Spain's relations with Argentina (by extension with Latin America) and the UK (by extension with the European Community) in the period from 1982 to 1992, requires different theoretical approaches.[51]

First, the elaboration of Spanish foreign policy during the 1982 war corresponds to Spain's circumstances at the time, the country's lack of definition in foreign policy matters together with the lack of an established bureaucratic system. The analysis of Spain's behaviour during the war leads to two conclusions of a general nature. First, Calvo Sotelo's government acted ambiguously throughout the war. On the one hand, it acted according to a rational pattern, with a clear preference for the negotiations with the EEC, but on the other hand, it was affected by belief systems which,

50. In spite of Spain's capital being chosen as 'the negotiating space', the Spanish government has nothing to do with the initiative and development of the said meetings.

51. For the elements of foreign policy analysis, theories and methods mentioned in these conclusions, see J. Greenaway, S. Smith and J. Street, *Deciding Factors in British Politics - A Case-Studies Approach*, London: Routledge, 1992.

due to the clearly pro-Argentine public opinion, had an effect on the decision makers. This ambiguity, together with the lack of resources of the Spanish government (stemming from not being a member of the Community) completely invalidated the Spanish proposals to adopt the role of mediator between Europe and Latin America throughout the crisis. The war was used as a pretext by the opposition parties who, as in any model of adversarial politics, took advantage of the occasion to counteract Calvo Sotelo's attempts to orientate his foreign policy. The opposition made the Falklands War yet another episode in the internal political battle, and even an issue within the party in power, the UCD, resulting in the PSOE winning an absolute majority in the October 1982 elections.

Second, the follow-up phase of Spanish policy with regard to the Falklands conflict, from the time the socialists came to power, was framed simultaneously within the whole set of relations of Spain with Argentina and Latin America, and with the UK and the European Community. Four additional conclusions of a general nature can be drawn from this. First, the debate between the Spanish political parties, because of the war in the South Atlantic which fitted the model of adversarial politics, meant that the coming to power of the opposition (PSOE) would imply a change in policy with regard to the Falklands and Argentina. The change was one of orientation, since the Latin-American policy of Felipe González was initially marked by ideological elements (democratization) and not by traditional historical elements as in earlier stages. This made Argentina, after the fall of the military junta one of the main partners of the Spanish government in Latin America. Within this privileged relationship between Spain and Argentina, the subject of the Falklands played a symbolic role as a strengthening factor for Alfonsín's government.

Second, the González government, like the Calvo Sotelo government, aspired to make foreign policy decisions on rational grounds in terms of calculating national interests. This led Spain to consider the European Community as the preferred space in all senses (economic, political, and a framework that would facilitate the solution of the Gibraltar conflict), but at the same time it was influenced by the belief systems of Spanish society that made Latin America 'a world in itself'; hence the rhetoric of the Spanish socialists on the role of Spain as a bridge between Latin America and the European Community.

Third, the González government through the ten years that followed the 1982 war fashioned a model that would articulate Spain's relations both with the European Community and with Latin America. Thus following Spain's entry into the Community (1986) there is a twofold process of European influence on the Spanish government's Latin American policy and, the articulation, thanks to Spanish diplomatic activity, of a Latin American regional identity in Europe. In the first case, the European influence on Spanish policy in Latin America meant that Spain would have to renounce its own policies, as in Nicaragua after 1983,[52] but at the same time it made Spain the spokesman of the Latin Americans in the framework of European Political Cooperation.[53] In the second case, the will to promote a regional Latin American space took shape, based on a socio-political reality rather than an economic one. This political reality was based on a positive identity (historical, sentimental and cultural) and on a negative identity (the need to be different from the Anglo-Saxon world).

The Spanish objective to foster the creation of a Latin American region meant greater complexity and bureaucratization in foreign policy making. Especially after 1985, Felipe González orientated his personal agenda towards relations with Europe, to the detriment of his personal contacts in Latin America; most particularly after Morán was replaced by Fernández Ordóñez, the cabinet government policy exercised by Felipe González in Latin America led to a situation of bureaucratic decentralization.

This bureaucratic decentralization meant that the King had to assume the symbolic content of Spanish policy in Latin America. The monarch thus became the spokesman of an ideological-cultural apparatus, the Latin American Community of Nations.[54] At the same time an institutional structure was created which united international cooperation and Latin America, including a Secretary of State for International Cooperation and Latin America, the Spanish Agency of International Cooperation and the Annual Plan of International Cooperation. The parallel existence of various bodies in charge of relations with Latin America in these last few years, with each of them in the hands of a different group (the advisors of Felipe González, diplomats from the Ministry, members of the Socialist Party in charge of the cooperation machinery), has complicated the organizational process to such an extent that the events of 1992 such as the Seville Exposition, the 500th Anniversary celebrations and the Second Latin American Conference of Madrid, became the framework for power struggles between the different interest groups in charge of elaborating Spanish policy for Latin America.

Finally, the experience of the years of Spanish foreign policy after the 1982 war, illustrates that in spite of Spain's undisputed preference for aligning itself in every sense with the European Community, we should not underestimate the weight of general belief systems, particularly in the cultural-sentimental space of Latin America, in times of crisis; this was seen

52. J. Grugel, 'Spain's Socialist Government and Central American Dilemmas', in *International Affairs*, vol. 63, no. 4, 1987, pp. 603-15.

53. E. Barbé, 'El año español de la Cooperación Política Europea', *Anuario Internacional CIDOB 1989*, Barcelona: CIDOB, 1990, pp. 109-20.

54. R. Mesa, *La idea de Comunidad Iberoamericana: entre la Historia y la Utopía*, Madrid: Cedeal, 1989; C. del Arenal, *España e Iberoamérica, de la Hispanidad a la Comunidad Iberoamericana de Naciones*.

yet again during the United States intervention in Panama in 1989. On that occasion, Spain broke away from the voting discipline of the EC in the General Assembly of the United Nations to condemn, together with the Latin American countries, the action of the United States. Ten years after the Falklands War, Spain – the great defender of European ortho-doxy – continues to be a potential dissenter in Western Europe whenever the crisis in question affects Latin American countries.

Conclusions

Stelios Stavridis

This chapter attempts to provide a general conclusion by summing up the main lessons to be drawn from the preceding empirical studies. It covers seven main areas, deriving from both the dimension of comparative foreign policy analysis and the substantive experience of European Political Cooperation.

Comparative Foreign Policy Analysis

In taking a comparative approach, this book in the eyes of some will be inherently positivistic and therefore subject to all the limitations of positivism. This is not the view of the editors, who assume that comparisons open up issues rather than predetermine conclusions. It is an open question as to whether events are 'unique' or whether lessons can be learned from them. Furthermore, in seeking to analyse the dual impact of on the one hand, the international system, and on the other hand, the domestic characteristics of individual states, we are looking inherently at the dividing line between common and unique experiences. The case has been made for such an approach in both the Introduction and in the discussion in Chapter 1 of FPA as a sub-discipline of the field of International Relations.

The reason for repeating this at the beginning of the concluding chapter stems from the fact that *only* this kind of approach makes it possible to ask such questions and to reach the subsequent conclusions. In other words, the view that each event is *sui generis* does not necessarily explain why the European Community member states reacted the way they did to the Argentine invasion of the Falklands in April 1982; nor does it explain any of the developments that followed, especially in the 'dissenting' countries, be they internal (Italy, Ireland) or external (Spain) to the EC at that time.

Finally, not to have included a comparative dimension would have ignored a fact that cannot be dismissed by any approach, namely, the existence of the European Community and European Political Cooperation as common frames for decision which clearly impact on national foreign policies. Comparing the reactions to the Falklands conflict of those states that belong to the EC is therefore not only desirable but necessary, as their membership implies that there is an additional dimension to their foreign policy-making process which is lacking from that of other states. The fact that the EC, and by implication EPC, is an organization quite unique in the world makes such an exercise all the more desirable. This dimension was examined not only in the decisions taken by the individual states but also in the chapter on the European Community's reaction (Chapter 2 by Geoffrey Edwards). This is not to say that other international organizations did not suffer from a lack of a coherent response, as was the case with NATO from the time Spain joined in June 1982, but, in the case of the European Community and EPC, the events in the South Atlantic represented, as was mentioned in the Introduction, an invasion of EC territory, the first time – and only time to date - that this has happened. Thus, a comprehensive study of the Western European reactions to the Falklands conflict could only consist of an analysis of the collective reaction of the EC and of the individual reactions of the member states of that organization.

Crisis

Let us first look at the nature of the problem that faced the European states in 1982. Before considering the conclusions that can be drawn on the question of whether, in addition to the UK, the Falklands represented a crisis for the other members of the European Community, one should note the wider context in which the Falklands incident occurred. It is possible to argue that the Falklands conflict added itself to a general feeling of doom and gloom in Europe and in the rest of the world. There were a number of international factors such as a difficult economic situation, the dispute over EC farms prices and President Reagan's talk of an evil empire, which created a sense of general crisis and pessimism.[1] It also meant that the outcome of the diplomatic, and then military, struggle in the Falklands created an environment conducive to (unrealistic?) expectations of a fast, coherent, and effective set of decisions at the European level as well as at the British and other individual national centres of decision making.

The question of whether the Falklands represented a crisis for Western European countries other than the UK can now be answered following the various case-studies in the book, which have shown how difficult and often controversial this issue was in 1982. However, to say that the events which occurred between early April and the middle of June 1982 represented a crisis for the whole of the Community does not necessarily mean that it was the same crisis for all the separate states concerned. There is little

1. For more on the decline of détente and the rise of the second Cold War, see F. Halliday, *The Making of the Second Cold War*, London: Verso, 1983.

doubt that for each it was a different type of crisis than the one experienced in Britain.

The theoretical literature has identified the following four factors as key elements of a crisis: time constraints, an element of surprise, a threat to basic values and the possibility of war. All these factors were present, albeit the last two directly applied only to the UK.[2] In other words, the events in the South Atlantic represented a typical security and national domestic crisis for the United Kingdom.

But the Falklands conflict was a crisis for Britain's partners all the same because, as with most international events, the Argentine invasion forced the various EC members to think about the costs and benefits of a joint reaction. It was a crisis of European unity which partly reflected national preferences over what kind of political process the European Community is in the first place, and partly a domestic crisis for those countries which were more directly affected by the developments in the conflict in general and by the military events in particular (such as the sinking of the *Belgrano*). The dilemma of belonging to two distinct but related historic communities through blood, language and affinity was particularly strong for Italy and Spain, but also affected Ireland and Denmark. It should also be noted that a similar dilemma existed in the United States (witnessed by the dispute between Weinberger and Kickpatrick). The added dimension of a classic EC crisis over farm prices reinforced the sense of a crisis of European unity despite the many efforts made by the British to try to detach these two issues.

The more general implications of the Falklands crisis for the question of how and why a crisis affects European unity can be summarized as follows: in any given international crisis, the perceived interests of the individual members of the Community almost automatically create a debate over where EC interests lie; whether or not they gel into a common interest which can be easily identified remains another question. In other words, every international crisis has an impact on the Community as an entity, be it positive or negative; the closer the crisis is to the national interests of a particular member state, the greater its impact on EC cohesion. If in addition there exists a clear difference of opinion between at least one member state and another (usually bigger) member state, then the emergence of a common European stance becomes all the more elusive because it acquires a confrontational tone. The recent developments in ex-Yugoslavia, more particularly the recognition of Slovenia and Croatia, and the Greek stance on the Former Yugoslav Republic of Macedonia (FYROM) are yet more examples of how divergent national interests affect Community cohesion. As was noted in the Introduction, the timing of the events in the

---

2. R. Lebow, *Between Peace and War – The Nature of International Crisis*, Baltimore: John Hopkins University Press, 1981, pp. 10–12.

South Atlantic was all the more critical in 1982 only a few months after the London Report had been adopted, following among other things the rather pathetic EC reaction to events in Eastern Europe and the Soviet invasion of Afghanistan in the late 1970s. Last but not least, the international perception of the Community as a more or less unified and coherent actor will be powerfully affected by its conduct during external crises.

European Foreign Policy

This leads us directly to the lessons that can be drawn from the Falklands episode for European foreign policy. Christopher Hill identified in the Introduction three different levels of assessment: first, the general level of cohesion; second, the question of linkage politics and procedural arrangements; and, finally, the level of common principles.

At the level of EC cohesion, Sophie Vanhoonacker's hypothesis in Chapter 4 that 'when there are serious domestic pressures, solidarity among the EC member states is severely tested' proved to be correct in the case of the Falklands. Even if the Community began rather well with a swift and coherent condemnation of the Argentine invasion and the imposition of economic sanctions, there is little doubt that any semblance of cohesion quickly dissolved. For a variety of reasons intrinsic to national circumstances, which were described and analysed in detail in this book, EC cohesion did not last very long and succumbed to several centrifugal forces. This collapse in European solidarity materialized when only seven of the Ten renewed EC sanctions and Denmark continued with sanctions but at the national level. If one adds to the equation, as this book has done, Spain's opposition to Britain, whatever the Spanish government of the time said or did to disguise this fact, EC cohesion would have been even less than it was with only ten members. Of course it could be argued that, once inside a club, departure from the common stance is very costly, and therefore Spain as an EC member might have behaved differently, especially at an early stage of membership when 'good behaviour' is needed to justify accession in the first instance. But this view fails to take into consideration the fact that two (and one-half) EC member states did break ranks, and that PASOK's early years in power in Greece (1981–5) showed that membership is no guarantee of toeing the line in foreign affairs. Moreover, if a country like Spain had been an EC member and had broken ranks, it would not be totally inconceivable that a Rome-Madrid axis might have developed with a strong anti-British stance on the Falklands within the Community, a stance which no Rome-Dublin axis could ever possibly produce.

It is worthing adding that Vanhoonacker's hypothesis applies equally for events after 1982 as, between 1982 and 1988 (the last year in which there was a vote at the UN General Assembly on the question of the Falklands) EC cohesion slowly dissipated in New York. During this time, once the military conflict was over, domestic pressures which had been suppressed or controlled in 1982 could take the upper hand and alter the position of some governments on the issue. This drift away from the British view first materialized in 1985 when France, Italy and Greece joining the permanent 'dissenter' (Spain),[3] with the Netherlands joining in for the final three years when the issue of the Falklands was discussed (1986–8).

A further point must be made about EC cohesion, which stems directly from what has just been said about the voting pattern at the United Nations; the short duration of the conflict in 1982 might have been a factor strengthening EC cohesion. In other words, and somewhat paradoxically, a crisis situation means that it is more difficult to 'take cover' or hide behind the views of more important and influential partners.[4] A quick and coherent stance must materialize immediately and be justified. In the longer term, however, such a centripetal force disappears with the end of tension. This explains in part what happened at the UN;[5] but it also means that the very fact that EC cohesion did not survive the start of the shooting war in 1982 further emphasises the absence of a common European position.

The question of EC cohesion also raises the related issue of how much power the EC expected to exert as a collective entity in 1982. Of course, 1982 is not 1995 and there was no debate over the new international role that the now renamed European Union might (or should) play, but such a question deserves some attention all the same, if only to provide an interesting snapshot. In 1982, the European Community as a whole was the first supplier and second buyer of Argentina's products. The conditions for the application of 'civilian (i.e. economic) power' through the imposition of sanctions were perfect; hence, the swift decision to impose sanctions and also to ban arms exports to that country. De Vree's view (quoted in the Introduction) that Europe should generate at least as much power as the superpowers if it wanted to be taken seriously on the international stage is worth considering at this stage because there is little doubt that in many quarters in Europe, not least in the European Commission, it was believed that Argentina would cave in to European economic pressures, and that the EC would therefore demonstrate a real form of power. On the other hand, there was an ongoing debate over the general effectiveness of

3. In fact Greece returned to its 1982 position, for more details see Chapter 4.
4. For the alibi function of EPC, see C. Hill (ed.), *National Foreign Policies and European Political Cooperation*, London: Allen & Unwin, 1983.
5. See Appendix B, for a summary of how the EC states and Spain voted on the Falklands at the UN General Assembly between 1982 and 1988, the years when there was a vote on that issue.

sanctions, and even when the Americans added their weight by deciding to join the EC ban once the Haig mission was pronounced dead, Buenos Aires did not in fact respond. In short, the imposition of economic sanctions against Argentina added to the international stature of the European Community without achieving its primary goal[6] of an Argentine withdrawal. But one should look at the trees hiding in the forest; at the end of the day, EC cohesion on sanctions evaporated.

To continue along the same line of argument, but this time from the perspective of the procedural arrangements followed during the 1982 crisis, the imposition of sanctions against Argentina meant a positive development for European foreign policy ('positive' in the sense of fostering EPC; no value judgment is attached to this word). The use of Article 113 (instead of Article 224) meant that the final decision had to be taken at the Community and not the national level. Article 113 is a symbol of a more *communautaire* approach to imposing international sanctions at the European level. Clearly this was a new development in the history of European integration; obviously a price had to be paid at some stage, and it was paid when Denmark went its own way and more importantly when Italy and Ireland broke ranks, but the fact that (in addition to the domestic factors elaborated upon in the respective national chapters) the fighting had actually started can be seen as an equally important factor in explaining the shift away from support for the British.

On the other hand, informal linkage of the Argentine sanctions with the row over the renewal of CAP prices in May 1982 showed the 'negative' implications that the Falklands conflict had for procedures and eventually for cohesion. Whether there was such an informal linkage is hotly disputed by the British, but one cannot ignore the fact that in the view of those less enthusiastic about supporting the British in the first place, such as Claude Cheysson to name but one example, the lack of flexibility over farm prices was very much like the straw that broke the camel's back. Certainly the other Nine showed no willingness to allow Britain to have it both ways.

In terms of principles, although it is quite easy to say that the Community as a whole and its member states both individually and collectively condemned the use of force in the conduct of international relations, it is not possible to argue that clear and unambiguous international principles for the European Community did actually emerge, mainly for the reasons presented so far. The generally accepted UN principles of condemning

6. See J. Barber, 'Economic sanctions as a policy instrument', *International Affairs*, vol. 55, no. 3, July 1979, pp. 367-84. Barber distinguishes between three types of goals for any given decision to apply international sanctions: primary objectives concern the target state; secondary objectives concern the imposing state; and tertiary objectives concern the broader international considerations such as the international system.

international violence, especially when unprovoked, not carried out in self-defence, and at the behest of a military *junta*, constituted only one element in a much wider interplay of domestic and international forces which eventually prevented the continuation of a common European reaction to the events in the South Atlantic. On the other hand, the nature of values subscribed to by the EC and the member states made it impossible for any one state to approve of Argentina's invasion, and therefore much easier for Britain to achieve its crucial early consensus on sanctions and on Security Council Resolution 502.

Some emerging principles were reinforced all the same, such as the imposition of sanctions being possible even when no direct national interest has been under threat, and imposed for political reasons. The creation of a precedent for the future can also be seen as a positive development for a European foreign policy in the long term, as a number of member states can refer back to the Falklands episode if they wish to do so (France over the territorial integrity of its DOM-TOM overseas territories, West Germany over the status of West Berlin – admittedly only until 1989, and even Spain despite its ambivalence in 1982, over its North African enclaves of Ceuta and Melilla). In her memoirs, Margaret Thatcher mentions the question of creating a precedent quite plainly, adding somewhat ironically that when she asked the Foreign Office for a brief over worldwide territorial disputes in order to make a stronger case during the Versailles G7 summit, 'it was a lengthy document'.[7]

One also needs to add that EPC then still very much resembled, in the phrase of Wallace and Allen, 'procedure as a substitute for policy'.[8] Progress towards a European foreign policy is not a linear process. If one looks at the initial reaction to the Argentine attack in early April 1982 it is quite easy to see that the European Community reacted quickly and in unison; if instead one looks at the later stages when a partner state began to use force itself, then obviously there was no coherent and consistent European reaction, neither procedure nor policy. What this shift signals is that no clearly identifiable European principles had emerged, beyond the general principles to which all states pretend to adhere (democracy, freedom, and human rights), which are sufficient to overcome different domestic constraints.

All this has implications for the future of European foreign policy under its new name, CFSP. As noted in the Introduction, this was the only instance to date of an attack on EC territory that did not lead to the kind of support expected from a genuine community of states (*Gemeinschaft* rather than

7. M. Thatcher, *The Downing Street Years*, London: Harper Collins, 1993, p. 192.

8. W. Wallace, D. Allen, 'Political Cooperation: Procedure as a Substitute for Policy', in H. Wallace, W. Wallace, C. Webb (eds), *Policy Making in the European Communities*, 1st edn, London: John Wiley and Sons, 1977, pp. 227-48.

Gesellschaft, and Deutsch's security commmunity).[9] Of course solidarity broke down only after the armed war began and, thirteen years ago, discussions on the political and economic aspects of security had only just begun in the EPC context; defence was still a taboo. But one should not underestimate the fact that even the most loyal supporters of Britain during the Falklands conflict expressed important doubts over the general line of British foreign policy in the South Atlantic. Sovereignty and security issues arouse strong political emotions: France did not hide its strong reservations concerning the legitimacy of the UK's claim to the islands, and West Germany made it clear that its own economic interests in the region meant that unlimited sanctions could not be imposed (instead, as was seen, the Germans successfully pushed for limited sanctions, both in scope and in duration). If the then 'external' dissenter, Spain, had been part of the EC at the time, one would have expected an even weaker expression of solidarity with the UK, as the NATO experience showed when Spain's entry into the Atlantic Alliance on 1 June 1982 brought the Alliance's unreserved support for the British to an unceremonious end.

National Foreign Policies

Closely related to the evolution of European foreign policy is the question of national foreign policies. From the other, national, end of the telescope, what can be said of the respective impact that the member states had on the overall EC reaction to the Falklands events? It seems quite clear from the case studies in this work that national viewpoints ultimately prevailed. This was the case not only for the dissenting states (Italy, Ireland and Denmark) where it is obvious that national foreign policy traditions constrained a common European foreign policy to the point of negating it, but is also true to a lesser extent of those states that supported the UK all the way through the 1982 conflict. The overall EC reaction had to accommodate the pluralist views that existed in those countries as well as factors such as the pressure of economic lobbies in West Germany (the major European economic partner of Argentina) which resulted in the restricted nature of the EC sanctions, or the many reservations in most other countries about the validity of the British claim to the islands (in France, for example).

The different national foreign policy traditions that exist among the member states of the EC can also be seen in the variety of reactions that have been examined in detail here. The difference in status (economic as well as political, but also from a security perspective), together with differences

9. See P. Taylor, *The Limits of European Integration*, London: Croom Helm, 1983, p. 3.

in culture, style and approach (general 'mood'), meant that the British had to convince not only a varied domestic public opinion, but also the many varieties of opinions within their partner countries. Added to this problem, one should mention the fact that different foreign policy actors reacted in different ways according to the state to which they belonged. In other words, not all political parties of the same ideological affiliation reacted in the same way, nor did every manifestation of public opinion matter in the same way.

This study has also emphasised the dilemmas posed by the Falklands in relation to the more general question of the reorientation of foreign policy. This was particularly true of the case of Spain, which although it was not an EC member state at the time, happened to join NATO at the time of the conflict. Moreover, Spain was an applicant EC country in all but name, and indeed in the eyes of many NATO membership was seen as a prerequisite for EC membership. The Spanish government's reaction to the events in the South Atlantic was but one of the first important signs that Spanish foreign policy had begun to look towards Europe even if it still wished it could play a bridging role between Europe and Latin America. As Esther Barbé points out, the ambivalence of the Spanish reaction can be seen as part of a wider and general reorientation towards Europe (symbolized by EEC membership) while also retaining ties with Latin America, which, once in power, even the Socialist PSOE accepted as the necessary and welcome new future for democratic Spain.

Foreign Policy Decision Making

With respect to the question of what lessons we can draw from this study, one should refer to the exisiting theories of decision making which, as Michael Clarke said in Chapter 1, should always be tested by empirical studies. In some areas this study has reinforced the existing theories on national foreign policy making: for instance, the Gaullist preponderance of the French president in foreign affairs was confirmed once again, as was the fact that the German system appears to be more decentralized and responsive to economic interests. Such a claim had not actually been tested before with regard to the specific case of the Falklands episode.

On the three models of foreign policy making referred to by Clarke, namely the rational actor, the administrative and the bureaucratic models, the following comments can be made now that a detailed comparative study has taken place. In more detail, each of these three models has shed some light on why states behave in the ways that they do.

The first model is particularly relevant because although its main assumption of a rational unitary centre of foreign policy decision making only partially reflects reality (such as the President's pre-eminence in French foreign policy), it allows for a useful discussion on what the term 'rational' actually means: how purposive is any foreign policy decision in the first place? Or, rather, how much purpose can one identify in it? In Hill's phrase, were the states in this crisis 'autistic rational actors' with no values attached to their decisions, a mere reflection of technocratic procedural arrangements (SOPs, or standard operating procedures, in Graham Allison's seminal work on foreign policy analysis)?[10] The answer seems to be a clear vindication of a more thoughtful approach stressing a complex, interacting set of actors influencing foreign policy according to their own agendas. In some cases, the final choice was quite clearly purposive, as for instance in Italy, where perhaps the most important of all the reasons for breaking EC ranks was the need for the Italian coalition in power to survive domestically. As one of its main partners, the Socialists, was against sanctions, the Italian Christian Democrats had to face a clear and rational choice: either agree with their junior partners or see the end of their government.

Similarly, but this time in a country which stuck with the sanctions line, namely France, a clear purpose of the Mitterrand position was that the Falklands could be used as a precedent, if a French overseas territory was to be attacked in the future. This came about not only because of the traditional presidential preponderance in French foreign policy since the beginning of the Gaullist Fifth Republic, but also because the opponents of such a stance (as represented by the Foreign Minister of the time, Claude Cheysson) did not win the argument until the end of 1985 when finally, as was analysed in Chapter 3, France decided to shift its voting behaviour at that year's United Nations General Assembly.

As for the administrative model and the bureaucratic models, both seem to offer less of an explanation for what happened in 1982, probably because of the limited time that the conflict lasted, and are more applicable in the case of Britain (see Chapter 1). They also seem to confirm the view that they are of no real use to explain the foreign policy-making process of small(er) countries as the respective studies of Ireland and Greece seem to suggest. In other words, this empirical study seems to confirm the view that bureaucratic politics play a greater role in larger states and over a longer period of time than they do in smaller states and/or over a short period of time.

This brings us to the role played by the overall political structure and culture of each country. This book has examined the various member states of the EC and Spain at the time of the 1982 conflict in some detail, and it is now possible to confirm that the belief systems of the leaders did

10. G. Allison, *Essence of Decision – Explaining the Cuban Missile Crisis*, Boston: Little Brown & Co., 1971.

play a role in the way those states reacted: for instance in France, President Mitterrand's emphasis on the fact that France owed a continuous debt to the UK because of the latter's role in freeing France during the Second World War prevailed. Similarly, the ideological dimension (democracy versus dictatorship) of the conflict tipped the scales in favour of Britain for many a politician who might have preferred to stress the imperialist dimension of the task force, even though a cynic could argue that such a factor did not appear to be an important foreign policy element prior to the invasion of the islands in April 1982 (important arms sales to the Argentine junta took place before and after the invasion). This was, as we have seen, especially true of the still new democracies of Greece and Spain.

Equally, history and culture also played important roles in the opposite direction, in Italy, Ireland and Spain. But this study went beyond mere intuitive explanations as it analysed in detail not only the reasons behind the dissenters' reactions, but also why their dissent did not materialize immediately. Even if no clear overall generalization appears to be possible, it is fair to say that decision-making models do tell us something about the way foreign policy is made. Individually, no one model offers a comprehensive explanation of what happened, but put together, they do offer insight into and indeed reflect the complexities of foreign policy making.

Domestic Pluralism

Christopher Hill's point in the Introduction with respect to the pluralist context of decision making in foreign policy can be summed up by the question of whether 'foreign policy begins at home', or, *per contra*, whether domestic factors only complicate foreign policy. This study has shown that there is a constant interaction between domestic and external factors. In West Germany for example, the wider pluralist model of foreign policy, which logically follows on from bureaucratic approaches by focusing on interest groups, seems to have been particularly relevant where the economic lobbies worked well to prevent comprehensive, retroactive and unlimited sanctions which would have damaged German economic interests quite dramatically.

Leaders are always influenced by their country's history and culture, which affect their views on foreign policy and subsequently their decisions. As their decisions are not taken in a vacuum but in the domestic political system, these create reactions from the main political actors, namely the parliaments, the media, public opinion and pressure groups. This book has shown various degrees of reaction and various types of reactions in these countries. But even in countries where foreign policy decisions remain the *domaine reservé* of the executive, a debate did take place and various lobbies tried to influence the final decision made by the government. The furore that followed Ireland's initial siding with the British, or the tension generated by the events in the South Atlantic in Italy, especially after the sinking of the Belgrano, are but two examples that one can take from the various empirical studies contained in this book.

Similar political affiliations led to a variety of reactions as it is not possible to say that there was a clear dividing line on the crisis between left and right (between French and Spanish Socialists, for instance). Moreover, a number of dissenting voices on each side of the political spectrum (widely defined) could also be heard (such as Cheysson and Mitterrand). Such a variety of opinion also existed in the UK, especially after the end of the military conflict, although some critical views such as those of Tam Dalyell or Tony Benn were voiced early on. This is not the place, nor is it the intention of this work, to try and pass a final judgment on who was right in the first analysis, but there were a number of varied views and opinions which influenced the final decision taken by all EC governments on whether or not to support the British. Such influence did not stop after the initial decision to impose a trade embargo and it continued over the numerous occasions of renewing them, indeed until well after the end of the military operations. It can also be argued that, once democracy was restored in Argentina, the very existence of domestic pluralism in Britain and its EC partners meant that eventually a rapprochement between the two belligerent countries was inevitable. One could mention here the visits by the then new Argentine Foreign Minister Caputo to Paris, Strasbourg and Rome in April 1984, President Alfonsín's visit to Madrid in June 1984 and the visit to the Argentine Senate by three British parliamentarians from the Conservative, Labour and SDP parties in late June 1984.[11] Admittedly, there also were government-to-government behind the scenes negotiations that led to the aborted Bern talks in July 1984 (and then again in August 1989), but neither this fact nor the failure of negotiations should lead us to underestimate the role played by non-governmental actors in the long and sometimes painful process of reconciliation that culminated only in October 1989 in Madrid.[12]

11. MPs Cyril Townsend, George Foulkes and Lord Kennet respectively. 'SDP' stands for the now-defunct Social Democratic Party.
12. What follows is not comprehensive but will give a good idea of the kind of non-official and official contacts that led to Madrid:
  – Alfonsín's address to the European Parliament in Strasbourg in October 1984,
  – his meeting with Keith Best, Conservative MP for Anglesey at a conference of parliamentarians in Athens in February 1985,
  – a three-day conference at the University of Maryland, USA, again in February 1985 where both Argentine and British parliamentarians participated,
  – a similar exchange of views at the Bonn-based Foreign Policy Institute, the following month,

It is also possible to argue, without pursuing the point extensively, that parties in opposition are naturally less responsive to a sense of international responsibility. They can promise almost anything under the sun because they do not have any real influence; this is particularly true in political systems where the party in power does not have to consider the opposition's views until the next general election. In cases where there is a coalition government, the opposition views become much more important, especially if they find a responsive chord in one of the parties forming that coalition (see Chapter 6). On the other hand, there is always a pressure towards bi-partisanship in foreign policy where vital national interests are concerned. Thus in Britain there was far more cross-party consensus over the Falklands than in other EC states.

Britain and the Western European Reactions

The British reaction was not included in this work because, as noted in the Introduction, a huge literature already exists on this subject, and the problem here is essentially how the other member states react when one of them requires urgent support on a matter of vital interest in foreign policy. However, the way in which Britain reacted to the reactions of its allies in the European Community deserves some attention, if only with a view to assessing the importance of the EC context as perceived by London.

As Geoffrey Edwards noted in Chapter 2, Mrs Thatcher had bitterly complained in 1985 when the UN vote on the Falklands issue resulted in an increasing number of EC member states siding against the United Kingdom. The British Prime Minister has since been rather dismissive of European reactions during the 1982 war, and in her memoirs she expressed gratitude only to François Mitterrand whom she called a 'staunch' ally[13] (see also Chapter 3). She also went to great lengths to show how much personal contact there was in her efforts to secure the support of other EC leaders during the conflict. This clearly reflects the fact that she deemed it important to try and get support from Britain's closest allies. She also

– Alfonsín's talks with Neil Kinnock in Paris and with David Steel in Madrid in October 1985,

– the February 1986 visit by Argentine parliamentarians to London,

– another parliamentarians meeting in Mexico-City in April 1986,

– Alfonsín's visit to Rome in December 1987,

– González's visit to Latin America in April 1988, and

- the European Parliament's Latin American Delegation visit to Buenos Aires on 31 August 1988 including talks with President Alfonsín.

(source: press review Chatham House 1984-9 including *The Times*, *The Independent*, *The Guardian* and *Le Monde*).

13. M. Thatcher, *The Downing Street Years*, p. 227.

Conclusions

contrasted the EC's eventual lack of consensus to the 'very supportive' stance of the Commonwealth, with the exception of India, and chastized the Irish (and to a lesser extent the Spaniards) time and time again for making her job, especially at the UN, more difficult.[14]

In a television programme which accompanied the publication of her memoirs, Mrs (now Baroness) Thatcher preferred to concentrate on the more constructive role played by the Americans, and only indirectly referred to the EC states that did not back her with the comment that 'appeasement is wrong'.[15] Admittedly, the role of the United States was of greater importance to the course of events in the South Atlantic in 1982, but European reactions cannot be ignored for a number of reasons: first, the UK needed EC support at the UN, initially in the Security Council in April and May 1982, and then in the General Assembly when the Falklands were put back on the agenda between 1982 and 1988; second, Britain needed a coherent EC decision on sanctions to increase its diplomatic pressure on Argentina, especially at the time when the USA was still ostensibly taking a neutral line (during the Haig mission); third, a common EC stance also increased pressure on the USA as a united European front meant that Britain's stance was being legitimized by its partners; and fourth, because of the *de facto* linkage of the foreign policy issue with internal EC politics (such as the CAP) in the minds of some, a mutual understanding of the two rather separate situations would have been easier without any intra-EC controversy over the Falklands episode.

It is also important to note that the price paid by the UK for failing to secure EC support was also paid by the countries which dissented from the prevailing European line. In short, this meant that Italy and, more importantly, Spain (see Chapters 6 and 8), disqualified themselves from being mediators in the conflict when it would not have been at all surprising to see them take the lead in the field of negotiations. Of course, such a price might seem insignificant in relation to the consequences that Britain had to face, but considering the timing of the conflict it would have been an important and useful diplomatic coup if, for example, democratic Spain had managed to offer a peaceful solution where the USA had failed. For Italy, this could have led to that higher profile in international affairs which it still lacks; it is worth adding that, when Mrs Thatcher visited Rome in January 1984, Italian Prime Minister Bettino Craxi told her that he could see a special role for Italy following the fall of the Argentine *junta* and the coming to power of a new democratic government in Buenos Aires (Raul Alfonsín took office in December 1983). The British Prime Minister replied that the Falklands was a British matter. The varying roles played by each European Community partner were not forgotten by Mrs Thatcher,

14. Ibid., p.191 and pp. 216, 223, 225 and 231.
15. Interview on *BBC1*, 27 October 1993.

but equally, the lack of progress on the Falklands meant that no break-through on trade and economic issues between the EC and Argentina could take place. It is no mere coincidence that the 1990 EC-Argentina agreement materialized a few months after the success of the UK-Argentina talks in Madrid.

Conclusions

This book has sought to demonstrate the value of policy analysis for our understanding of both national and European foreign policies. Structuralism, by contrast, as was argued in the Introduction, is too general a view to do justice to the idiosyncracies of the Falklands War of 1982. It could not have explained the Western European reactions to the Falklands because the show of solidarity which did occur, admittedly for a limited period, cannot be squared with the structural realist's view that different national interests always prevail. Similarly, liberal structuralism, with its emphasis on economic interdependence and solidarity, cannot explain the hard decisions that had to be taken, first in support of Britain (imposing sanctions) and then, for some, against it.

A structuralist would perhaps argue that these reactions did not matter, as Britain made its decision to fight, and fought and won on the basis of power. What mattered was American support, and after an interlude to allow Haig's shuttle diplomacy (a waste of time in some realist views), the UK got full support from the American administration because, for Washington, Galtieri was dispensable but Thatcher was not. Such a view ignores a number of important facts, such as the lukewarm diplomatic support for Britain caused by the division within the American administration due to the clash between Caspar Weinberger's Pentagon and the 'Latinos' represented by Jeanne Kickpatrick. American support was probably important in military terms, at least in the short term, but there is an ongoing debate over how crucial it was. However, this question falls beyond the scope of this book, as does the matter of the 'luck' enjoyed by the British task force given that no ship of vital military or symbolic importance such as one of the two small aircraft carriers or the liner *Queen Elizabeth II* was sunk.

A second point that a structuralist might want to make is that the EC reaction did not affect the UK's ability to fight and win the war. However, such an approach would ignore the simple but important fact that this is not the same as saying that the EC states, as a collectivity and as individual members, did not influence at all the British policy in the South Atlantic. Indeed, power and influence are not the same thing. More importantly perhaps, the British government did pay a price for ignoring the reservations expressed by some EC states and the growing discontent over UK military actions: the very ending of the EC consensus when Italy, Ireland and to a lesser extent Denmark, broke ranks is the best evidence of this, at least insofar as European support was regarded as important. The failure to prevent CAP prices rising can also be seen as an indirect consequence. The overall European image of the UK also greatly suffered, as some of Claude Cheysson's caustic comments to the media at the time clearly demonstrated. Admittedly, the eventual victory restored some lost pride, but in the long term, the small doubts of a limited number of British individuals over the wisdom of the 1982 war have been much larger in some European and international quarters where it was not uncommon to perceive British actions as an anachronistic colonial gunboat diplomacy; this was partly reflected in the progressive shift in the annual vote (1982-8) taken at the United Nations General Assembly over the Falklands where more and more EC states moved away from backing the *status quo*.

In sum, a structuralist approach, be it realist or liberal, completely fails to explain the varied reactions of the EC states towards UK policy, let alone their shifts over time. Such a straitjacketed view of foreign policy making does not reflect reality. There is some truth in such an approach in that EC behaviour was marginal to the outcome of the war, given the defections of some states on grounds of national interest, but as a whole, this tends to blur the overall picture rather than clarify it. Even in a short period of time (the two and one-half months from early April to mid-June 1982), significant shifts in the national foreign policies of EC states took place. Foreign policy analysis in general and the analysis of European foreign policy in particular are the only ways of explaining why such shifts occurred. We have tried to illustrate the inadequacies of so many of the crude, system-wide generalizations which pass for explanations of foreign policy in international relations, without thereby obscuring and complicating the basic issues of how states cooperate and defect in foreign policy, and how domestic issues affect the process of cooperation. It is to be hoped that other systematic comparative studies of European foreign policy will follow in the future.

Appendix A

UN Security Council Resolution 502 on the Falkland Islands (Malvinas) situation (3 April 1982); UN Security Council Resolution 505 on the Falkland Islands (Malvinas) situation (26 May 1982).

	Resolution 502	Resolution 505
China	Abstention	Yes
FRANCE	Yes	Yes
Guyana	Yes	Yes
IRELAND	Yes	Yes
Japan	Yes	Yes
Jordan	Yes	Yes
Panama	No	Yes
Poland	Abstention	Yes
SPAIN	Abstention	Yes
Togo	Yes	Yes
Uganda	Yes	Yes
Soviet Union	Abstention	Yes
UNITED KINGDOM	Yes	Yes
United States	Yes	Yes
Zaire	Yes	Yes

Source: *Index to the Proceedings of the Security Council – Thirty seventh year 1982*, New York: UN, 1983, pp. 71–2.

Appendix B

UN General Assembly Resolutions on the Falkland Islands (Malvinas) 1982–8 (after 1989 decision to defer consideration of the question); details for EC member states (ten in 1982; twelve by 1986).

	Res.37/9 (4.11.82)	Res.38/12 (16.11.83)	Res.39/6 (1.11.84)	Res.40/21 (27.11.85)	Res.41/40 (25.11.86)	Res.42/19 (17.11.87)	Res.43/35 (17.11.88)
Yes	90	87	89	107	116	114	109
No	12	9	9	4	4	5	5
Abstained	52	54	54	41	34	36	37

Appendix B *continued*

	Res.37/9 (4.11.82)	Res.38/12 (16.11.83)	Res.39/6 (1.11.84)	Res.40/21 (27.11.85)	Res.41/40 (25.11.86)	Res.42/19 (17.11.87)	Res.43/35 (17.11.88)
Yes	Greece Spain	Spain	Spain	Spain Greece France Italy	Spain Greece France Italy The Netherlands	Spain Greece France Italy The Netherlands	Spain Greece France Italy The Netherlands
No	Britain	Britain	Britain	Britain	Britain	Britain	Britain
Abstained	Belgium Denmark France Germany Ireland Italy Luxembourg The Netherlands Portugal	Belgium Denmark France Germany Ireland Italy Luxembourg The Netherlands Portugal Greece	Belgium Denmark France Germany Ireland Italy Luxembourg The Netherlands Portugal Greece	Belgium Denmark Germany Ireland Luxembourg The Netherlands Portugal	Belgium Denmark Germany Ireland Luxembourg Portugal	Belgium Denmark Germany Ireland Luxembourg Portugal	Belgium Denmark Germany Ireland Luxembourg Portugal

Source: Various UN documents (General Assembly) & EC documents.

Index

Index

Index

Index

Index

Index

Index

Index

Index